D1553755

RATIONAL LANDSCAPES AND HUMANISTIC GEOGRAPHY

Rational Landscapes and Humanistic Geography

EDWARD RELPH

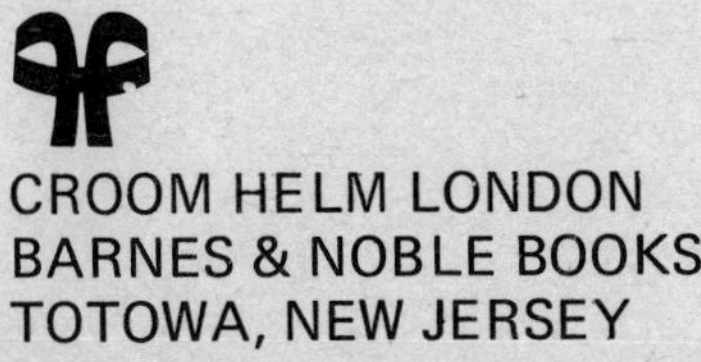

CROOM HELM LONDON
BARNES & NOBLE BOOKS
TOTOWA, NEW JERSEY

Croom Helm Ltd, 2-10 St John's Road, London SW11

British Library Cataloguing in Publication Data

Relph, Edward
Rational landscapes and humanistic geography.
1. Anthropo-geography
I. Title
909 GF41

ISBN 0-7099-0016-3

First published in the USA 1981 by
BARNES & NOBLE BOOKS
81 ADAMS DRIVE,
TOTOWA, New Jersey 07512

ISBN 0-389-20237-1

Printed and bound in Great Britain
by Billing and Sons Limited
Guildford, London, Oxford, Worcester

CONTENTS

PREFACE

Humanism is the conviction that men and women can best improve the circumstances of their lives by thinking and acting for themselves, and especially by exercising their capacity for reason. This conviction has deeply influenced the character of many of the buildings, towns and landscapes that have been constructed since the Renaissance. It has, however, become increasingly detached and rationalistic, and its associated landscapes have been ever more systematically controlled so that they will serve the limited ends of material comfort and technical efficiency. Humanism now seems inclined to restrict rather than encourage reason, and instead of being expressions of hope and commitment the landscapes of humanism are unintentionally being turned into vast yet subtle prisons.

In this book I examine these changing relationships between landscapes and humanism with particular attention to modern built-environments. This was not my original purpose. In its earliest stages this was to have been a manifesto for humanistic geography, but then I discovered that there have been no explicitly humanist geographers and that the philosophical perspective of humanism is very confused. My thinking underwent a metamorphosis and the book that has finally emerged is critical of humanism and has little to say about geography. Instead I have drawn together the work of architects, historians, artists, landscape architects, geographers, poets and philosophers, as well as my own observations of modern landscapes; and I have made particular use of the landscape ideas of the Victorian art critic John Ruskin, and Martin Heidegger's thinking about guardianship and appropriation.

So this is an eclectic book, one that does not fit neatly into any conventional category or discipline. I hope this does not consign it to some academic netherworld. It has to do with how places and landscapes are made, lived in and thought about, and it should be of interest to anyone who, for whatever specific reason, has wondered why modern landscapes are as they are and whether they could be made more sensitive to a full range of human concerns.

I have not self-consciously followed any philosophical or methodological system, phenomenological or otherwise. I have simply tried to make a coherent argument that accounts for the paradoxical fact that modern built-environments meet all our material needs but lack other intangible qualities. This argument has three entwined strands. The first demonstrates that the ideas of humanism and the forms of landscape have a shared history that has culminated in the comfortable yet restrictive character of modern landscape; the second is a criticism and rejection of humanism; the third is a proposal for an attitude that can perhaps grow out of the debris of humanism, and which I call 'environmental humility'. This promotes guardianship rather than control of environments and communities. I do not expect it to hold any great sway in planning or environmental management; it is only my attempt to identify a way of seeing and thinking that is just, careful and non-authoritarian, and which might help to disclose the means for making places that will bear the signs of individual human skills and commitments.

I have tried to express my ideas in non-technical language but this has not always been possible, most notably with the concept of 'appropriation'. The terms 'place', 'landscape' and 'environment', unless qualified, refer equally to urban, rural and natural settings.

I wish to acknowledge several people who, often unwittingly, have helped me in the writing of this book. I have quietly gleaned ideas and references from Michele Bouchier, Mike Bunce, Peter Cave, Pauline Chan, Bill Cowie, Chuck Geiger, Deryck Holdsworth, Alan Jeffrey, Diana Liverman, Katie Oliver, Rick Peddie, John Punter, Mark Schroeder, Doug Sherman, Hugh Sloan, Rod Watson and Miriam Wyman. Dick Morino not only lent me most of his extensive library on Heidegger but helped to clarify my thinking. Nigel Thrift suggested that I might write a book on humanistic geography and therefore initiated the entire project. David Harford of the Graphics Department at Scarborough College did what he could to make my illustrations presentable, and Marje Kimmerley and Carol Tuck helped me to acquire a grant from the University of Toronto to defray some of the costs. I am grateful to Barbara Holst for typing part of the manuscript. My wife, Irene, typed the rest under less than ideal conditions and also sustained me whenever my spirits weakened. Lexy and Gwynnie keep academic work in its proper perspective. And my mother generously gave not only encouragement but shelter and an environment in the Welsh Marches that was conducive to writing.

Ted Relph,
The Narth, Gwent

ACKNOWLEDGEMENTS

I wish to acknowledge the following for giving permission to reproduce illustrations: Figure 2.2 Maritshuis, The Hague; Figure 2.3 The British Museum; Figure 2.11a The Architectural Press; Figures 2.8 and 2.11b The MIT Press, Cambridge, Mass.; Figure 2.12c is by Malcolm Carder, by permission of Theo Crosby; Figure 4.1 The Bodleian Library, Oxford; Figures 9.1 and 9.2 © 1981 Cosmopress, Geneva and ADAGP, Paris.

PART ONE

LANDSCAPE

'Do we want to be strong?—we must work. To be happy?—we must be kind. To be wise?—we must look and think. No changing of place at a hundred miles an hour, nor making of stuffs a thousand yards a minute, will make us one whit stronger, wiser or happier. There was always more in the world than men could see, walked they ever so slowly; they will see it no better for going fast.' (John Ruskin, *Modern Painters*, Vol. III, 1856, p. 331)

1 INTRODUCTION: LANDSCAPES AND THE AMBIVALENCE OF HUMANISM

The landscapes, buildings and urban environments that have been created in the twentieth century have met with scant praise and widespread condemnation. We are told in countless books by architects and historians that cities have become formless malignant growths, and that the pretentious towers of glass and steel within them demonstrate all the design qualities of cardboard boxes covered in graph paper. These office blocks are apparently reoccupied daily by armies of clone-like organisation men and women, issuing from the suburban blandscape wherein lives a race of uniformly bland suburbanites, striving to indulge their materialistic tendencies in the latest model of video-recorder, a package tour to Spain or, at the very least, in the ineffable sameness of the umpteen-billionth hamburger.

Such is the picture painted by the critics of modern society and its landscapes. They would have us believe that this new world is ugly, that it does not work well, that the individuality of persons and places has been overwhelmed by mass culture, and that the traditional values of aesthetics and ethics have given way to the facts of material comfort and efficient industrial production. Their arguments are supported by photographs taken from the air and at ground level, by the results of social surveys, by detailed studies of inefficiencies in design, and by comparisons with the architectural and town-building achievements of other ages. These arguments and facts constitute a compelling case for a recent decline in the quality of built-environments and ways of life. However I find that they do not fit exactly with my own experience.

I live in a suburban area of Toronto that has been almost entirely created since 1945 (everything older has been more or less systematically obliterated). I shop at automobile-oriented plazas and climate-controlled enclosed shopping centres, and I work in a late-1960's poured-concrete building that has been certified as a modern megastructure by the architectural historian Reyner Banham (1976, pp. 133-5). Much of the downtown area of Toronto has been thoroughly overhauled since about 1960 with the construction of high-rise office buildings, and it is overlooked by a telecommunications tower reputed to be the tallest in the world. In short, my life is lived mostly in new surroundings. There is nothing at all remarkable in this; there are hundreds of millions of others in North America, Europe, Japan and Australia who live and work in similar modern landscapes.

If the critics are correct our lives should somehow be diminished because of their modern contexts, and in some unspecified sense we should be incomplete people. Yet I find it strangely difficult to identify how I have been deprived. On the contrary it is the case that the new man-made environments, with all the ingenuity and technical achievements that lie behind them, have made it possible for me and my neighbours to enjoy standards of health and convenience that were until recently unattainable. There are few clear indications in modern landscapes that industrial culture has taken a downturn, but there is ample evidence that our lives have less hardship, and more opportunities for education, recreation and travel than those of any of our ancestors.

This, then, is the paradox which modern landscapes present to us: intellectual and academic condemnations of modern environments contradict the directly experienced evidence that these are invariably comfortable and convenient to live and work in. A number of explanations can be advanced to account for this discrepancy. Perhaps we who live in the midst of the modern are an illustration of the remarkable human ability to adapt to any situation, no matter how bad. Perhaps we have been deluded by advertisers and propagandists for developers into believing that our actually monotonous and repressively manipulated environments are attractive and liberating. As we have gratified our sensual and materialistic desires perhaps we have evolved a sort of blindness to the world around us. Perhaps we are simply less sensitive to our surroundings than Lewis Mumford, Peter Blake, Ian Nairn, or the other critics of modern landscape. Or perhaps the critics have been carried away with the force of their own ideas; probably they live in elegant Georgian houses surrounded by antiques and expensive books and know nothing of the real lives of office workers, factory employees and suburban families.

There is an element of truth in each of these explanations, but none of them goes to the heart of the paradox. The fact is that it cannot be explained away. Both the criticisms of modern landscape and my experiences are correct. It appears that recent improvements in the everyday conditions of life are derived from ways of thinking and doing that necessarily undermine long-held aesthetic, ethical and spiritual values and inexorably destroy the well-established patterns of familiar landscapes.

Modern landscapes are therefore profoundly ambivalent. On the one hand they are obvious manifestations of technical accomplishment and widespread material prosperity – obvious because we know and appreciate them for these qualities in daily life. On the other hand they reflect aesthetic confusion, ethical poverty and a disturbing degree of dependence on technical expertise, but these are subtle and can only be identified by a deliberate effort of observation and reflection. The source of this ambivalence can be traced directly to humanism, the philosophical perspective which encourages the exercise of human reason for human benefit. Humanism not only paved the way for countless social and economic reforms, it also has led to the development of powerful rationalistic techniques for manipulating environments and communities regardless of the values or qualities which might be displaced in the process. The benefits which derive from humanism are manifold, measurable and tangible. The losses, too, are manifold, but they are immeasurable and intangible. In modern landscapes the obvious gains and subtle losses of humanism are conjoined.

Landscape and Humanism

The ideas of landscape and humanism have been intertwined since the early seventeenth century, though the meanings of both terms have changed frequently since then. The tenets of humanism, such as detached observation, concern for the welfare of others and the primacy of man over nature, have been given visible form in landscape gardens, the orderly planning of towns, and in the engineering of natural environments to meet human ends. In the present century, however, these relationships and expressions have become increasingly complex and obscure. This is in part because modern landscapes are so different from all their predecessors. In the nineteenth century a gothic revival was possible because there was still some slight continuity with the societies and craft traditions of the middle ages, if only in the minds of artists and architects. It would be silly to suggest reviving such styles in the late-twentieth century, too much has changed too drastically. We have new sources of energy, innovative technologies and original designs. Humanism is now merged with attempts to use scientific and technical knowledge for human welfare, and its landscape manifestations are implicit in self-consciously designed and planned environments.

Modern landscapes, that is those made since about 1900 and looking to the present or the future rather than to the past for their design inspiration, are the result of a fusion of technical methods of analysis and construction with philosophies which promote improvements in the efficiency and material conditions of life. Since these methods and philosophies have almost universal currency with international corporations and centralised governments, any particular landscape is likely to be representative of a wide range of modern built-environments. Clearly this means that the individuality of a place is now taken to be far less important than its general properties. What is less apparent is that these techniques require that various moral issues and political freedoms are overlooked in the interests of increased productivity and efficiency. Ours is not a culture so much as a superculture run by a class of highly trained experts and professionals using methods that are insensitive but effective. Authority and techniques are imposed gently and with benevolence, so that laymen acquiesce willingly as responsibilities are wrested from them. In the exclusive newness of suburban developments, leisure centres, fast-food outlets, shopping malls, international airports and geometric office blocks, people are treated less as autonomous beings than as pets—they are housed, exercised, fed, cajoled, moved and used. All of this, needless to say, is for their own welfare.

Humanism, Humanistic Geography and Confusions

Humanism is the conviction that human beings are alone responsible for their circumstances and their destiny, and that we can put our faith or find excuse neither in God, nor fate, nor some invisible hand. It is maintained in humanism that only by using our capacity for reason can we understand and control the conditions of our lives.

Humanism is an unaligned philosophical perspective that has been central to Western traditions of thinking and doing for the last four hundred years, though it has never been precisely formulated and has undergone many transformations in that time. It has been explicitly associated with several, and sometimes opposed, philosophical and political traditions, including atheism, Christianity, Marxism, liberalism and existentialism. It has, however, been especially well linked with the progress of science presumably because science also questions dogma, and stresses free enquiry and the use of disinterested reasoning. This link has taken a double form. First, scientific knowledge has been accepted as the highest human achievement; and then, even though it is assumed to be neutral, scientific method is taken to be the only truly effective means of explaining and resolving problems of nature, society and even psyche.

This all seems quite marvellous, and the more earnest advocates of scientific humanism have long believed that the new, benevolent, efficient, scientifically-based and comfortable society is at hand. Cancer will be cured, colonies established in space, poverty eliminated, starvation eradicated and, with scientific research directed to human needs, world peace and prosperity will be assured as soon as the irrationalities of politics and emotions can be overcome. There is, however, a deep flaw in this vision of scientific humanism, a flaw that is exposed, for instance, in recent attempts to promulgate humanistic geography.

Geography offers accounts of the ways in which places and environments are or can be ordered, and superficially there seems to be considerable scope in this for the perspectives of humanism. However, philosophical perspectives tend to come belatedly to geography and it is only in the last few years that there have been attempts to develop an explicit humanistic approach in the discipline. These attempts argue variously for a deeper appreciation of the value of the humanities, for phenomenology and for a revitalised social science, but they are united in their desire to develop an alternative to what can be called 'scientistic geography'—that is the unthinking and uncritical use of scientific method to study all the human and social matters of interest to geographers. This seems logical enough: humanistic geography opposes scientistic geography as humanism opposes the orthodoxies of scientism. The difficulty is that scientism is a direct extension of the humanist principles of free enquiry and rational thought, an extension in which these principles have become dogmatic and inflexible, and therefore deny themselves. In humanistic geography humanism is challenging its own extension, not as an act of self-awareness but through the confusions that beset it and make it so difficult to know just what humanism stands for.

This is, furthermore, only one of several serious weaknesses in humanism. Through its associations with technical expertise humanism has developed a contempt for ordinary knowledge, and through its anthropocentrism is has promoted the domination and exploitation of natural environments. Humanism has failed to live up to its own hopes and goals of eliminating man's inhumanity to his fellows and of creating a humane, just and equitable world; indeed, because of its involvement with rationalistic technology humanism has been party to the manufacture of instruments of enormous and horrible brutality. Given such confusions and inadequacies there really is little justification for continuing to encourage humanism. It was once a constructive and viable philosophical position; now it is tarnished and inclined to vitiate its own best principles.

Environmental Humility

It is a common habit to condemn the new as demonstrating a deterioration in the quality of civilisation. Whether or not the modern world represents a decline of some sort is arguable, but it is always wise to remember that pre-industrial existence was rarely idyllic and that most people's lives then were neither happy nor long. The application of the humanist ideal of reason has undeniably helped to improve the everyday circumstances of living. This means that, having rejected scientific humanism, it is not then sensible to advocate a return to some arbitrarily selected pre-industrial era of craftsmanship and to abandon the material benefits to which we have grown accustomed.

What I wish to suggest is that, for much of the world's population, standards of living are now quite adequate and that further attempts to develop and apply rationalistic techniques of design and planning will result at best in incremental improvements. Indeed, with the continuing arrogation of responsibility to specialists, coupled with all sorts of remote and unanticipated consequences stemming from new technologies, they will probably do far more harm than good. There is already a widespread sentiment that natural environments and inherited man-made landscapes are being sacrificed for dubious increases in standards of living; nuclear power stations and factory farms should be universally welcomed for the immediate comforts and conveniences they bring, yet are bitterly opposed for their distant effects and detached cruelty. And it is not insignificant that many best-selling books in Europe and North America have to do with sex and diet while the less-developed nations grapple desperately with the chronic problems of high birth-rates and starvation. We have enough technical knowledge. It is time to reconsider matters of quality, value and distribution.

About a hundred years ago John Ruskin wrote in the preface to *The Crown of Wild Olive* of the rubbish and pollution in a stream in south London, and he observed that it would take a few men only a day's work to clean it away. Then his attention was drawn to a decorative iron-railing outside a public house and he reflected on the work that had gone into its manufacture; there was 'cramped and deadly work' in the mine, 'fierce and exhaustive' work at the furnace, 'foolish and sedentary' work of ill-taught students making bad designs. All of this to produce something neither attractive, nor useful, nor even profitable, for the public house across the street had installed a grander ornamental railing with which to attract the attention of potential customers. Ruskin concludes (p. 14) from his observations of stream and railings that: 'It matters little, ultimately, how much a laborer is paid for making anything; but it matters fearfully what the thing is which he is compelled to make.' The work that produced the useless iron-railings could have cleaned and maintained the river and hence produced useful and enduring results. So long as iron-railings are manufactured then payment must matter; but if work could somehow be redirected so that fresh air and clean water are not defiled and are maintained by a deliberate effort, then it would be care and responsibility for environments that would be of first importance. Of this Ruskin saw no possibility.

Higher productivity, more scientific research and greater specialisation, even if they are superbly efficient, may not be good in themselves or in their consequences. They can and do produce useless objects and trite results, and they seem to be able to clarify or contribute little that grapples with the problems of the modern era. The pressing aim, now as when Ruskin was writing, is to discover attitudes and ways of thinking which attend to the values and qualities of what is made and of what exists already. The challenge is to learn how to protect and care for these, and then to ensure that they are distributed fairly. These are tasks of ethics, aesthetics and politics. Scientific humanism has declared its neutrality with regard to such matters and therefore has nothing to contribute to the debate.

'Humility' has the same etymological root as 'humanism' and preserves some of the principles of tolerance and responsibility that were to be found in the original impulses of humanism. However it reverses the arrogance and confronts the anthropocentrism of humanism. This reversal can be stressed and given a specific orientation by thinking in terms of 'environmental' or 'geographical humility'.

Environmental humility is not an attitude of self-effacing contrition, lauding the virtues of nature, condemning the destructiveness of humans and advocating abject subservience to the supposed laws of ecology. Nor is it a recipe and methodological guide that can be applied to resolve all the defects of modern landscapes; to suggest that would be perversely arrogant. It is instead a direction for a way of thinking, and perhaps doing, that respects what there is in the world and seeks to protect it and even enhance it without denying its essential character or right to existence. This could conceivably have some indirect and implicit effect, as humanism has had, on the appearance of landscapes. Environmental humility is marked by a concern for the individuality of places, and this requires a careful and compassionate way of seeing that can grasp landscapes as subtle and changing, and as the expression of the efforts and hopes of the people who made them. To learn this way of seeing we must allow ourselves to be appropriated by environments and situations. In other words we have to come to accept places, buildings, people and objects for what they are and as they are, not merely because of their resource potential or research significance. Appropriation means accepting that everything has value simply by virtue of its existence, and recognising that this acceptance further implies an obligation to protect and guard what exists so that this value is not destroyed or diminished. In this there is neither domination nor subservience, but a deliberate effort to exerçise a responsible sense of humanity which embraces not only human beings but literally everything.

If environmental humility and appropriation are to be expressed in some form in landscapes this will require an environmental ethics which can provide some consistent directions for good and bad designs and developments. And rather than planning for goals of efficiency and least-cost, planning would have to respond genuinely to the needs of the most sensitive users of built-environments, especially children and the elderly. However, one of the consequences of environmental humility is that the spiral of proposing more planning controls to correct the problems created by planning would be broken by recognising local autonomy and returning responsibility for making and managing places to the people who live and work in them.

The paradox of modern landscapes and built-environments is that they have provided material comforts and conveniences at the expense of the aesthetic qualities inherent in craftsmanship, and by displacing ethical standards and the small freedom of taking responsibility for the place in which one lives. The origins of this paradox lie in humanism, and especially in scientific humanism which advocates the ever greater use of rationalistic and technical knowledge in order to manage environments and the affairs of society. This knowledge has been instrumental in creating landscapes of such awesome scale and harsh angularity that they often seem to be dehumanised. But they are not dehumanised; they are in fact an expression of the failed possibilities of humanism, they are excessively rationalised and therefore excessively humanised.

It is difficult to condemn rationalism without being labelled as irrational, or to criticise humanism without being accused of advocating the inhumane. Environmental humility may offer a possible way of transcending the paradox of modern landscapes without exposing oneself to these charges. Environmental humility may seem quaint and impractical, and it is unlikely to open avenues of research and employment. It is simply a suggestion for a way of seeing and thinking that is responsive to the best qualities of landscapes and which promotes guardianship and custodianship of environments both natural and man-made. This may seem to be too difficult or imprecise or idealistic in comparison with scientific methods and the technical achievements of planning and engineering. As a response I can do no more than to repeat the hope and caution expressed by John Ruskin over a century ago (1856, vol. III, p. 319):

> The great mechanical impulses of the age, of which most of us are so proud, are a mere passing fever, half-speculative, half-childish. People will discover at last that royal roads to anything can no more be laid in iron than they can in dust; there are, in fact, no royal roads to anywhere worth going to.

2 THE INTERRELATED HISTORIES OF THE IDEAS OF LANDSCAPE AND HUMANISM

I generally use the word 'landscape' to refer to everything I see and sense when I am out of doors. This includes clouds, houses, streets, transmission lines for electricity, rain and rainbows, valleys and vehicles, tourists and the litter which they leave behind them. My idea is that landscape is the necessary context and background both of my daily affairs and of the more exotic circumstances of my life. The Bauhaus architect Walter Gropius used the word 'design' in much the same way; in *Scope of Total Architecture* (1955, p. 20) he wrote that: 'The term "design" broadly embraces the whole orbit of man-made visible surroundings, from simple everyday goods to the complex pattern of a whole town.' Design has to do with visible form, but landscape includes this and the evidence of senses other than sight. The smell of gasoline fumes, the feel of the wind and remembered experiences can all be a part of landscape.

I happen to think that it is useful to have a word which encompasses environments in terms of the way in which I experience them, and landscape seems eminently suitable. However, I am being eccentric in this for landscape has a number of conventional definitions and they are all much more technical and narrowly proscribed than mine, usually referring only to the fixed and enduring objects of the world we see. Using such definitions a landscape can be accurately depicted in a snapshot or sketch which omits smells, sounds, associations and, not infrequently, people as well. Though they are limited to enduring and visible objects, these meanings are historically accurate for the idea of landscape is basically an invention of artists and gardeners of the seventeenth and eighteenth centuries. The origins of the word can be traced to Anglo-Saxon, in which it meant simply a tract of land, but it seems to have gone out of use until it was revived around 1600 by Dutch painters to refer to the pictorial representation of a scene either as a subject in its own right or as the background to a portrait. Landscape soon came to designate the view or prospect itself as well as the painting, and by the middle of the eighteenth century seems to have been an essential term in the working vocabulary of poets, artists, gardeners and gentlemen.

Subsequently, the idea of landscape had undergone several transformations and divisions. Throughout these changes, and in its earlier more stable phase, its fortunes have been intertwined with those of humanism. Humanism is the philosophical position which understands men and women as responsible beings, masters of their own fate and free to think and act for themselves. It has ancient and diverse roots, but in the form it adopted in the Enlightenment and has since maintained it is associated with the exercise of reason and the progress of science and secularism. The ideas of humanism and landscape appeared on the stage of Western history at about the same time. They have since complemented one another in many different ways and have been instrumental in creating the forms of landscapes of the late-twentieth century.

The history of the idea of landscape has to be traced in the works of poets and artists, for it is only in the present century that there has been any technical or academic discussion of the meaning of landscape as a concept. By studying the subjects chosen by painters and poets, and the manner in which these are depicted or conveyed, it is possible to recognise the main shifts in the meaning of 'landscape' from about 1500 up to the end of the nineteenth century. Of course, at any one time the meaning would not have been completely consistent—individual artists anticipated trends or held idiosyncratic opinions—yet in order to satisfy their patrons or to sell their works most conformed to whatever attitudes and styles were fashionable. If this seems to be an elitist and limited approach it is so because in those four centuries landscape was primarily a concern of the affluent and ruling classes. Max Friedlander (1963, pp. 13-14), a German art historian, has observed that: 'The peasant knows the land which he cultivates, which nourishes him; he looks up at the sky, sender of light and rain, but the landscape hardly affects him at all; the relishing eye cannot emerge where hard necessity and harder use predominate.' Landscape was for long an aesthetic concept that required leisure and training to appreciate.

The history of humanism is even more difficult to follow with certainty, in part because it has only been explicitly identified as a philosophical position since the mid-nineteenth century when the word 'humanism' was first used. Nevertheless, the ideas and thinking to which this word refers have existed since the Renaissance even if they had no explicit name (Renaissance scholars of Greek and Latin did call themselves 'humanists', but apparently did not self-consciously expound a coherent philosophy of humanism). The assumptions and arguments of humanism have changed over the centuries so that the term in its present usage incorporates an entire stratigraphy of meanings. These include not only the authority of human reason and the spirit of free enquiry but also a general sympathy for the welfare of mankind, a specific caring for the condition of those less fortunate than oneself, and an anthropocentrism which gives value to things only in so far as they are related to man. To recognise these sorts of associations when they are not so identified by their authors is of course an act of interpretation. But where there is explicit discussion of the supremacy of reason, or the circumstances of humanity, or of human and public welfare, or of man's needs and abilities, such an interpretation is not, I think, unreasonable. Furthermore, the frequency of such discussions suggests that humanism has been a fundamental, if largely implicit, component of the popular conception of the order of things that has prevailed in the Western world since the seventeenth century.[1]

Landscape Painting and Cartesian Philosophy

Prospects and views began to insinuate themselves into the backgrounds of religious pictures in the early fifteenth century. These were usually symbolic or imagined, rarely showing either a particular or a geographically typical scene, but they do suggest some awakening of pleasure in views of the countryside. By the first half of the sixteenth century the balance had shifted so that it was not uncommon for the 'background' scenery to be the dominant feature, if not the focus, of a picture. In the later paintings of Pieter Bruegel (1525-69) the subject matter, almost for the first time, was secular rather than mythical or religious, though his pictures of various seasons and peasant activities are often a combination of social fact and landscape fantasy (Figure 2.1). His paintings tell a story, they are packed with incident and event for which the setting of Dutch vernacular architecture and Alpine peaks provides both a familiar and a dramatic context. There is little attempt to convey a particular and total scene accurately, so mountains can be depicted in Holland.[2] Nor is there any attempt to show landscape as detached from the events which are taking place; they are utterly integrated so that we see peasants and villagers skating or cutting wheat *in* this setting which is the context for their activities. They are not looking at the landscape and admiring its formal qualities.

In the poetry and drama of the same period setting and event are similarly intertwined. Shakespeare's 'blasted heath' and Forest of Arden are always part of a scene, helping to establish its mood. In Ben Jonson's poem 'The Forrest', published in 1616, the Sidney family estate at Penshurst is described in the following way:

Figure 2.1: Hay-Making (July) 1565, *by Pieter Bruegel. Imaginary topography and a fusion of human activities with the natural setting that characterises the period before the invention of the idea of landscape. (Source: National Gallery, Prague)*

Thy copp's, too, nam'd of *Gamage*, thou hast there,
That never failes to serve thee season'd deere,
When thou would'st feast, or exercise thy friends.
The lower land, that to the river bends,
Thy sheepe, thy bullocks, kine and calves doe feed:
The middle grounds thy mares, and horses breed.
(Jonson, 1616, section II, lines 19-24)

No doubt a little praise was good for patronage, but what is significant here is that Jonson's description moves from detail to detail, event to event, each with its specific setting. There is no larger scene, no detached view of the whole landscape.

If Bruegel's paintings and Jonson's poems convey as Kenneth Clark (1949, p. 28) suggests 'an all-embracing sympathy with humanity', the landscape paintings and poems created only a few years later were pervaded with a quiet detachment. In the early 1600s Dutch artists began to paint what were for the first time explicitly called 'landscapes', and these were not merely appropriate settings for other subjects, nor were they filled with mythological and imagined trimmings. They were paintings of the land or the scene itself, in its own condition or state of being (the suffix -scape derives from the same root as -ship, as in friendship, and means state of being). They were topographically accurate, depicting typical and often recognisable scenes in which people and events had become merely incidental, and they were popular souvenirs for merchants from other countries travelling in Holland.

This was a dramatic change – from implication and involvement to impersonal and precise representation. It is almost as though the discovery of the word 'landscape' allowed the artists to see for the first time the scenes and prospects around them. Nowhere is this more clearly conveyed than in Johannes Vermeer's *View of Delft* painted in 1658; seen from across the river a fragment of the view has been isolated for its pictorial qualities and depicted with precise lines and in a clear light (Figure 2.2). It is, the author of a catalogue for an exhibition of paintings on Dutch cityscapes suggests (Amsterdams Historisch Museum, 1977, p. 22), a portrait of a city that embodies a broad collective social expression rather than an individual vision.

The reasons for this change in style and subject from Bruegel to Vermeer can be sought in several places. Clark (1949, pp. 29-30) gives three possible explanations. One is artistic, the previous mannerist styles had been worked out. A second is sociological, the bourgeoisie and merchants wanted art to portray experiences and places which they could recognise, especially the land of the recently united territory of Holland; furthermore, many of these artists had no particular patrons and were selling to the highest bidder, and that encouraged them not merely to paint for the demand but also to avoid paintings that showed only one property. The third explanation is a philosophical one; this was a period of scientific upheaval, the observations and theories of Galileo, Huyghens, Newton and others were tantamount to a new perception of nature, and the landscape painters too were adopting that precise and detached perception of the world.

It may have been coincidence, but at the very time the Dutch artists were developing their new objective and generalised approach to landscape, the French philosopher René Descartes was living in Amsterdam. It was here that he wrote his enormously influential philosophical study *Discourse on Method*, a study which spelled the end for medieval theology and was the foundation stone for the Age of Reason and the subsequent development of scientific humanism.

Descartes, a French nobleman and a Jesuit, went to live in Holland

Figure 2.2: View of Delft about 1658, *by Jan Vermeer. The precise and detached pictorial representation of a specific landscape is typical of paintings made in the seventeenth century after the invention of the concept of landscape. (Source: The Hague, Maritshuis)*

in 1628 and stayed there without significant interruption until 1644. His motives for leaving France are not clear, but they probably had to do with the relative isolation and independence he could gain by moving away from Paris. Some of his ideas could easily have been judged heretical and there existed in Holland a tolerance for religious minorities which could not have been unattractive to him. The biographers of Descartes have found no indication that he was interested either in the beauties of nature or in the art and artists flourishing in and around Amsterdam at the time he was living there. Nevertheless, there is a remarkable similarity between the detached clarity of the landscape paintings and Descartes' argument for adopting a detached attitude for an understanding of the world and man's place in it. I do not intend to imply that there was any direct connection between them, only that both the idea of landscape and its representation and Cartesian philosophy spring from the same geographical, social and historical context. If Johannes Vermeer and others painted for the fashion of their times, Descartes formulated and focused its philosophical character. This character rested above all on faith in the capacity of disinterested human reason to describe and to account for the order of things.

The importance of Cartesian philosophy can hardly be overestimated. It provided a basis and justification for science that involved no appeals to animating souls or spiritual forces, but required solely the power and certainty of human thought. The method which Descartes developed in his meditations was one of progressively doubting the existence of things. This led him to the recognition that he could not doubt his own existence, for 'I who thought thus must be something' (1637, *Discourse 4*, p. 53). This gave the famous proposition 'I think therefore I am', which in turn led him to maintain that while 'I could pretend that I had no body and that there was no world or place that I was in . . . I could not, for all that, pretend that I did not exist' (Ibid., p. 54). In short, the mind that reasons and thinks is certain, and is distinct from and superior to body, world and matter because they do not think. However, Descartes did not put man with his powers of reason above everything, and offered proofs that God existed on the grounds that the idea of perfection which is manifest in God could not have come from an imperfect being like himself. Implicit in Cartesian philosophy, then, is a chain of being, with God as perfection, human mind or reason as imperfect yet superior to and separate from body, creatures and matter. Mind is an indivisible unity, but matter or nature is divisible into parts, and functions strictly according to the certainties of mathematical laws. This is the Cartesian dualism which is at the basis of all detached and objective science—the human mind has the role not only of disclosing the mechanical and mathematical character of nature but also of dominating its surroundings.

It is instructive that Descartes titled his work *Discourse on the Method of Properly Conducting One's Reason and of Seeking the Truth in the Sciences.* Although he was not a humanist in that he was arguing quite expressly against the scholastic form of education which depended only on the study of the humanities, his philosophy is profoundly humanistic in the emphasis it puts on the exercise of human reason to overcome false opinions and habits of thought. And in linking this exercise to the discovery of scientific truth he established the connection between humanism and science that has persisted to the present.

After Descartes there could be no easy return to the attitudes of involvement in the world and of implication in the facts and fantasies of particular settings. Just as mind had been separated from matter so viewer had been separated from landscape. For the first time landscapes were objects for contemplation by the human mind, their facts were to be represented with attention to outline and clarity. That the discovery of landscape and the formulation of the pre-eminence of human reason were contemporary events in Western history may have been coincidental or it might have resulted from the mood of the times. Whichever was the case, the idea of landscape and the belief in the authority of reason progressed together into the eighteenth century, though it was in England rather than in Holland that their association was most completely expressed.

Landscape Gardens and Enlightenment Humanism

In 1642 a poem with the title 'Cooper's Hill' by a minor English poet, Sir John Denham, was published. This poem inaugurated, according to no less an authority than Samuel Johnson, 'a species of composition that may be denominated local poetry, of which the fundamental subject is some particular landscape, to be poetically described, with the addition of such embellishments as may be supplied by historical retrospection, or incidental meditation' (cited in Kenner, 1964, p. 398). Denham's poem was quite unlike Ben Jonson's account of Penshurst written less than thirty years earlier. The author assumes a position on a hill in Surrey overlooking the Thames Valley and proceeds to describe the view spread out before him; he was a spectator commentating on the landscape with special attention to its pictorial qualities and with occasional controlled flights of imagination.

> My eye descending from the Hill, surveys
> Where *Thames* amongst the wanton vallies strays.
> *Thames*, the most lov'd of all the Oceans sons,
> By his old Sire to his embraces runs,
> Hasting to pay his tribute to the Sea,
> Like mortal life to meet Eternity.
>
> (Denham, 1642, lines 159-64)

Denham's poem was the first in this descriptive manner. It proved to be a popular form and was repeatedly imitated in the next one hundred and fifty years. Indeed in eighteenth-century England, when landscape contemplation became one of the chief pursuits of the cultivated, wealthy and fashionable members of society, there were countless such poems written. Inevitably the author recounted the view on a clear day from some convenient hill, probably overlooking the country estate of the person who had commissioned the poem. The prospect was filled with 'verdant fields', 'lofty hills' and 'soft winding streams', described with a tone of muted bucolic hyperbole and clothed in frequent classical and emotional analogies.

John Barrell (1972) in his account of *The Idea of Landscape and the Sense of Place, 1730-1840* is particularly concerned with the poetry of John Clare, but he also identifies the main features of the idea of landscape that prevailed in the eighteenth century. The word had achieved a wider currency than in the previous century and was now used in a general sense rather than to refer solely to particular prospects. Thus it was possible to speak of 'the landscape' as well as 'a landscape', and this meant especially inland *rural* scenery. This was not a restriction that had applied to the Dutch landscape painters who had painted rural and urban scenes with equal accomplishment. A further innovation in the meaning of landscape was the stress on visual composition and the formal qualities of views. Barrell argues that English landscape tastes were deeply influenced by Claude Lorrain (1600-82), the Roman painter of landscapes whose pictures were distinguished by a high viewpoint, a view of tremendous depth well framed by great trees in full leaf and some incidental figures involved in some event from classical mythology or history (Figure 2.3). Kenneth Clark (1949, p. 64) writes of Lorrain's paintings: 'They are a perfect example of what old writers on art used to call Keeping. Everything is in Keeping: there is never a false note. Claude could subordinate all his powers of perception and knowledge of natural appearances to the poetic feeling of the whole. The world of his imagination is so clear and consistent that nothing obtrudes, nothing is commonplace, nothing is done for effect.'

There can be no better account of what English gentlemen and ladies looked for in the landscapes of Georgian England—a composed unit in which everything is simultaneously remarkable and in keeping, with distant prospects and marvellous trees. Of course one did not come upon such scenes nor the ability to appreciate them easily. On the one hand it was necessary to create such landscapes wherever money and circumstances permitted, and on the other hand the contemplation of landscape required that it be reconstructed in the imagination according to principles of composition that had to be learnt.

If the development of the general sense of landscape and the stress on formal qualities were new, there were also aspects of the eighteenth-

Figure 2.3: Landscape with Erminia and the Shepherd, *by Claude Lorrain (1677). Lorrain's views of leafy trees and distant prospects had a great influence on eighteenth-century English landscape tastes. (Source: Liber Veritatis 196, British Museum)*

century attitude to landscape that were derived from seventeenth-century philosophies. Landscapes maintained their remoteness and detachment – they were to be looked at or down on in exactly the way in which we look at a framed painting. Landscapes were regarded as ordered and systematic manifestations of nature. In his poem of 1730 called *The Seasons*, James Thomson could write that their passage is 'not eccentric once – So pois'd and perfect is the vast machine' (Thomson, 1730, Summer, lines 41-2). This machine view of nature had become the prevalent one. It owed a great deal to Newtonian physics which was popularly admired, and also, though a little more remotely, to the Cartesian mathematical view of nature. According to this perspective the order of the material world could be derived from a few general and certain principles of mathematics, the truth of which Descartes believed he had established and the effectiveness of which Newton had demonstrated with his discoveries of physical laws. In the wider poetic world-view God remained as the Prime Cause, for the mechanical world presupposed the existence of a mechanic, but as soon as He had started the clockwork and had nature moving efficiently He retreated from the scene. The world was therefore perfectly ordered and in it man was pre-eminent. The character of this hierarchical order was clearly stated by Alexander Pope in his *Essay on Man*, and he summarised it precisely in 'The Argument of the First Epistle' (section vii) (i.e. Table of Contents) for that poem.

> That throughout the whole visible world, an universal order and gradation in the sensual and mental faculties is observed, which causes a subordination of creature to creature, and of all creatures to Man. The gradation of sense, instinct, thought, reflection, reason; that Reason alone countervails all the other faculties.

Here again is the humanistic attitude that had been formulated in Cartesian philosophy and which emphasises the primacy of human reason. In the eighteenth-century English idea of landscape it was still fundamental, though its outlines had been blurred by the fashionable concern for pictorial qualities and pleasant compositions in scenes. But there was no conflict or contradiction between the exercise of reason and the pleasures of imaginative contemplation; instead they seem to have been taken as complementary. In a poem written about landscape at the end of the century, R.P. Knight summarised this synthesis of a mechanical understanding of nature, aesthetic appreciation and reason:

> Whate'er its essence, or whate'er its name,
> Whate'er its modes, 'tis still, in all, the same:
> 'Tis just congruity of parts combined
> To please the sense and satisfy the mind.
> (Knight, 1795, Book I. lines 37-40)

Yet this is not the complete story of eighteenth-century concepts of landscape. Descartes had written that his philosophical method would make men 'masters and possessors of nature', and the English gentry were in a sense fulfilling his prophecy in their careful contemplations of landscape. Yet it was not always enough to reconstruct landscapes in the imagination according to learned principles of composition. Thinking a dead tree or asymmetrical bush or peasant hovel out of the scene was not quite enough. It was thoroughly in accord with the temper of the times, with humanistic attitudes of the Enlightenment that asserted the primacy of human reason over nature, to reconstruct the actual landscape to achieve a pleasant and satisfying composition.

Hence the development and practice of landscape gardening, which in Georgian England went hand-in-hand with landscape poetry and painting. Alexander Pope, for instance, designed his own landscape garden for his house at Twickenham, wrote landscape poetry and owned many landscape paintings (Mack, 1969).

The reconstruction of landscapes on a grand scale in order to make them into gardens was not, of course, an English invention of the 1700s. Huge gardens had been constructed around Italian villas during the Renaissance, and in the previous century the gardens of Versailles and many French chateaux had been created. In these French estates reason falls in straight lines—they are utterly geometric, an extension of contemporary urban and architectural design into the garden. Descartes, had he had an eye for such things, would have approved for he had written favourably in *Discourse on Method* (1637, pp. 35, 37) of 'orderly towns which an engineer designs at will on some plain' and 'the plumb-line of reason'. The English landscaping Descartes would not have appreciated for it took its inspiration from nature and tamed that into gardens. There were other influences too; the principles of composition which Claude Lorrain had invented can be recognised in carefully contrived prospects, and his groups of figures engaged in mythological activities were realised as statues. There may also have been some Chinese influence, since trade with the Far East had resulted in a familiarity with Chinese tastes for irregularity and asymmetry in gardens, but whether these were self-consciously adopted is a matter of dispute (Tunnard, 1978, pp. 76-87).

Whatever the aesthetic sources for English landscape gardens their order is an extremely subtle one, with carefully sited trees, great expanses of grass, ponds that are clearly man-made, yet none of the predictability and certainty of lines and circles (Figure 2.4). The order is one that is based on but transcends the natural scene. Barrell (1972, p. 46) suggests that William Kent, the first of the English landscape gardeners in this mode, created his gardens not as faithful copies of the natural landscape, but that 'he looked on natural landscape as striving to realise the ideal he created in the gardens he improved'. So there was no brutish mastery of nature or imposition of forms but a working with the landforms and vegetation that existed so that everything was in 'keeping'. Pope gave precise advice on how to proceed:

> Consult the Genius of the Place in all,
> That tells the waters or to rise, or fall,
> Or helps th'ambitious Hill the heav'n to scale,

Figure 2.4: The landscape garden at Burghley House near Stamford, Lincolnshire, 1977. This garden with its ha-ha (in the foreground), artificial lake (in the middle distance) and carefully articulated groups of trees, was laid out by Capability Brown between 1757 and 1760.

> Or scoops the circling theatres the vale . . .
> (*Epistle to Richard Boyle*, lines 57-60)

and so on. The result was to be an improvement by subtle manipulation of the parts until the right sorts of compositions and prospects were achieved. Though contemporary admirers claimed that these landscape gardens were scarcely distinguishable from nature, it is difficult now to consider them as anything but contrivances, no matter how attractive. The gardens were meant to be seen from specific temples or viewpoints for it was from these that the composition was correct. And of course the gardens were only gardens—scenes for contemplative leisure on the grand country estates of the landed gentry. The gardeners took a pictorial and arbitrary ideal of landscape and made it real for their wealthy clients.

The idea of landscape that prevailed in eighteenth-century England was doubly detached. It was detached in that landscape was regarded as an object to be looked upon and enjoyed if its arrangements were right, or reworked to make them right if they were not. It was always subject to human reason and human will, and indeed those landscapes most admired for their aesthetic qualities were exactly those which had been redesigned to accord with human sensibilities. It was detached also in that it was an aristocratic and bourgeois notion that had nothing to do with working farms or cottages or the lives of the vast majority of the population. The Enlightenment idea of landscape embraced a belief in the primacy of human reason, an acceptance of the principles of mechanistic science, an adoption of artistic fashions of composition, and the possibilities for ideal contemplation that are provided by affluence.

Romantic Landscapes and Sympathetic Humanism

From the time Descartes formulated his philosophy to the end of the eighteenth century reason reigned supreme in art and science as well as in the detached and pictorial concept of landscape. About 1800 this supremacy came into serious question and a profound change in world view seems to have taken place. Michel Foucault, in his enquiry into the ways in which some fundamental assumptions of modern Western thinking have developed, *The Order of Things* (1970, p. 318), asserts that: 'Renaissance "humanism" and classical "rationalism" were indeed able to allot human beings a privileged position in the order of the world, but they were not able to conceive of man.' He means that there was no epistemological awareness of people and human problems, there was no domain of study which had as its focus human or social problems, no sense of individuals who live, work and speak. Everything happened, as it were, in the third person and not in the first person. However, in the nineteenth century there emerged a sense of subjectivity and a concern for social and human problems that was manifest in the development of sociology, psychology and economics.

It was the poets and artists of the Romantic movements who first effected this change of outlook. William Blake believed Newton and Descartes to be apostles of the devil and he railed passionately against the Cartesian method of doubt:

> He who doubts from what he sees
> Will ne'er Believe, do what you Please.
> If the Sun & Moon should doubt,
> They'd immediately Go out.
> (Blake, *Auguries of Innocence*, p. 70)

Wordsworth also reacted strongly against the values of the Age of Reason, perhaps because he was thoroughly disillusioned by the outcome of the French Revolution for which he had had high hopes, but also because he was inclined by temperament to favour insight and intuition over rationality. In a poem to his sister written in 1798 he declared:

> It is the hour of feeling.
> One moment now may give us more
> Than years of toiling reason.
> (Wordsworth, 1798, p. 23)

Unlike Blake, Wordworth phrased many of his reactions against the previous age in the context of landscapes—the Lake District, the Alps, the Wye Valley, London. In his poems the idea of landscape underwent a dramatic change. It ceased to be something detached, pictorial, mechanical and man-made and took on a spiritual force that could be apprehended by those who were sensitive to it. In his poem *Tintern Abbey* he writes of the Wye Valley on the border of England and Wales:

> These beauteous forms
> Through a long absence, have not been to me
> As is a landscape to a blind man's eye:
> But oft, in lonely rooms, and 'mid the din
> Of towns and cities, I have owed to them
> In hours of weariness, sensations sweet
> Felt in the blood, and felt along the heart.
> (Wordsworth, 1798, p. 66)

Landscapes, and that meant primarily the landscapes of nature and of rustic villages and excluded the 'mean and vulgar works of man', were a manifestation of God's presence, so a faith in nature became a sort of religion in which landscapes had a purifying and uplifting effect on those who were willing to open their senses to them.

Something similar can be seen in the paintings of John Constable, for although he followed many of the principles of composition that had been held in the previous century, his driving motivation seems to have been the idea that nature is a manifestation of supernatural powers. Kenneth Clark (1949, p. 78) writes of Constable's work: 'naturalism is raised to a higher mode by his belief that since nature was the clearest revelation of God's will, the painting of landscape, conceived in the spirit of humble truth, could be a means of conveying moral ideas.'

If this romanticism and adoration of the spiritual in nature seems far removed from the Cartesian humanism of reason, well so it is. Yet there is in the art of Romanticism an element of something which, from a twentieth-century perspective, must be considered humanistic. Wordsworth, again in his *Tintern Abbey* poem, wrote:

> For I have learned
> To look on nature, not as in the hour
> Of thoughtless youth; but hearing oftentimes
> The still sad music of humanity,
> Nor harsh nor grating, though of ample power
> To chasten and subdue.
> (Wordsworth, 1798, p. 68)

This is no celebration of human reason but a generalised sympathy for the condition of mankind. Wordsworth set out deliberately to avoid the mannered style and language of the poetry of the previous age, and to write in 'the real language of men' about 'incidents and situations from common life' (Wordsworth, *Preface to Lyrical Ballads*, 1798, p. 210). This seems wholly consistent with a concern for humanity, though it must be remembered that he always looked through these incidents of common life and through particular places and landscapes to something universal. The object of poetry, he claimed, is truth 'not individual and local, but general and operative; not standing upon external testimony, but carried alive into the heart by passion' (Ibid., p. 223).

The distinctive contribution of the Romantic artists to humanism was the sense of feelings shared with others, of sympathy for their suffering and involvement in their joy. It was not a personal sharing, however, but a generalised and perhaps even slightly sentimental participation in mankind. This could be achieved, among other ways, by attending to the picturesque and sublime landscapes of nature and seeing in them a spiritual and moral presence. Landscapes were deeply subjective, preserving and reflecting memories and emotions (both Wordsworth and Constable drew inspiration from the scenes of their childhood), yet were shared; others could see them and have similar spiritual experiences. By being open to the qualities of natural and rustic landscape it was possible to get some feeling of association with all of mankind.

Ruskin's Moral Interpretation of Landscape and its Sentimentalisation

The Romantic notion of landscape was refined and clarified by John Ruskin, the influential Victorian art critic, whose book *Modern Painters* (1856) contains what is probably the first explicit discussion of the *idea* of landscape. Ruskin argued from his studies of the history of painting and poetry that there had been significant changes in attitudes towards landscape in the previous century or so. For several thousand years before that men had been anxious to know something of their ancestors, their heroes and the gods, but had shown little interest in the external world. But then a shift had occurred: man was still aware of the existence of gods but '*now* he is capable of going through life with hardly any positive idea on this subject, and doubting, fearing, suspecting' (Ruskin, 1856, vol. III, p. 164). Spirituality had been cast out of the world and a mechanical and materialist universe substituted; the aridity of this universe had effectively driven the Romantics to natural scenery both as a source of beauty in contrast to the ugly and false world of men, and for its intimations of divine order.

Landscape for Ruskin meant especially, though not exclusively, natural scenery and paintings and poems of this. Though he understood a love of landscape to be a substitute for a sense of the presence of gods it was in no way trivial. His own life was in fact centred on experiences of landscape, for he declared that: 'The gift of taking pleasure in landscape I assuredly possess in greater degree than most men; it having been the ruling passion of my life' (Ruskin, 1856, vol. III, p. 316). Seeing landscapes with sensitivity and imagination could provide people with a sense of humility, a feeling of something other than themselves that was profoundly important, as well as considerable pleasure. Indeed the 'pure landscape instinct' he thought to be 'inconsistent with every evil feeling . . . but would associate itself deeply with every just and noble sorrow, joy or affection' (Ibid., p. 318). To take pleasure in landscape was therefore a sign of moral perception, and to that extent landscape had a moral character (Figure 2.5).

Ruskin's writings on landscape are filled with the same sort of humanism that imbues Wordsworth's poetry—not the humanism of reason, but one of sympathy for his fellows that is based on an attempt to grasp all aspects of what it means to be a human being—spiritual, moral, emotional, aesthetic and rational. The landscape instinct, as a love of truth and beauty in one's surroundings, was a clear expression of the character of human nature. He wrote at the end of *Modern Painters* (vol. V, p. 190) that 'all true landscape whether simple or exalted,

Figure 2.5: Lake, Land and Cloud, *(near Como), by John Ruskin. This is the Frontispiece to Volume III of* Modern Painters, *published in 1856. Later in this volume (p. 318) Ruskin wrote that 'pure landscape instinct . . . would associate itself deeply with every just and noble sorrow, joy or affection'.*

depends primarily for its interest on connection with humanity'. This connection he saw as being threatened by science and industry; scientific truth he claimed was 'the truth of husk and surface, hard and shallow' (cited in Herbert, 1964, p. 14). He wanted to root understanding in human imagination and human hope. In *Modern Painters* (vol. III, p. 49) he stated that the proper business of human beings in the world was to know themselves and the existing state of things, and to be happy, and to mend themselves and the existing state of things in so far as they were mendable. To do these required above all an effort to see clearly, to observe things as they are and not through some gloss or veil. By such clear seeing it might be possible to grasp the essence of a life 'which all men recognise for the human life of all time' (Ibid., p. 100). This, Ruskin argues, was just what Shakespeare achieved and not because he sought to present directly some universal human truth, but because he represented honestly and precisely what he saw in the particular men around him. The essence of being human lay in real and immediate experiences that have always been possible, not in abstractions and material comforts. Almost as a manifesto he wrote:

> To watch the corn grow, and the blossoms set, to draw hard breath over ploughshare or spade; to read, to think, to love, to hope, to pray – these are the things that make men happy; they have always had the power of doing these, they never will have the power of doing more. The world's prosperity depends upon our knowing or teaching these few things; but upon iron, or glass, or electricity, or steam in no wise.
>
> (*Modern Painters*, vol. III, pp. 332-3)

Ruskin's argument for the validity and moral force of landscape fell on deaf or uninterested cars, or perhaps worse was listened to selectively without attention to his careful arguments and distinctions. He emphasised repeatedly the necessity to observe well, to treat landscape with respect because of its moral force, and not to misrepresent what was observed by endowing it with imagined and sentimental qualities. Victorian industrialists were, however, not inclined to let such faint-hearted concerns stand in the way of the factories and railroads which Ruskin had despised and had hoped were but a passing fever. Nevertheless, the businessmen and engineers had no objection when their families turned scenes of no particular economic value into the subjects of leisurely, sentimental and largely undiscriminating pleasure. Ruskin had argued passionately that taking pleasure in landscape was not a trivial and easy experience, but it was just such a slight and superficial idea of landscape enjoyment that came to dominate in the late-nineteenth century. A few individuals did struggle to maintain a depth in landscape perception; Gerard Manley Hopkins developed his mystical idea of 'inscape' to express the unique and spiritual identity that pervades particular scenes (Grigson, 1962, pp. 21-3). And Paul Cezanne struggled for years to paint the very essence of a landscape, and to identify himself with it completely. 'The landscape thinks itself in me', he announced mysteriously, 'and I am its consciousness' (cited in Merleau-Ponty, 1964, p. 17). Hopkins and Cezanne were exceptional; for most artists and certainly for the general population in the late-nineteenth century, landscape was nice scenery that made a gentle or fashionable impression upon their senses.

In 1890 a book by P.G. Hamerton called simply *Landscape* was published. This was inspired by many of Ruskin's ideas but managed to reduce them to simple aesthetic experiences. 'Landscape' Hamerton defined simply as the 'visible material world' or 'a piece of the earth's surface that can be seen all at once' (p. 10). He suggests that what we perceive in landscape is a reflection of our moods and idiosyncracies, and his central thesis has to do with what might be called subjective felicific formalism. He suggested that 'Each of us has some idiosyncracy related in a mysterious way to a certain class of scenery, and when we find ourselves in a scene answering to our idiosyncracies the mind feels at home in them' (p. 27). The aim presumably is to match mood and landscape, for 'one of the greatest elements in happiness is to live . . . in the midst of scenes that are exactly adapted to our needs' (p. 29). So there are strong men's places of mountains and torrents and wild grandeur, and weak men's landscapes of gentle valleys and softness and amenity. This Darwinian landscape psychology is not well developed, however, and most of Hamerton's book is a description of the formal aesthetic qualities of various categories of landscape—lake shores, lake surfaces, lake islands, and so on.

Hamerton's arguments were not particularly profound and they seem to be little more than a popular and sentimentalised version of Ruskin's ideas. They are representative of those common late-nineteenth century attitudes which understood landscape as an object for casual contemplation and the development of sentimental associations, something to be indulged especially by daughters of the nouveau riche (Figure 2.6). Landscape had become only its appearance, and it required no special sensitivity or education in the principles of composition to appreciate it, for it was seen through penny-dreadful or superficial categories and conventions of picturesqueness. Such attitudes foreshadow the twentieth-century concept of landscape which manifests itself in coffee-table books and in tourism to look at pleasant scenery.

The Origins of Landscape Architecture

The romantic idea of nature and its sentimental derivations were not the only ideas of landscape to develop in the nineteenth century. There was a very different yet parallel tradition—that of landscape architecture.

THE QUEEN'S ROYAL HOTEL.

Figure 2.6: The lakefront at Niagara-on-the-Lake, Ontario, seen through the artist's pallette, 1886. Contrivance and sentimentality came to play a major role in landscape experience and depiction in the late nineteenth century. (Source: Barlow Cumberland, The Northern Lakes of Canada, *1886, p. 28)*

The romantic poets and painters had reacted against the intellectual rationalism of their predecessors: they saw themselves not as minds detached from the world and contemplating it, but as implicated in and learning from the landscapes of nature. The works of man were no better than a 'rash assault', to use Wordsworth's expression, on the existing scene. The romantics had moved against rationalism and had taken the idea of landscape with them, and had implicitly modified the notion of humanism to fit with their new philosophies. In contrast the landscape architects of the nineteenth century, though they could not be entirely aloof from the popular fashions of picturesque romanticism, were in a direct line of descent from the landscape gardeners of Georgian England. Their task and achievement was to create parks and pleasure-grounds for the use of the general public rather than some aristocrat and his friends, and this they did with all the technical skills and principles of picturesque composition they had at their disposal.

The expression 'landscape architecture' and the manner of its practice were both American inventions, specifically attributable to the architects of Central Park in New York City, Frederick Olmsted and Calvert Vaux. Of course their ideas and techniques were not entirely without precedent. Humphry Repton, the last of the Great English landscape gardeners, had devised a system of before-and-after design sketches to show a landscape as it was and as it would be after improvement. It was but a short transition from this to formal blueprints and plans designating the location of paths, trees and facilities. This progress to planning was accompanied by another change, a social one, from designing parks for gentlemen to designing public parks. Up to this time landscape had been exclusively an elitist idea, something to do with affluence and leisure. In a sequence of events in the first half of the nineteenth century, culminating in the opening of public parks in every town and city, it became a popular fact. The exact sequence is not clear, but it seems that gentlemen had missed their country estates when they were living in their city houses, and had small private parks laid out for themselves in squares and crescents like those of Bloomsbury. The advantages of these for providing shade (perhaps these parks were also the origin of the fashion of planting street trees) and for relaxation was apparent to a wider audience. In the 1840s public parks open to all were developed in London's east end and in Birkenhead, and were subsequently widely copied.

Olmsted visited Birkenhead Park in 1850 and was undoubtedly influenced both by its design and by the fact that it was open to the general public. In the late-1850s Olmsted and Vaux won the competition for the design of Central Park, and the success of their plan was so great that over the next few decades they were commissioned to design parks in many of the largest North American cities, including San Francisco, Boston and Montreal. And the parks which they did not create themselves were deeply influenced by their ideas of mixing public facilities, open meadows, lakes, a variety of more and less dense woodland and spaces for both formal and informal recreation (Newton, 1971, ch. XIX). The term 'landscape architect', which they first adopted in 1863, was to show that they bore towards landscape the same relation that an architect bears towards a building – in short the vegetation and landforms with which they worked were capable of manipulation and reconstruction and were objects of professional and technical concern.

These designs for public parks were comprehensive plans, rationally conceived, laid out in advance on maps and plans as though seen from the air (Figure 2.7). Olmsted's approach to landscape was a scientific one. He stressed a clear spatial geometry in his designs, sought to achieve a maximum efficiency of use by means of such devices as grade separations between roads with vehicular traffic and those for pedestrians, and systematically attempted to meet the wide range of public demands for recreation in parks.

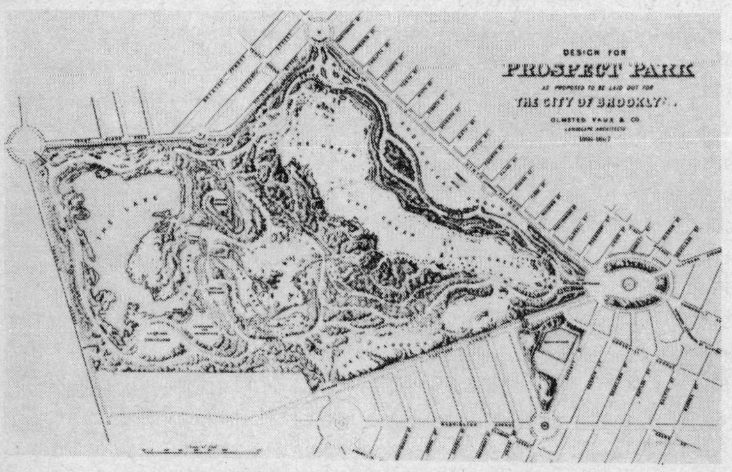

Figure 2.7: The design by F.L. Olmsted and C. Vaux for Prospect Park, Brooklyn, 1866-7. These two landscape architects initiated the use of professional expertise in park and landscape design for the public welfare. (Source: Newton, 1971, figure 190)

In using his special abilities as a landscape architect for public welfare, Olmsted was practising what might be understood as yet another form of humanism – philanthropic or paternalistic humanism. The shift from private to public service of landscape gardeners was a specific expression of the recently developed concern for the living and working conditions of the lower classes of the population. This was perhaps derived in part from the romantic sympathy for mankind, but confrontations with the horrendous slums and factories of industrial cities had translated this into practical attempts to promote the building of humane environments. These attempts took two forms. There were utopian proposals for entirely new types of communities, and there were reform movements seeking to make specific changes to legislation and technology in order to improve living conditions (Benevolo, 1967). Landscape architects were not aloof from these, and in line with the reformers they apparently came to see themselves as public servants who could resolve at least some of the horrors and disparities of industrialisation by the appropriate use of their expertise. That there was an element of paternalism in this can hardly be doubted, but its beneficial effects were very real. The new parks were considered to be the lungs of the cities—essential in providing oxygen and reducing epidemics. Be that as it may, they provided much needed green space and facilities for healthy recreation, and they certainly helped to alleviate some of the inhumanities of nineteenth-century city development.

Professional expertise used for the public good has been an essential element of the character of landscape architecture (and all planning) since the mid-nineteenth century. The approaches have in fact become increasingly detailed and technical. Ecological and botanical researches, detailed site surveys, the precise calculation of grades to allow for easy maintenance by motor-mowers and satisfactory drainage, are now undertaken as a matter of course (Figure 2.8). There are even serious attempts to measure landscape resources by determining their attractiveness according to the proportion of a view occupied by 'distant zone, intermediate zone and immediate zone', or some other similar device, and to develop from these measurements some sort of predictive model to anticipate the impacts of changes on scenery (Zube *et al.*, 1975, has several examples). At the same time the humanistic concern for meeting people's aesthetic needs has remained central. For instance Eckbo begins *The Landscape We See* (1969) with a quotation to show that his concerns are firmly set within the context of the humanities—those disciplines which embrace whatever influences conduce to freedom and enlightened choice. More specifically J.O. Simmonds, in a textbook on *Landscape Architecture* (1961, p. 200) announces that the needs of human beings are always basic—needs for a rich variety of spaces, health and convenience on an hitherto undreamed of plane,

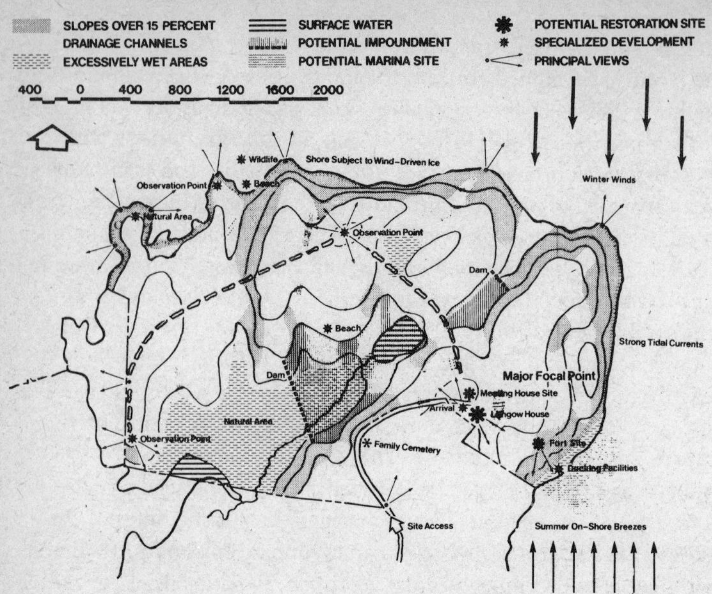

Figure 2.8: Landscape as an object for technical research and analysis. This is an example of a preliminary site evaluation. When considered in sequence with Repton's before and after sketches and Olmsted's detailed site plans, this diagram demonstrates the progression towards abstraction that has occurred in landscape gardening and architecture. (Source: Lynch, 1971, p. 21)

order and sources of inspiration, stimulation, refreshment, beauty and delight. It is presumably the task of the landscape architect to attempt to provide these, using neither experience gained through apprenticeship nor intuition, but the expertise that comes from a sound academic training.

The landscaping around an institutional building or the headquarters of some multinational corporation, the sweeping lawns and rounded hillocks and carefully selected trees, is quite directly a manifestation of the scientific humanism that involves the application of special expertise for human benefit and pleasure. Both in its style and in the idea it expresses it is in a direct line from the landscape gardens of the eighteenth century, but it has carried the attitude of detachment and authority over nature to a new and sophisticated level. The idea of landscape in modern landscape architecture is that it is an object comprising many subtle and complex ecological systems, which can be investigated in a logical and scientific manner, so that the forms of the landscape can be remade to meet human needs efficiently and to satisfy human pleasure without disturbing the balance of nature. Alexander Pope and the landscape gardeners of Georgian England would have understood this even though they may have disliked the specific compositions. But for Wordsworth and Ruskin this would have seemed an amoral and spiritually empty approach to landscape.

Academic Landscapes

The traditions of landscape poetry and painting in which the idea of landscape had developed did not survive into the twentieth century (at least not as representational art forms), though the technical and professional practices of landscape architecture have continued up to the present day. From its reintroduction by Dutch painters about 1600 until 1900 the word 'landscape' had been used unselfconsciously, that is with few explicit discussions of its meaning and without landscape being treated as a subject of investigation in its own right. But in the twentieth century, even as it has lost much of its appeal for artists and poets, landscape has become a subject for academic consideration and investigation. Its meaning as a concept, its components and qualities, people's perceptions of types of landscape, have been examined by geographers, historians, architects and critics of literature. The philosopher of art Susanne Langer (1966, p. 36) has warned that the effects of landscape are not measurable, yet in these recent studies there is little doubt demonstrated that landscapes can be examined and assessed objectively and that we can thereby explain something of ourselves and our society. This detached analysis is new, but it is also the case that in some of these discussions landscape is given the meaning it held for a time in the seventeenth century of either natural or man-made, urban or rural environments. This is a valuable recovery of meaning.

Much of the recent academic writing has to do with how people relate to landscapes, either individually or through culture, and how landscapes have been and can be modified in a rational way to improve the quality of human life. So once again the idea of landscape has come to be associated with attitudes of humanism, though this link is rarely made explicit and seems to involve many humanisms lumped together. There are hints of humanistic rationality in arguments for the disinterested investigation of landscapes, there are romantic expressions of sympathy for those who live in environments less comfortable than one's own, and there is a general assumption that the expertise of a planner or architect or some other professional can be used to improve the landscapes and lives of others. But the humanism associated with landscape has been absorbed and become completely accepted as part of a general consciousness that man is the measure of things. This is apparent in a widespread concern for humane environments and humanising influences like that expressed by the Bauhaus architect Walter Gropius (1968, p. 7): 'In our technological society we must passionately emphasise that we are still a world of human beings and that man must stand in his natural surroundings as the centre point of all planning and building.'

Geographers' Landscapes

The geographical approach to landscape is neutral. It is neutral socially, historically, politically and aesthetically, for it tries to embrace all these. The special concern of geographers has been the 'cultural landscape' understood as the patterns and forms produced by the interaction of people, that is culture, with natural environment. Since culture includes technologies, customs and beliefs, and environment incorporates geomorphological, climatic and botanical factors, this is indeed a grandly synthetic approach. What is important in it is that while sometimes the role of people is stressed and sometimes that of environment, the two are always seen as conjoined and interacting. However, it is not usually particular scenes and situations which are described and analysed, but generalised ones. This sets the geographical notion of landscape sharply apart from that of art and landscape architecture, in which the chief concern has been with specific settings. The American geographer Carl Sauer wrote in 1925 in a very influential article on 'The Morphology of Landscape' that 'The geographic landscape is a generalisation derived from the observation of individual scenes' (p. 322), and that the individual scene is only of interest as a type or variant from type in a generic or morphological taxonomy of landscapes. Using this generalised geographical concept it is possible to refer to and describe the 'landscape of New England' or the 'landscape of Wales', meaning by these an imagined aggregation of the more typical topographical features, settlement forms, building types and other elements of landscape. There are of course regional variations, but one can none the less envisage the mountains, moorlands and valleys of Wales, with small stone cottages and chapels and mining towns, and can recognise that there is a distinctiveness to these and to their patterns which could only be Welsh. It is this sense of what is typical yet regionally distinctive that is the basis of the geographical idea of landscape.

This process of generalisation works both spatially and temporally so that, just as local variations are overlooked in order to see the regional landscape, seasonal variations and all things ephemeral are somehow ignored in favour of what might be called 'the average annual landscape'. The result of these combined generalisations is that descriptions of cultural landscapes have an abstract quality that can be seen as fragments in particular views, but which can nowhere be exactly recognised.

This abstract idea of cultural landscape has provided a datum for three types of geographical enquiries. There have been attempts to describe regional landscapes and to account for them in relatively straightforward terms as the product of interacting historical, cultural and natural factors. A second and defunct approach was to try to formulate regional patterns and systems of landscape features so that classifications could be made. The third use of the idea of cultural landscape has been rather different, and has greater significance here than the others, for it treats landscape as a clue to culture and as an expression of human values and practices. Whereas the other two approaches are confined to description or some sort of narrative explanation, this allows for interpretation. It is held in this third approach that what people do and what they make are often more honest expressions of beliefs and attitudes than what they write about themselves. From this perspective landscape can be understood as a cultural artifact that is as valuable and informative as literature, art or architecture (Figure 2.9).

The clearest explicit summary of this way of considering landscape as a clue to culture is a paper by the American geographer Peirce Lewis on 'Axioms of the Landscape' (1976). His argument is that all landscapes, no matter how ordinary, have cultural meaning and that this meaning can be apprehended by reading landscapes as though they are books. Of course such meanings are not always self-evident, and some skill and experience are often needed to decipher a particular situation. Lewis maintains that human landscapes represent a considerable investment of time, effort and money, that they look as they do for a reason, and that they will not be changed unless there is an even better reason to do so. Furthermore, and in contrast to the biases so often found in art and architectural history, he proposes that virtually everything, no matter how unique or commonplace, reflects culture in some way. Hence fast-food outlets are no more or no less important as expressions of culture than architect-designed megastructures.

Figure 2.9: Landscape as a clue to culture – Georgian row housing with recent infill development, Society Hill, Philadelphia, 1979. Lewis and Marsh (1979, p. 28) describe these streets as 'still very European, with their close-packed row houses . . . On the other hand, the grid-pattern street plan is American – not in origin, of course, but in spirit.'

These axioms for reading landscape suppose that landscapes are like great documents spread out around us, informing us in countless subtle and obvious ways about the values of our culture if we can be bothered to attend to their messages. The disinterested (though profoundly engaged) intelligence of those geographers who are interested in landscape can render these messages clear, elaborate their implications and elucidate their meanings.

An Historian's Landscape

Historians, too, have been involved in examining landscapes, trying to use them as a source of information about life in former periods. Since so much money and effort is expended on making landscapes, on laying out roads, erecting buildings, making villages and towns, they tend to endure and hence to form a visible record of the decisions and practices of the time when they were created. Some historians have treated landscapes as an extension of the archives, but for W.G. Hoskins, the English local historian who is perhaps the dean of the tradition of landscape history, archives are an extension of landscapes. In his masterpiece, *The Making of the English Landscape* (1955), he traces the development of

English field patterns and settlement forms, asks why various landscapes have come to assume the shape and appearance they now have, and 'why the hedgebanks and lanes of Devon should be totally different from those of the Midlands, why there are so many ruined churches in Norfolk or so many lost villages in Lincolnshire' (p. 13). So he sets himself the task of unravelling the complex scenes he encounters. Even the view from his room in his house in Oxfordshire 'contains in its detail something of every age from the Saxon to the nineteenth century' (p. 300). The omission of the twentieth century is significant in this, for while most of his investigations are undertaken with an admirable scholarly detachment, he cannot bring himself to say anything about the landscapes of this century—they actually repulse him. 'Since the year 1914 every single change in the English landscape has either uglified it or destroyed its meaning or both' (p. 298). So landscape history, like representational landscape art, seems to come to an end at the beginning of this century.

Figure 2.10: Landscape as a record of history. This winding, sunken road in Herefordshire was made some time before the parliamentary enclosures of the eighteenth and early-nineteenth centuries created the geometric fields which are now alongside it.

Aesthetic Townscape

The socially and politically neutral sense of landscape that prevails in Hoskins' work and in most geographical writings is found also in landscape studies that take a formalist and aesthetic approach. Gordon Cullen in his famous study of *Townscape* (1961) examines the qualities identifiable in the landscapes of towns, such as the sequence of views as one walks along a street, the enclosed and open spaces, the variety of signs and materials and textures. His interest is in the pleasures to be gained from a visual environment that has been well put together, and how to recognise and perhaps make such an environment. His bias is towards medieval, picturesque townscapes and, like Hoskins, he pours scorn on modern landscapes, especially those which are the result of planning.

Robert Venturi and his associates (1977), in tone and content not only a continent but several centuries away from Cullen, have surveyed the visual merits and defects of one of the great commercial strips of America, that of Las Vegas. Cullen uses precise black and white photographs and beautifully drawn ink sketches of the medieval townscapes he praises; Venturi uses colour photos, all sorts of maps and symbols and photo sequences, rough sketches, catchy language and half-explained diagrams, studio notes and cartoons to construct his investigation of commercial streetscape at its archetypal best (Figure 2.11). Yet his effort to look 'non-judgementally at the environment' (p. 3) has much in common with Cullen's approach to landscape. Certainly he challenges in dramatic fashion the historians' bias against the modern, but he nevertheless adopts an aesthetic approach that separates method from social values.[3] His concern is with grasping the character of landscape forms and with whatever may be visually appropriate, so that he can claim with equanimity that 'the analysis of a drive-in church in this context would match that of a drive-in restaurant' (p. 6) and can compare the space of supermarket parking lots with the spaces of Versailles. The approach adopted by Venturi and his co-authors recognises that people do get pleasure from pleasant or exciting landscapes, and that popular notions of what is pleasant or exciting do not necessarily conform to stale academic opinions which are probably lodged somewhere in the Renaissance. Their approach also encourages the development of a greater sensitivity to our visual surroundings, and can offer design proposals to enhance and make more attractive existing landscapes by means consistent with what is there now. Not avenues of trees along commercial strips, but better designs for fast-food outlets and shopping malls and service stations.

(a)

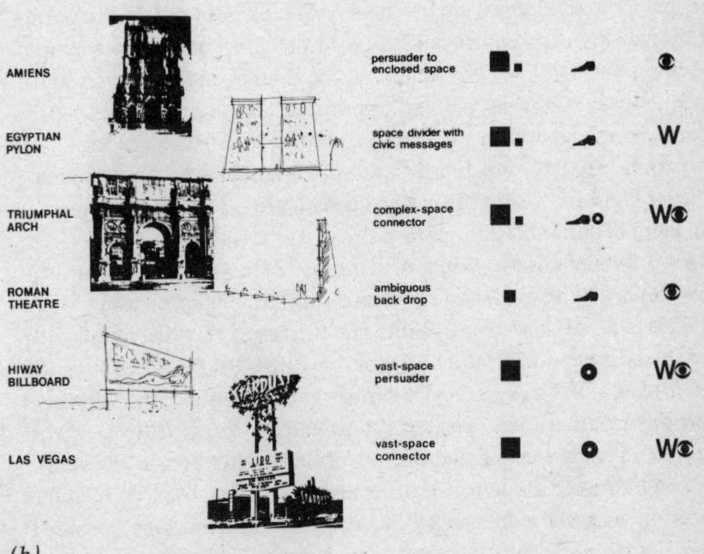

(b)

Figure 2.11: Aesthetic interpretations of landscape.
(a) Gordon Cullen (1961, p. 147) used pen-and-ink sketches of a village street to show how 'kinetic unity' can be destroyed by the improper use of lighting poles.
(b) Robert Venturi et al. *(1977, p. 17) used all sorts of devices in this attempt to analyse the visual impact of billboards and buildings.*

Ideological Interpretations of Landscape

The orthodoxy of disinterested interpretation that characterises the approach to landscape of many geographers, historians and architects has been challenged on the grounds that method cannot be so neatly divided from context, nor values from techniques, when dealing with the environments in which we live. Whatever methods of investigation are used, no matter how objective they may be, landscapes themselves are not neutral. Indeed to separate the forms of landscape from the motives of those who own and control them is to mask an essential reality and ignore important political issues. Thus Raymond Williams, in his study of *The Country and the City* (1975) as they have been treated in English prose and poetry, sees landscape primarily as an expression of property ownership and argues that the real history of the English countryside is centred on problems of property. The landscaped country estates and the aesthetic and humanistic sensibilities of eighteenth-century gentlemen and women were all very well, but these same people passed unseeing by the labourers whose toil and suffering was required to make those landscape gardens. It was not uncommon for houses and even parts of villages to be destroyed in order to contrive splendid views; Capability Brown, perhaps the best known and most admired of the landscape gardeners, removed parts of villages at Chatsworth, Audley End and Richmond Park, and even destroyed a village at Warwick Castle so that he could landscape both sides of the river there (Tunnard, 1978, p. 84).

'A working country', writes Williams (1975, p. 149), 'is hardly ever a landscape. The very idea of landscape implies separation and observation.' This is a strong truth. The origins of the idea of landscape lie in its separation from the hustle and bustle of daily life as something to be looked upon and painted. In most of its subsequent meanings and mutations landscape has been seen as something separate, to be admired, observed, modified, explained or interpreted. Williams uses the term very much in the eighteenth-century sense of a composed view, and separation was especially marked in that particular meaning because it involved both detached contemplation and the ownership of landscape gardens by the wealthy few. The concept of landscape has since changed and taken on less distinct associations with a ruling class, though the point that it is not just appearance, but an expression of the values of those who have the money and power to dictate the patterns of its forms, is no less true now than then.

This recognition requires that landscapes be understood not simply as more or less attractive scenes, nor as some neutral clue to culture, but from a politically committed attitude which looks for explanations in the demands and values of specific groups. Boris Pushkarev (1966, p. 88) has written that the environment does not automatically reflect a common denominator of cultural values in a society, but is shaped by relatively small groups professionally engaged in the field whose interests should be mediated by democratic processes to ensure that the highest possible standards are achieved. This ideal has not worked well, he suggests, because even these elite groups exercising their skills on behalf of the society as a whole are not sure of their own values and standards for beautiful landscapes. To resolve this uncertainty and so again to make attractive landscapes requires an intellectual effort to reunite technology and art, to re-establish the aesthetic standards of the designers.

Most writers taking an ideological position and recognising the role of elite groups in making landscapes have a far less charitable view of democratic process as it currently functions. Adopting a Marxist or socialist viewpoint they understand man-made landscapes to be expressions of vested interests which exploit the rest of the society. Landscapes for them are systems of signs and symbols that serve to impose the world-view of a dominant class as though it is the natural and inevitable way of things. For instance, this world-view may proclaim that the architecture and gardens of great country houses are beautiful and provide the standards to which we should all aspire, but ignore farm labourers' and miners' row-houses as having no architectural significance.

Paul Kurtz (1973), in a series of critical essays on modern American landscapes, argues that beauty cannot be seen in the objects of environment alone, but must always be related to the motives of those who made those objects. He wants to 'restore moral judgement to the aesthetic evaluation of built-environment' (p. 6) and this necessarily involves examining social consequences, motives and reasons as well as visible and tangible forms. In other words the world we see is the expression of deep and often subtle social and political processes, and if we wish to understand or change landscapes then we will have to consider the underlying social and political system.

The character of this system as it applies in Britain has been analysed by Theo Crosby in what was initially an exhibition and later a book called *How to Play the Environment Game* (1973). The game analogy is by no means as frivolous as it sounds, nor, I believe, is its appropriateness limited to Britain. At the risk of distortion by summary his

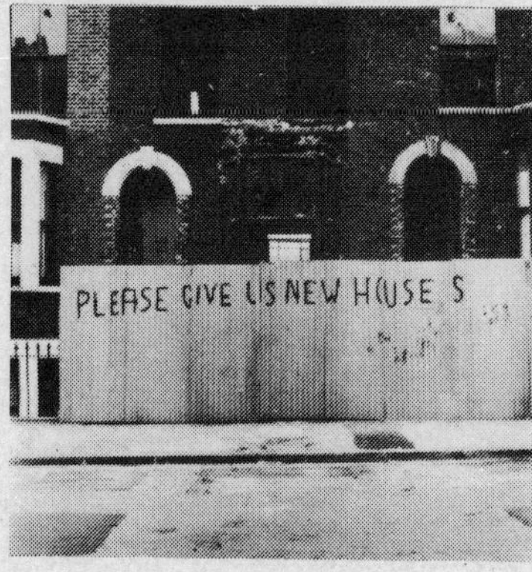

Figure 2.12: Ideological landscapes. Three examples of explicit ideology in landscape – 'Free Press, Free People' is in Red Wing, Minnesota, 1976; 'You can take it with you' was in suburban Toronto in 1979, but the sign has now been taken away; and 'Please give us new houses' is from Theo Crosby's book How to Play the Environment Game, *1973, p. 252.*

argument is this: Modern landscapes and built-environments include a substantial inheritance from the past, but are none the less continually changing. A number of interested parties, especially government and business, have stakes or investments in landscape and they react to any changes, first by using more or less technology according to whether they think technology is beneficial or harmful, second in order to preserve and perhaps increase their stakes. Several strategies are open to them—planning, taxation, lobbying, confrontation and so on, and these are applied to basic resources which include people, land, energy and food, according to rules of law, safety, habit and economics. So modern landscapes, as probably all former ones, are a dynamic and constantly changing expression of competing interests following more or less conventional strategies which are governed by limiting rules. Modern landscapes are above all an expression of the growing authority of those who hold the largest stakes, namely governments and large corporations. Individuals and communities are allowed only a minor role. This concentration of authority, Crosby suggests, is disguised by the seductions of consumerism and material comfort. The final message of *How to Play the Environment Game* is an encouragement to expose these seductions, confront authority, become obstructive and slow down change, and to participate actively in making the built-environments and landscapes in which we live.

In this instance, and in most of the recent political writing, the idea of landscape has gained a new set of meanings. Instead of being something separate and detached, to be viewed for its visual content and qualities, or for what it can tell us about our culture, it has become something with which we are actively involved. Landscape is the visual context of our lives. It has to matter to us because our social identity, perhaps even our personal identity, is bound up with it. In Crosby's account, as in that of Kurtz, this involvement is primarily a political one; they maintain in effect that we are responsible for our own landscapes and environments and if we neglect that responsibility, allow it to be taken from us by the agencies of government or by developers and business corporations, then we are abandoning part of our freedom. But behind, or perhaps within, this sense of political implication another involvement is inferred, an existential one which suggests that our very identity as individuals and as participants in a community are tied to our landscapes and to the places in which we live and work. Jacob Wasserman, a German novelist, has written of this (1947, p. 322): 'The landscape in which a person lives does not merely frame the picture. It enters his very being and becomes part of him.'

In this sense of a visual environment in which we are existentially and socially implicated the idea of landscape appears to have come almost full circle. It has lost much of the suggestion of detachment and separation which it acquired in the eighteenth century, it has lost its romantic association with natural and wild scenery, it has lost its landscape architecture connotation of manipulable open space. In this specific meaning, and it is of course only one among several current meanings, landscape is perhaps beginning to regain some sense of the particular settings and situations in which we are all necessarily and deeply involved in our everyday lives. And it is, of course, just such a feeling of implication that is apparent in the paintings made by Bruegel and others before the idea of landscape was even invented.

Landscape and Humanism: A Summary

'Landscape is an attractive, important and ambiguous term' Donald Meinig has written (1979, p. 1). Attractive because it conjures up pleasant images of scenes and views, important because it involves matters of professional interest and public concern, ambiguous because it is used in so many different ways. The fact is that in its four-hundred-year history the idea of landscape has taken on many meanings but left few behind, so that while there is some continuity in its sense it has acquired a cumbersome baggage of artistic, popular, technical and academic associations. Of course many of these ideas of landscape overlap and interpenetrate one another, so it is little wonder that the term is ambiguous. What is clear, however, is that it is quite impossible to take a simple dictionary definition of 'landscape' and make it universal. The word has a multiplicity of meanings and making sense of them depends mostly on the context in which it is being used.

The relationship between the ideas of landscape and the philosophical perspective of humanism has a similarly varied history, and one that is further complicated by the fact that it is largely implicit. The pictorial origins of landscape were contemporary with the development of Cartesian philosophy and the adulation of reason which is central to much humanism. Certainly the notion of landscape that prevailed in the eighteenth century was closely tied to a humanism which stressed the authority of human reason over nature. This attitude has been preserved in scientific, technical and some academic approaches to landscape up to the present day.

The romantic reaction against reason manifested itself in the formulation of a new concept of landscape as wild and picturesque scenery invested with spiritual forces. This was tied to a complex new humanism that embraced a desire for self-knowledge through spiritual experiences of nature, a recognition of the entire range of human feelings and emotions, and a sympathy for all of mankind. The development of the technical methods of landscape architecture, however, involved a return to detachment and rationality and an association with a paternalistic humanism which assumed that one's professional expertise could be used especially to improve the circumstances of those less fortunate than oneself.

Twentieth-century notions of landscape have a blend of all these attitudes of humanism. It now seems to be taken for granted that landscapes are primarily for the benefit and pleasure of men and women, that they can be understood by the application of disinterested human intelligence, and that they can and should be altered to meet better the needs of human beings. Above all the humanism involved in modern landscape is paternalistic and scientific -- research, and rational design and management techniques are used to improve the settings of our lives, to plan a rich variety of built- and natural environments, to accommodate all the requirements necessary for sound physical and mental health, and to provide all those other things that are 'conducive to the living of the whole, full life' (Simmonds, 1961, p. 200).

That there is a humanistic aim in landscape study and landscape making would not, I think, be generally questioned. There is, however, deep disagreement about how it should be achieved. There are those who maintain that landscapes are primarily aesthetic and that appropriate changes in forms and arrangements are all that is required to make them pleasant and conducive to the full life. This is a matter chiefly for the experts who know about such things. Conversely, there are those who argue that such changes can only be cosmetic; planting trees around nuclear power stations or landscaping the grounds of the head-offices of multinational corporations is like going to 'Elizabeth Arden for a cancer cure' (Nelson, 1977, p. 2). They maintain that landscapes, especially the landscapes of built-environments, cannot be understood apart from ethical and political considerations, for they are not merely scenes waiting for our passive appreciation but active declarations of the values of those who have authority over us. Landscapes must be engaged in and authority challenged.

This is a deep division of opinion. On the one side are the landscape neutralists and aesthetes who stand for reason, contemplation and the use of disinterested intelligence to explain and to improve the visual quality of human environments. On the other side are the landscape moralists and socialists who see landscape in ethical and political terms and capable of change only through committed thought and action. It was a similar problem which John Ruskin confronted over a hundred years ago when he wrote *Modern Painters*, though his specific task was to establish whether the pleasure to be gained from appreciation of landscapes and landscape paintings could be anything more than trivial and fleeting. He demonstrated to his satisfaction that it could indeed be something more than trivial, for landscape had a moral and spiritual value. The content of Ruskin's argument is not especially relevant here—much of it had to do with Turner's paintings—but the structure of it can be borrowed to attempt to resolve the division, or at least to decide between aesthetic landscape and political landscape.

There are three main elements in Ruskin's arguments which are important. First, he proposes that truth and beauty are quite distinct, though related, because truth has to do with statements and beauty with objects. In the context of landscapes this would mean that we can comment on appearance and yet imply nothing about the truth or honesty of a landscape. To assess truth requires some understanding of motives and intentions—'An artificial rose is not a false rose', he wrote. 'It is not a rose at all. The falseness is in the person who states or induces the belief that it is a rose' (Ruskin, 1856, vol. III, p. 35). So a dishonest landscape is one which pretends to be something which it is not—for instance a suburb masquerading as a Tudor village. And an honest landscape is one which makes no pretentious claims and is simply itself. But more important is that there is a grave dishonesty involved in representing something as other than itself, as unusual when it is ordinary, or as the greatest and best when it merely flatters the tastes of a few influential people. To avoid such dishonesty requires close observation and careful reporting of things as they are.

Secondly, Ruskin distinguishes 'great and mean art' according to its 'nobleness of end', and not because of its detail or skill or boldness (Ibid., p. 24). Great art has to do with love, admiration, joy or their opposites—hatred, horror and grief. We may not necessarily agree that these alone constitute nobleness of end, but that the intentions of the artists, or in this case of those making landscapes, are fundamental to our assessment of worth is indisputable. If someone's motives in making attractive and comfortable environments are primarily to make money for themselves or to display their present affluence conspicuously, it is difficult to see those environments as great human accomplishments (unless we too hope to make lots of money in the same way). Conversely, if someone's motives in making quite simple and crude places are primarily ethical and to improve or express the meaning of life, then those landscapes have 'nobleness of end'. It is rare, however, for motives and intentions to be quite so clear cut, and it is often difficult to impute such intentions from man-made forms—an architect with the best intentions may utterly lack the skill to translate them into reality. Nevertheless, the assessment of motives must be central to any understanding of landscape.

Thirdly, Ruskin observed that 'It is evident that a curiously balanced condition of the powers of the mind is necessary to induce full admiration of any scene' (Ibid., p. 309). Too little thought leads to a vacant and superficial experience; too much thought makes us forget the visible world around us. So in understanding landscapes we must try to balance our appreciation of forms and appearances with a knowledge both of their implications and consequences, and of the motives of their owners and makers. Thus the country houses of England are attractive despite the facts that their origins are based in the exploitation of rural labourers and their styles are an expression of authority and wealth. It is entirely possible to enjoy the appearance of a landscape and yet to deplore the circumstances of its making and the oppression it represents. Similarly one may detest the ugliness in a soot-grey townscape of row houses but be in total sympathy with the needs and values of the people who make their lives there. Certainly there is an ambivalence in such attitudes, but many landscapes are themselves ambivalent and paradoxical. There is nothing to be gained by denying or suppressing this; indeed that would take us into exactly the sort of falseness which Ruskin condemns, for we would be denying the evidence of our own senses. Rather we should seek this 'curiously balanced condition of the powers of the mind' and acknowledge both our feelings and our thoughts about landscapes, even if they are contradictory.

In May of 1854 Ruskin was in Amiens and while there he went for a long walk along the banks of the River Somme. In his diary he mentions how vivid the spring flowers were against the blackness of a dyer's back-yard who had been dying black all day, he comments on the fearful houses of rotting timber, the filthy stream, a flamboyant Gothic church. These were 'all exquisitely picturesque, and no less miserable . . . As I looked today at the unhealthy face and melancholy mien of the man in the boat pushing his load of peats along the ditch and of the people, men as well as women, who sat spinning gloomily at their cottage doors, I could not help feeling how many suffering persons must pay for my picturesque subject and happy walk' (1856, vol. IV, pp. 11-12n). It is always pleasant to look upon attractive scenes, but their social and moral implications matter too. There are no simple ways to understand and appreciate landscapes, no neat categories into which all our thinking and evaluations can fit. Any landscape can be understood and experienced in countless different ways. It is in some measure an historical document, a demonstration of social and ecological processes, an expression of authority and of time and money committed, and a comment on the values of the culture of which it is a part. To consider landscape from any of these perspectives is justifiable. But above all landscape is the visual context of human existence and therefore partakes of all the subtleties, possibilities and ambiguities of human life. In every beautiful place there is some sadness and suffering, and in every ugly landscape there are signs of hope and happiness.

Notes

1. The development and main types of humanism are considered more completely in Part Two of this book. In this chapter I am concerned only with the main forms of humanism as they have overlapped with ideas about landscape.

2. Like all generalisations this statement can be argued. Bruegel's field sketches and drawings often appear to be accurate topographical representations without human figures. Furthermore, many of the Dutch landscape painters of the following century did mix and match their scenes. All of which merely indicates that this change in style about 1600 was not a completely unanticipated revolution and that there was some continuity in both style and subject matter.

3. These sorts of criticisms of Venturi's work are addressed briefly by one of his co-authors, Denise Scott-Brown, in the preface to a revised edition (1977, p. xv). She thinks they are unfair, perhaps because the Las Vegas study represents a remarkable attempt to grasp the character of a modern landscape in its own terms and one cannot be expected to do everything. She refers to an article which elaborates this rebuttal but does not say where it is published. In any case judging solely from the book, which is all I have to go on, *Learning from Las Vegas* is not a social and political statement, but an aesthetic one.

3 THE CHARACTER OF MODERN LANDSCAPES

At the beginning of the twentieth century, after three hundred years of enchantment with it, artists and poets suddenly abandoned landscape. They ceased to be interested in imitating and representing its forms and appearances and began to experiment with abstractions of the essential qualities of whatever they experienced. Kenneth Clark (1949, pp. 131-43) suggests that this was because there was 'a common impulse' that the old approaches had been worked out, and also because traditional notions about the order and unity of the universe had been undermined. Landscape had quite simply become too obvious to warrant serious attention, it offered no challenge to the imagination when compared with the microscopic and macroscopic worlds of elements and forces which were being revealed by scientists. Of course the fact that partists were no longer interested did not mean that the idea of landscape had completely lost its value—it has persisted in various professional and academic meanings and in the popular sense of pleasant scenery. Nevertheless, the sudden disappearance of landscape as a serious subject in art does suggest that there was a contemporaneous and significant change either in the character of actual man-made environments or in the cultural attitudes and processes of landscape-making.

I believe that in the first two decades of the twentieth century there were indeed dramatic shifts in the technologies, cultural attitudes and aesthetic fashions of the Western world. The result has been that modern landscapes—those made in the twentieth century—are qualitatively distinct from their predecessors. They differ in function, in meaning and, most obviously, in appearance. It is therefore entirely appropriate to write and speak of modern landscape as a distinct and coherent category which demands its own modes of description and interpretation.

What is less clearly the case is that in spite of their distinctiveness, these modern landscapes are an expression of attitudes similar to the paternalistic humanism which emerged as part of the nineteenth-century reform movements, and which are an extension of the Enlightenment faith in the powers of human reason. Such attitudes are manifest in continuing attempts everywhere to improve efficiency of operation and production, and in the expanding use of professional expertise to solve problems of human environments. However, it is not easy to recognise these attitudes and processes of rationalism and humanism at work in modern landscapes, nor to grasp their subtleties and intricacies, except by the close investigation of particular situations. I take only two cases here—the landscapes of fast-food and of suburban housing. Both are considered with specific reference to Toronto, but there can be little doubt that they are widely representative because the procedures used to make and maintain these landscapes are well-nigh universal. There are many other examples that would illustrate these procedures equally well, for example the cityscapes of high-rise offices, international airports, shopping malls and new towns all reflect in various ways the current pressures for efficiency and control. But such examples would add only details to the central arguments of the case studies of fast-food and suburban development which establish that modern landscape-making with its relentless rationalism denies feelings, ignores ethics and minimises the responsibility of individuals for the environments in which they live.

It is paradoxical that while analytic and rational methods of research, organisation and planning have been demonstrably beneficial, for they have helped to improve living standards and to increase material well-being, they have also resulted in the creation of landscapes which are frequently judged to be inhumane or dehumanising. In fact such judgements are quite wrong—but not because modern landscapes are without deficiencies. They are wrong because those deficiencies, cloaked though they are by comfort and convenience, are the product of too much rationalism and an excess of humanism.

The Distinctiveness of Modern Landscapes

A danger in isolating the age in which one lives for special consideration is that it opens the way to charges of bias towards the present and of insufficient awareness of historical continuities. In the instance of modern landscapes there is undeniably an enormous inheritance from before 1900, but the forms and materials of this inherited landscape are quite different from those which are now used. Craft techniques and social hierarchies which had existed for generations have come to play only a minor role in landscape-making. Country houses have become tourist attractions open to the general public, folk houses are preserved in architectural museums, while office buildings, power stations, fast-food outlets and microwave transmission towers are constructed in materials and to serve functions that were inconceivable a mere century ago. Susanne Langer (1966, pp. 43-5) has argued that in the industrial revolution and subsequently the invention of materials, products and methods of production has been associated with abrupt shifts in design and with the emergence of unfamiliar forms for everything from kitchen utensils to bridges. In the course of a single life-time there was a change from horse-drawn carriages to automobiles, from steam engines to nuclear power stations. 'We are witnessing', she claims, 'the transition from one order of human existence to another.'

It is undoubtedly the case that in the last hundred years the appearance of many everyday objects has been transformed—consider clothing styles, bathrooms and kitchens, highways and store-front signs. But landscapes, it could be argued, are many-layered records of history, manifestations of the continuities of culture and cumbersome in their overall response to change. A landscape does not respond to short-term swings in fashion as do automobile and clothing styles (except in so far as these are part of landscape), nor does it have a clear historical beginning like steam engines and electricity. Landscapes none the less reflect larger scale modifications in technology and philosophical outlook, and hence record major discontinuities in cultural history. These discontinuities are, of course, relative—a speeding up in the rate of change and the breakdown of established patterns and traditions.

Such a discontinuity occurred early in this century. It did not happen spontaneously, but was the culmination of the industrial and economic developments of the Victorian Era. Methods of mass production for textiles, iron, even bread, had been invented and refined; a mechanised and capitalistic system of production had been introduced; exploitation of the working population had attained cruel excesses and had already been countered in part by social and political reforms. Radical changes had, in fact, been underway for decades and as early as the 1850s Ruskin had written that the age he lived in was quite distinct from its predecessors. It was both dark in a literal sense—'we build brown brick walls and wear brown coats' (1856, vol. III, p. 275); and in a more fundamental sense—'Man *was* invariably sensible of the existence of gods . . . *Now* he is capable of going through life with hardly any positive idea of this subject—doubting, fearing, suspecting, analysing—doing everything, in fact, but believing.' (Ibid., p. 164.)

Perhaps so, but such deep transformations were for long hidden by habits of practice and thought and by revivals of medieval and Renaissance ideals. Wrought iron and brick were moulded into floral designs copied from the middle ages, railway stations were made to look like ancient cathedrals and the churches flourished even as belief waned. What happened shortly after 1900 was that the profound changes that had been slowly working for the better part of the nineteenth century found an appropriate aesthetic expression – a clean and unornamented style that reflected the properties of the new materials, machines and energy sources. At the same time the products themselves began to become available and affordable to a much larger segment of the population than hitherto. This was the beginning of what Reyner Banham (1960), an architectural historian, has called evocatively 'The First Machine Age'; an age characterised by the reduction of machines to a human scale and by their introduction to the home; an age in which for the first time machines became constant and necessary companions for human beings. The techniques of mass production *by* machines had suddenly been translated into the mass consumption *of* machines, and of all the other consumer goods that were now being mass-produced.

Reyner Banham is quite specific in dating this cultural revolution around 1912, and perhaps for his particular concerns with architectural history this is valid. But from the larger perspective of cultural landscape it is the entire period from 1900 to 1920 that is important, with the First World War – the first machine war – capping the social and economic and other changes of the preceding years and making them irreversible. In those years Einstein formulated and published his general and specific theories of relativity, thus transcending the Newtonian conceptions of the universe that had held sway for two centuries; Picasso painted his first cubist pictures, Marcel Duchamp exhibited his ready-mades in New York and Paris, and so a half millenium of imitative and representational art was left behind; the Wright Brothers flew the first aeroplane; Marconi sent radio messages; F.W. Taylor formulated the principles of scientific management for more efficient industrial operations; and Henry Ford introduced the assembly line into his automobile factory. Furthermore, many of these inventions and transformations reached all levels of society rather than being claimed by some aristocratic or affluent elite for exclusive uses. The mail order catalogues for 1900 were filled with quaint Victorian objects covered in floral designs and geared to an age of horses and coal; an equivalent catalogue for 1920 included talking machines (phonographs), radios, electric irons, toasters and washing machines, spare parts for automobiles and many of the accoutrements of daily life that are now taken for granted.

The new aesthetic evolved rapidly, in part self-consciously through the work and writing of artists and architects, in part unselfconsciously through modifications in industrial design. The self-conscious changes are carefully traced by Banham in his book *Theory and Design in the First Machine Age* (1960). It appears that in the first years after 1900 a number of European architects had begun to design buildings, especially industrial buildings, that employed the new materials of steel, glass and concrete in a very straightforward manner which seemed appropriate to the industrial activities which they housed. The principle that was developed in association with the design of these was explicitly stated by the Austrian architect and journalist Adolf Loos in 1908 in his maxim that 'the evolution of culture marches with elimination of ornament from useful objects' (cited in Banham, 1960, p. 94). In other words all decoration, all surface carving and painting and pattern were henceforth considered superfluous.

This set the tone for the new aesthetic. It was forcefully complemented in the ideas enunciated in the famous Foundation Manifesto of the Futurist movement that was published in 1908. This dismissed unequivocally all antiquarianism and backward-looking attitudes while extolling everything progressive, new and oriented to the future. The author, an Italian poet Fillipo Tomaso Marinetti, claimed that there had been a clean break with the past and he lauded the beauty of speed, the works of industry, the splendour of the masses; he praised automobiles, locomotives and 'the easy flight of aeroplanes, their propellors beating the wind like banners, with a sound like the applause of a mighty crowd' (cited in Banham, 1960, p. 104). Marinetti and Loos and their many contemporary admirers ushered in a modern attitude and style. Previously artists, architects and designers had looked to the past for inspiration; now, and for the first time, they looked to the future.

Still this philosophy did not achieve a full and coherent expression until it was realised in the works of the Bauhaus in the 1920s. The Bauhaus was an enormously innovative and influential school of art and design which involved distinguished artists and architects like Paul Klee, Walter Gropius and Mies van der Rohe, as well as furniture and textile designers, typographers and others. It began in 1919 under the direction of Gropius as an attempt to blend all these interests and to integrate the new machine technologies with the design qualities of craftsmanship. By 1923 this philosophy was seen to be impracticable and was replaced by a more realistic one which sought to create revitalised designs for an age of industrial technology. These designs were characterised especially by simplicity in outline and by clean and undecorated surfaces and forms. In 1925 the school moved into a new building in Dessau (the building itself also being called the Bauhaus), which had been designed by Gropius and which constitutes one of the clearest expressions of the Bauhaus style as well as being one of the most important buildings in the development of twentieth-century architecture. It was a complex of interpenetrating cubes of steel frames and glass that were meant to be walked around and experienced dynamically rather than seen from a single viewpoint (Figure 3.1). The

Figure 3.1: The Bauhaus, Dessau, 1925. In its rejection of stylistic imitation and ornament, and in its use of the new materials of glass and steel, the Bauhaus was one of the chief initiators of the principles of design that have dominated twentieth-century architecture. (Source: Gropius, 1935?, facing page 44)

building was a rejection of stylistic imitation and ornamental frippery, a demonstration of the qualities of the new architecture which Gropius was to describe a few years later as 'simple and sharply modelled designs in which every part merges naturally into the comprehensive volume of the whole' and in which walls are thrown open to admit fresh air, daylight and sunshine (Gropius, 1935?, p. 44).

This building is but one of countless influences on modern design that derive from the Bauhaus. Through its students and teachers the style of the Bauhaus has reached into almost every corner of our lives—chairs, cups, typefaces, office buildings, light shades, city plans—practically everything that we might casually refer to as 'functional' owes something to these designers (Figure 3.2). However Gropius cautions that functional is far too simplistic a description for designs which in their honesty to materials sought to achieve 'a satisfaction of the human soul which is a part of the unity of life' (Gropius, 1955, p. 62). Whatever is the case, by the time of its dissolution in 1932 the Bauhaus had effectively managed to invent and to popularise design forms which corresponded to the changes in aesthetic philosophy and in technology that had occurred in the first two decades of the century.

While the members of the Bauhaus were trying to conceive relevant designs for the modern age the new technologies were already changing the face of the landscapes of Europe and North America. The labour-saving domestic machines required electricity from generating stations that was sent along transmission corridors. Designs for these were often little more than straightforward engineering solutions to immediate problems, and when the designs were successful they have often persisted, for instance the pylons now used scarcely differ from those introduced about 1910. In America innovations in steel frame construction, elevator and heating technology, accompanied by various social and economic changes in cities, had made possible and worthwhile the construction of skyscrapers. Up until 1916 these were given various ornate neo-classical or Second Empire styles, albeit elongated, but thereafter were built in a relatively plain and unadorned manner. This may have been because the cost of carving the ornaments became prohibitive, but since nobody could see all the intricate details twenty or thirty storeys above street level they really were redundant. As this change in skyscraper style was taking place the first freeway, the Bronx River Parkway, was being constructed on the northern edge of New York City. Conceived in 1907 and constructed between 1910 and 1922 this was intended for recreational driving (hence 'parkway'). It established the fact that motor vehicles require their own special facilities and roads that are graded and curved for automobile speeds (Tunnard and Pushkarev, 1963, pp. 161-2). But while the development of skyscrapers,

Figure 3.2: Designs by the various members of the Bauhaus have infiltrated every area of modern life and landscape. These are product designs which were adopted as models for mass production, 1922-8; and working-class apartments at Dessau designed by Walter Gropius, 1928. (Source: Gropius, 1935?, facing pp. 33, 72)

expressways and other innovations has historical significance these were for the most part localised events. It was not until the new electrical and gasoline technologies began to filter down to the middle and lower classes that widespread effects on landscape began to be apparent. This happened in the 1920s and 1930s.

In 1928 Clough Williams-Ellis published his polemic on the destruction of the English landscape, *England and the Octopus.* To this he had an appendix titled 'A Devil's Dictionary' in which he listed alphabetically the things he found most offensive in terms of their landscape quality. His list includes Advertisements (billboards), Airfields, Archaeologists and Antiquaries (who are dangerous because they extol the past), Automobile Association, Broadcasting facilities such as radio towers, Borough Engineers, Bungalows, Electric Power Distribution Facilities, Golf-courses, Oxford and Cambridge (as symbols of academic insensitivity to landscape), Parkways, Petrol Pumps and Standardisation which appeared to be reducing diversity. What is particularly striking about this list is that many of these items are still widely commented upon and criticised, yet thirty years before Williams-Ellis was writing many of them had not existed. In other words, by the late 1920s the landscape manifestations of the First Machine Age had become sufficiently widespread to be perceived as a major threat to the identity of the English scene.

In America a similar impact was taking place. In the mid-1930s a survey of a 47-mile stretch of highway between Newark and Trenton in New Jersey counted 300 gasoline stations, 472 billboards, 400 other commercial uses and 165 intersections (Tunnard and Pushkarev, 1963, p. 162). This was the period of full mechanisation, of the general adoption of the new domestic machines, and of the first appearance of the undesirable consequences of these, such as roadside blight and the initial phase of twentieth-century suburban growth. Thus is was that by 1940 the landscape inherited from the nineteenth century had been deeply reworked and transformed into the landscape of the First Machine Age.

Yet this too has been changed. Reyner Banham claims that the 'cultural revolution that took place in 1912 has been superseded, but it has not been reversed' (1960, p. 12). It has been superseded because the First Machine Age, based as it was on electrical and gasoline power and the reduction of machines to a domestic scale, has passed into a Second Machine Age, based on domestic electronics and the products of synthetic chemistry. There is now scarcely a household in the Western world that has neither television set, transistor radio nor pocket calculator, and which does not have countless things made of plastics, man-made fabrics, detergents, foods with additives and preservatives. The effects of all this on landscapes are not clear except for the obvious forms of chemical plants and television aerials. In fact many of the consequences may be impossible to perceive directly. Just as the visible pollution of the nineteenth century—smoke and effluent from coal powered factories—has given way to invisible pollution—nuclear wastes and microwaves and DDT—so the influence of the Second Machine Age on landscapes has become increasingly subtle and imperceptible. Thus far it is the small things of life that have been obviously revolutionised, and changes in the larger environmental patterns are not yet evident.

The development of plastics, antibiotics, computers and televisions may mark the qualitative differences between the First and Second Machine Ages, but the period since the Second World War has also seen a quantitative change in the impacts of modernism. It is these quantitative extensions of processes that were already at work in the 1930s which are most important in terms of the present-day landscape. What has happened is that an electrical, mobile life-style has become available for everyone, virtually regardless of social status or economic class. Even the officially designated poor live in high-rise apartment buildings with central heating, a full range of electrical appliances and television. Car ownership is taken for granted; motorways, expressways, freeways, have been constructed in nation-wide networks; office buildings of steel and glass have risen in most city centres; the rapid increase in air traffic has required the construction of vast new airports and, in North America, about half of the total population lives in automobile-oriented suburbs built since 1945. And all these developments have occurred, furthermore, under the steady and all-seeing gaze of professional designers, planners and administrators. Of course there has been careful planning at other times in history, but there has never before been the extensive yet minute bureaucratic planning that is a fact of the Second Machine Age.

So the built-environments and man-made landscapes of the twentieth century stand sharply apart from those of previous ages. Writing specifically of architecture, but expressing ideas that are equally relevant for landscape as a whole, Walter Gropius (1955, p. 61) declared that 'a breach has been made with the past which enables us to envisage a new aspect of architecture corresponding to the technical civilisation of the age we live in; the morphology of dead styles has been destroyed and we are returning to honesty of thought and feeling'.

The landscapes in which most people now live, work and relax are distinctively different from any landscapes that were made in the past. To this extent I agree with Gropius. Whether we are returning to an honesty of thought I am less sure. If by that he meant that designs are subject to deliberate and rational analysis then this is indeed so; but if he meant that materials and functions are no longer disguised by stylistic pretensions and subterfuges then that is sometimes the case and sometimes not. Many modern landscapes are almost too painfully honest—oil refineries and expressways and international airports can hardly be contrived or given a facade; but new landscapes also have their share of restorations, reconstructions and copies, and even when these are charming they are lies. However, of a return to feeling I find virtually no evidence in modern landscape. In fact it seems that feeling has been removed with an almost surgical precision and its excision then cleverly disguised by contrivances of mood and emotion and the achievements of efficiency. Of this there is ample, though often subtle, evidence in the landscapes associated with fast-food and suburban housing.

Fast-Food and Factory Farming

At one of McDonald's restaurants in suburban Toronto there is a playground—McDonaldland—with larger than life-size models of the characters from the television commercials, Mayor McCheese, Ronald McDonald, the Hamburglar, and so on. Children get very excited when they see this playground, no doubt the bright colours and exotic characters suggest all sorts of adventures. For several minutes the newcomers leap onto the various pieces of play equipment, climb the towers, go down the slides. Then they seem to discover that there is nothing special in any of it, just the usual swings and slides with McDonald characters stuck on the top. As the hopes and expectations meet reality there are signs of disappointment, tears of frustration or quarrels to get on the equipment. The promise of magic and fantasy is suddenly denied; the playground offers no scope for exploration or creativity, the nice green ground-surface turns out to be indoor-outdoor carpeting over asphalt and there is a ten-feet high chain-link fence to protect the illusions of McDonaldland from real vandals (Figure 3.3).

For a long time I believed that McDonaldland epitomised everything to do with commercial strip development. In its brightness and its suggestion of fantasy that is not realised, in its superficial gloss to disguise

Figure 3.3: McDonaldland, Eglinton Avenue, Toronto, 1980

a very ordinary product, in its intimations of adventure and freedom that barely obscure a precise and rigid organisation, and especially in its obvious and seductive appeal for purely commercial ends – in all of these McDonaldland represented all the other enterprises of the strip. I thought that what was required for making more attractive and sensitive landscapes was a mollification of commercial attitudes and a greater concern for the details and subtleties of human behaviour.

I now realise that this interpretation was far too naive. The design of many of the buildings in commercial strips is of the highest quality, and environments like McDonaldland are honest attempts to provide fun. In particular the fast-food restaurants meet a real demand for convenience. Criticisms of modern commercial strip landscapes which are concerned only with appearances and arrangements must inevitably miss the point. These landscapes are merely the superficial manifestations of attitudes and processes that lie deep within not only North American culture but the cultures of all industrial and commercial societies.

Landscapes of Fast-Food Chains

At dusk on a commercial strip the signs of gas stations, automobile dealerships and fast-food outlets stand out vividly against the graying sky. The sight is always a dramatic one, especially from a moving automobile. The heraldic yellow and green of BP, the red, white and blue oval of Esso or Exxon, the benign face of Colonel Saunders revolving on its bucket, the curvaceous yellow arches of McDonald's which declare mysteriously 'Over Thirty Billion Served'. These glow evenly and cleanly in their primary acrylic colours. The flickering neon of the 1950s has already gone. The signs, the building styles, are new and precise, and any untidiness disappears into the gathering dark.

In full daylight some of this drama is lacking. The signs though still bright, no longer hang apparently unsuspended against the sky but stand on inelegant poles or rusty footings; unused spaces, garbage cans and litter on the ground all become obvious. Criticisms which maintain that these sorts of strips are 'whole strings of places, competing, clamouring, blasting your eye for attention' (Kurtz, 1973, p. 10) make more sense in daylight. There is little visual order, and if you are unfortunate enough to be out of a vehicle then the noise and smell of traffic and the windy openness of it all can be quite distressing. Yet the individual buildings are not so easily criticised. Fast-food outlets in particular have been designed to offer a wholesome and neat appearance to potential customers, and they are usually well maintained and frequently

Figure 3.4: Dyspeptic design does not promote sales: a carefully landscaped McDonald's outlet, Eglinton Avenue, Toronto, 1980.

landscaped with shrubs and flowers (Figure 3.4). Dyspeptic design does not promote sales.

This concern for attractiveness of outlets is a relatively recent development among the fast-food chains. The blatant 'look-at-me' or 'plonk-me-down-anywhere' styles are being replaced. In the new designs the whole package is considered carefully – the building itself both inside and outside, the landscaping, the signs and, in city centres at least, relationship to other buildings are all taken into account (*Restaurant Business*, March 1979, p. 136). In keeping with the design trends of the 1970s and 1980s most of the major chains have developed designs which are distinctive yet adaptable and muted, usually with brick and wood and shingles on the exterior. Interiors are efficient and clean and often have suggestions of a rather exaggerated kind of domesticity – carpeted floors, paintings on the walls, antiques. The recently constructed outlets for any of the major fast-food chains are not all identical though they do have a consistency in style. And they are certainly not garish and vulgar, but rather exemplars of that type of modern design which combines niceness, cleanliness, comfortable convenience and efficiency. However, since only ten chains in North America account for about half the total sales of 240 food chains

(Figure 3.5) the consistently designed outlets and uniform signs of these seem to be everywhere. They either reassure us with familiar symbols and products or annoy because they are apparently placeless and inescapable.

Chain	Numbers of units	Sales in millions of dollars
McDonald's	5747	5385
Kentucky Fried Chicken	5444	1669
Burger King	2439	1463
Wendy's	1818	1000
Dairy Queen	4860	926
Pizza Hut	3846	829
Big Boy	1100	750
Hardee's	1231	750
Arby's	928	430
Howard Johnson's	867	425
Total of top ten chains	28,280	13,627
Total of top 240 chains	59,928	24,591

Figure 3.5: The Top Ten Fast-food Chains. The figures include both US and international sales and units. (Source: Restaurant Business, *1 March 1980, p. 130)*

The merit of the fast-food chains is that they offer prepared food of consistent quality at reasonable prices. Though this food has been criticised for its blandness and poor nutritional value (criticisms denied, of course, by the chains) it is apparently what people want. In 1978 about 36 cents of every dollar Americans spent on food they spent in restaurants, and of this about 30 cents went to fast-food chains. It is expected in the industry that the expenditure on fast-food will rise to about 50 cents of the food dollar by the late 1980s, though competition from cook-at-home convenience foods sold in supermarkets may make this estimate unrealistically high. In short, whatever arguments may be made against fast-food there is no denying either its popularity, or that through powerful promotional campaigns and the development of drive-in, drive-to and drive-thru outlets of great visual prominence, fast-food has become a central trait of modern culture.

The restaurants with their signs are the most obvious aspect of the landscape of fast-food. They are, after all, meant to be seen. But none of them would exist were it not for highly efficient procedures of factory farming and the landscapes of broiler houses and feed lots. In these visual quality is of little concern, it is efficiency and maximum production per unit input that matters.

It is through investigating these procedures that it becomes clear that the costs of convenient fast-food are not so much economic and aesthetic as ethical. Behind the facade of pleasantly designed outlets lies the scientific production and systematic extermination of countless millions of steers and chickens. There is nothing brutal and malevolent in this. It is all done efficiently and with due concern for sanitary conditions and the quality of the meat product. It is also one of the consequences and manifestations of those attitudes of scientific humanism, or rationalism used to benefit human ends, which pervade modern Western culture.

An Example: Barbecued Chicken and the Broiler Industry

'Swiss Chalet' is a small Canadian restaurant chain which specialises in barbecued chicken and caters mainly to people between 25 and 40 years old. Its buildings are conservatively designed on a vaguely Alpine theme, with heavy timbers and gently sloping roof. The Swiss theme is not some contrived promotion but a reflection of the fact that the founder was a Swiss immigrant to Canada.

The fifteen Swiss Chalet outlets in Toronto consume about 30,000 chickens a week, or 1,500,000 chickens a year.[1] Since in North America there are about 5,500 Kentucky Fried Chicken outlets plus many smaller fried and barbecued chicken chains, at the Swiss Chalet rate of use the total annual consumption of chickens by these chains must be close to 1,000,000,000. This sort of consumption has been permitted only by the development of intensive poultry production techniques. Although these have served to meet food demands in general, they have been developed especially to meet the needs of the fast-food industry and its specific demands for consistency in the quality and size of chicken pieces (US Department of Agriculture, 1970, p. 58). In 1934 broiler chickens—those 7-10 weeks old—accounted for only 3.7 per cent of all chickens consumed in the United States; in 1976 they comprised 93.3 per cent of the consumption. This was made possible by a shift from many small barnyard flocks to a 'highly integrated, efficient industry' in which the eggs are hatched in incubators and the chickens are raised in 'windowless sheds under artificial lights' (US Department of Agriculture, 1977, pp. 1, 2, 44). In 1950 it took twelve to fourteen weeks to raise a broiler chicken, now it not only takes seven to eight weeks and this reduced time has been accompanied by a reduction in the conversion ratio of feed to weight of chicken from 4 to 1 in 1940 to about 2 to 1 in 1979.

Figure 3.6: The innocuous and sanitary exterior of a broiler chicken farm; there is even a cheerful chicken logo. Oldbury, Gloucestershire, 1980.

This remarkable increase in productivity has been achieved by skillful organisation and by the development of high energy diets. The chickens are housed at high densities in cages or sheds. An advertisement for the 'Tri-Deck Cage' system suggests the following possibilities: at an occupancy of four birds per 12 inch by 20 inch cage each bird has 60 square inches of floor space, or in a 16 inch by 20 inch cage six birds can be kept at 53.3 square inches per bird. In a three-tiered row about 250 feet long (the shortest they propose) there can therefore be as many as 24,000 birds. Using fully automated systems of feeding it is possible for one person to tend as many as 70,000 chickens.

In the first few weeks of life the birds are kept under continuous bright light since this encourages feeding and weight gain; thereafter the lights are turned on and off at two hour intervals since chickens are inclined to eat more after sleeping. Various drugs and chemicals are added automatically to the water supply to promote growth and reduce the incidence of disease, which spreads easily at these densities. A further problem with high densities is that the chickens often attack one another, thereby damaging skins and reducing meat quality. This is prevented by debeaking the birds at an early age—the top beak is clipped off.

When the chickens have grown enough to meet market requirements they are taken to the packers for slaughtering and evisceration. They are usually starved for a day before slaughtering for this makes evisceration cleaner and does not affect the weight of the bird. The killing and packing process is almost entirely a mechanical one: the live chickens enter at one end of the plant, are hung on a conveyor belt by their legs, killed, scalded, plucked, washed, eviscerated, decapitated, graded, packaged and shipped to the stores (Figure 3.7).

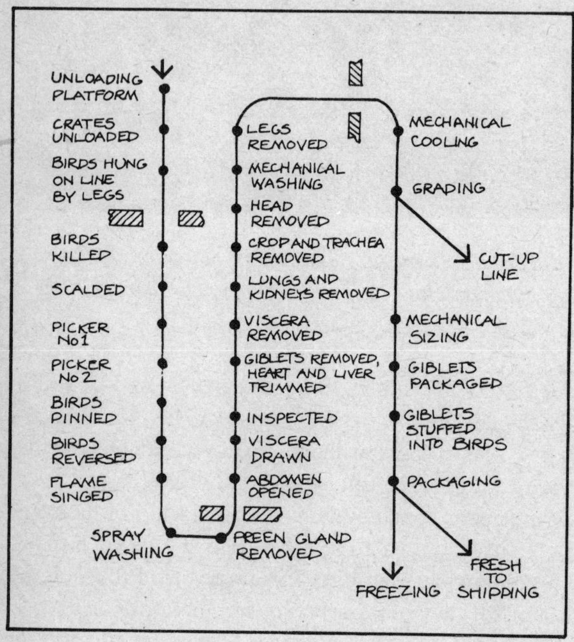

Figure 3.7: The sequence of operations in a chicken-packing plant. (Source: redrawn from Moncrieff and Rizvi, 1974)

Commentary: Animals as Machines for Human Use

The modern broiler chicken industry is efficient, based on scientific research and the development of precise techniques for feeding, disease control and management. It has kept the cost of chicken meat relatively low, and has led to a marked rise in the *per capita* consumption of chicken since 1950. In the production of beef and pork and other meats similar procedures have been instituted and have also led to great increases in productivity. In terms of all the criteria of efficiency —cost, total quantities produced, conversion ratios, consistency of the produce quality—these have been remarkable achievements. Yet there is another perspective from which to consider them.

Writing in 1940, when all these changes were just starting, the American essayist and sometime farmer E.B. White (1966, p. 127) suggested that 'The farm as a way of life has been subordinated to the farm as a device for making money. Somewhere along the line the thread has been lost; somewhere in the process of introducing vitamins and electric time-switches into his henhouse the farmer has missed the point of the egg.' The point is, presumably, that the egg represents a life, and therefore has a right to existence or at the very least to some small measure of respect. Instead it has been reduced to a mere thing, an element in a complex process governed by the dictates of efficiency. A chicken for Swiss Chalet or a steer for McDonald's has no more ethical status than a Sony television set or a Ford car. It is simply a machine for converting low-value feedstuff into high-value meat. It is produced and consumed and forgotten.

Sitting in the air-conditioned, quasi-domestic comfort of a fast-food restaurant contemplating one's uniformly-browned quarter-chicken and french fries, it is easy to forget the processes by which the food has reached the table. Birds in cages so small they cannot spread their wings or stretch their necks, behavioural control, growth-promoting chemicals and debeaking seem remote even if we know about them. And in any case such practices are required if we are to have our inexpensive and convenient meal; they are not so much cruel as efficient and necessary.

Since about 1970 several academic philosophers have been writing about the moral status of animals (e.g. Singer, 1975). They have levelled sharp criticisms at factory farming (and the use of animals in scientific research), criticisms that are doubly significant here because they are also condemnations of certain kinds of humanism. The basic question they raise is this: while science has made it possible to treat animals as objects, does this also mean we have the right to treat them thus and deny their lives and being?

The gulf between animals and men that allows us to treat animals as things is, Michael Peters argues (1972, p. 229), a feature of a particular kind of society that has developed since the Age of Reason. Ours is a society in which human reason has been arrogated to a position of supreme importance; man has a unique liberty while the rest of nature is conceived mechanically, as law-governed, or 'as material for our scheming' (Clark, 1977, p. 7). Such attitudes have a clear basis in the philosophical meditations of Descartes, for he argued that animals are automata: 'they do not have a mind, and . . . it is nature which acts in them according to the disposition of their organs, as one sees that a clock, which is made up of only wheels and springs, can count the hours and measure time' (1637, *Discourse* 5, pp. 75-6). This view was not accepted unquestioningly at the time, Voltaire at least took issue with it, but it accorded well with the development of science and industry and in due course was generally adopted. It offers a philosophical justification for the packing plants of the nineteenth century and for the factory farms of the twentieth century.

The implication of the Cartesian argument is this. By defining animals as machines, lacking mind or soul, human behaviour toward them and treatment of them is freed of all ethical concerns. Instead, an attitude of detachment and neutrality can be adopted, like that of a physicist contemplating matter or a miner digging coal. Thus the life and the death of animals can be mechanised without remorse or qualm because they are only objects which happen to be able to move. In *Mechanisation Takes Command*, Siegfried Giedion (1948, p. 246) provides this harsh description of a beef packing plant.

> The death cries of the animals whose jugular veins have been opened are confused with the rumbling of the great drum, the whirring of the gears and the shrilling sound of steam. Death cries and mechanical noises are almost impossible to disentangle. Death happens so quickly and is so smooth a part of the production process that emotion is barely stirred.
>
> What is truly startling in this mass transformation from life to death is the complete neutrality of the act. One does not experience, one does not feel, one merely observes.

Fast-food and Humanism

It is a long and improbable route from the meditations of Descartes to fast-food outlets in suburban Toronto. Yet the route exists. Of course the designers of abbatoirs, Tri-Deck cage systems for chickens and new restaurants are not literally translating Cartesian ideas into practice. Rather, the arguments for scientific humanism which are developed so clearly in Descartes' philosophy, and which assert the authority of human reason over all that is natural or non-human, have been deeply assimilated into Western culture and have been made technically and economically feasible by countless scientific discoveries and mechanical and chemical inventions. These inventions have made life healthier and easier for us – few people in Europe or North America suffer now from severe hunger or chronic protein deficiencies.

Precisely because of this it is difficult to make convincing criticisms of fast-food outlets and factory farms. Perhaps some quality of the lives of animals has been sacrificed to efficiency and the need to meet the demands of humans, perhaps the rights of farm animals to a reasonable existence are being denied, perhaps all this programmed breeding for mass extermination is disturbing. But there are no black villains who can be blamed for this, no malevolent research scientists or cruel farmers or heartless fast-food chain operators. Behind every McDonald's sign or Kentucky Fried Chicken bucket is a store manager struggling to maintain his sales and to pay off the debt he incurred in acquiring the franchise. And inside the pastel clean sheds of a broiler farm is a farmer worrying about how he can keep up the quality of his flock and maintain his quotas. These are not participants in some vast and evil conspiracy, but individuals trying to make something of their lives, and who are involved in a culture and a life-style which not merely condones, but actively encourages the logical and rational procedures which they are using to maintain efficiency and to provide convenience.

Nevertheless the convenience, quantity and consistent quality of fast-food have been achieved by treating animals as though they are machines. Indeed from the standpoint of efficient production, and in all of this no other standpoint is apparently of much consequence, machines that could be eaten would be altogether better. Possibly with cloning this ideal will soon be approached – thousands of chickens all laying an egg at precisely the same time, all eating at the same moment and of the same dead weight.[2] Since this is not yet the case it is necessary to make do with veal calves, pigs and chickens that are kept virtually immobilised, free from disease and fed on schedule. The living existence of the animal or bird is thus entirely subordinated to its technical and economic qualities and its productive capacity, and of course to its worth when dead. From a strictly Cartesian perspective, which understands human beings to be apart from and superior to all other living creatures, this is reasonable for it benefits humankind. But from an ecological view, that is one which sees a continuum of mind and body and nature, or from any view which does not arrogate human reason into a position of superiority, this is a practice which diminishes and confuses the meaning of life itself.

The bright plastic signs, the immaculate kitchens and fantastic advertisements for fast-food chains give few hints of the principles of rigorously efficient organisation on which they are based, and no indication at all of the systematic growth and slaughter of millions of cattle and birds for the hamburgers, hot dogs and chicken pieces. Scientific humanism, stressing as it does the authority of detached human reason, lies at the heart of the landscapes of fast food. 'What I detest', writes S.R.L. Clark in his study of *The Moral Status of Animals* (1977, p. 8), 'is humanism, which so far from being a humane and civilising influence has, in an enormous area of man's relation to the non-human, served merely to darken counsel.'

Suburban Hyperplanning

The use of rational techniques to improve the material circumstances of human life is by no means confined to the fast-food industry. Most elements of modern society and most of their landscapes are imbued with rationalism. Medicine, business, government and planning have all been deeply influenced by the use of scientific and technical knowledge to achieve higher levels of efficiency and success than were hitherto possible. And in all these instances the ambivalent character of scientific humanism, that it offers such marvellous tangible returns yet destroys something subtle and intangible, can be identified, though the specific forms of gains and losses differ from case to case.

In modern urban planning the gains have occurred almost entirely since 1945, for it is only since then that there has been effective planning legislation with the professional planners to implement it. The achievement has involved the adaptation of cities and towns to the new technologies, especially that of the automobile, and meeting enormous demands for new housing. In North America dwellings for about 100,000,000 people have been provided since 1945 (that is the number by which the population has increased). Furthermore, these houses and apartments, with central heating, garages and a full range of appliances, offer standards of comfort and convenience that were no more than parts of peoples' dreams before the Second World War.

In spite of these obvious accomplishments of city building, modern suburbs and their landscapes have been repeatedly criticised for their uniformity and blandness. Most of these criticisms miss the point. It is not the appearance of suburban areas that is the real problem, but the paternalistic humanism of planning and development which threatens to smother everything. What exists now is not planning so much as 'hyperplanning', enquiring into every detail, arranging things just so, eliminating the possibility of fundamental change, and drastically reducing the opportunities for individuals to become involved with their suburban places.

Criticisms of Residential Suburbs

It is a thoroughly accepted academic practice to condemn suburban landscapes and suburban living. Condemnations are usually accompanied by aerial photographs of little boxes sprouting from a treeless waste somewhere in the Los Angeles Basin (Figure 3.8). The caption may read something to the effect that 'Many urban problems are largely the result of unplanned, haphazard development' (Ehrlich, 1973, p. 148). This is misleading since such suburban growth has taken place at the very time when urban planning has reached its highest development, and the photographs invariably show a precisely regulated pattern of streets and buildings. Peter Blake, the architect and journalist, writing some years before Ehrlich, and remarkably using the identical photographs of the Los Angeles Basin, offers a more complex account of the suburban landscape. He recognises that it can be attributed in part to garden city ideas of democracy in which everyone has their own plot of ground, in part to the mass production of standardised houses, and in part to the straitjacket of planning regulations which specify the placement of the house on the lot, the curvature of the street and countless other details (Blake, 1964, pp. 107-8). So suburban landscapes are criticised for being demonstrations of too much planning and too little planning; in either case they are clearly open to scorn.

Peter Blake does not care for 'the massive monotonous, ugliness of most of suburbia' (Ibid., p. 17). Lewis Mumford is no less outspoken. In *The City in History* (1961) he notes that while cities have always had suburbs the scale of modern suburbs makes them the dominant force in urban regions. He does not like the way they look – they are a 'formless urban exudation' (p. 505) which consists of 'a multitude of uniform, unidentifiable houses lined up at uniform distances, on uniform roads, in a treeless communal waste, inhabited by people of the same class, the same income, the same age group, witnessing the same television programmes, eating the same tasteless pre-fabricated foods, from the same freezer' (p. 486).

These are powerful ideas expressed in persuasive language. Yet they have a deep flaw, for they are phrased in such general terms and have to do with apparently insubstantial matters. Compare Mumford's

Figure 3.8: Archetypal photographs of the suburbs; a housing development in the Los Angeles Basin about 1964. (Source: Blake, 1964, p. 107)

description of 'suburbia' or 'the suburbs', in which he never mentions a specific location, with nineteenth-century descriptions of urban situations and problems. For example Jacob Riis (1968, pp. 37ff) wrote in the 1880s of specific New York City tenement buildings and particular families of ten people living in two rooms, and of a couple who committed suicide because they were 'so tired'. Similarly the report of Charles Booth on *Life and Labour of the People of London*, which was written at about the same time as Riis' account of New York, described comparable conditions with equal precision, giving names and addresses of families with especially bad problems. Of Shelton Street off Drury Lane he wrote: 'In little rooms no more than eight feet square would be found living father, mother and several children . . . Fifteen rooms out of twenty would be dirty to the last degree . . . Not a room would be free from vermin, and in so many life at night was unbearable. Several occupants have said that in hot weather they don't go to bed, but sit in their clothes in the least infested part of the room.' (Booth, 1902, p. 47).

Booth and Riis had something really awful to describe; the overcrowding, the squalor, the suffering, were visible and extreme and their accounts of these were specific and precise. In contrast the criticisms Mumford, Blake and others make about modern suburbs are phrased in generalities, and are about the overall character of suburbia rather than this or that street. If their comments are based on detailed and careful observation we get no sense of that. And many of their criticisms of anonymity and uniformity are nebulous and conceptual and not of actual circumstances. They would mean little or nothing to the residents of suburbia, who are people proud of their house and car and swimming pool.

The issue is this. The difficulty that critics of the suburbs have in grounding their criticisms in particular contexts, or in giving them substance apart from the weight of polemic, or in identifying issues to attack other than questionable aesthetic inadequacies, is a reflection of the fact that these new environments do provide a very high standard of living for millions of people. And yet there is some elusive quality that leads to the frequent charges of uniformity and blandness. Such charges miss the point, however, for the real difficulties of suburbia are much more profound than these. They have to do with the use of all-embracing but precise procedures for development and planning, procedures that depend on technical expertise and which greatly reduce the opportunities for individual residents and communities to become seriously involved in making and maintaining the places in which they live. The quality that is missing in suburban landscapes is commitment, and it is missing not because of some shared deficiency of 'suburbanites' but because it is systematically denied by the ways in which these environments are developed and planned.

The Making of a Suburb

At the suburban front drastic changes in the landscape occur in a matter of months. Appropriately it takes only about nine months to create from fields and farms a scene of streets, sidewalks and neat houses with finished lawns and a car in every garage. The anatomy of this change reveals how completely individual involvement in making places has been displaced by rationalist procedures that impose new landscapes.

First come the signs – Land for Sale, or Application for Rezoning (Figure 3.9). Much has happened before these are posted, the land has been sold and resold, used for speculation, incorporated into master plans. But these signs are the first visible indication of the changes that are to come. They are a death warrant to the existing scene. Farming may continue for several years as zoning is appealed or economic circumstances delay development, but the fields are worked without conviction. Fences fall into disrepair, boards fall off barns and are not replaced, weeds begin to grow. The landscape loses its spirit.

The surveyors are harbingers of more radical changes. Their markers, wooden pegs with pink and yellow ribbons, are the means by which drawing-board plans are transferred to the ground. The pattern of pegs makes little visual sense since it denotes an order that is conceptual and in outline only. However, the drivers of bulldozers and back-hoes can read the outline well enough when they come to demolish the fences, and to strip the fields of grass and topsoil. It takes but a few days to eradicate a landscape whose forms had been developing for one-hundred-and-fifty years or more.

The scale and detail of the new suburban landscape that will emerge owe much to the size and power of the machines used. The land surface is entirely reshaped, graded to allow adequate drainage with slopes that are machine slopes smoothed to the width of a blade. Vegetation is destroyed except for a few mature trees. Indeed ecological sensitivity here must be measured in terms of these trees for they are the smallest objects which can be protected from the bulldozers. The streams are realigned and given geometric valleys that will help to prevent flood damage. Human artifacts suffer similar fates. If there are any buildings of architectural significance they will either be neatly sliced from their foundations and carried off on a trailer to a museum, or systematically disassembled and reassembled elsewhere. Their foundations and sites will disappear without trace. Buildings of no architectural importance are simply demolished for it is too inconvenient and expensive to incorporate them into the suburban design.

Figure 3.9: The radical origins of a suburb. From rezoning signs to occupation of the almost complete landscape takes about nine months. Suburban Toronto, 1979 and 1980.

The machines render the earth into a mud wasteland—a shapeless battlefield surface of pools and mud. Pipes and wires are laid as dictated by surveyors' stakes. Then fire hydrants are installed, the first recognisable elements of the new landscape. Block walls for basements are constructed in groups of eight or ten. To these wood frames are attached, covered with construction panelling and filled with insulation. Prefabricated stairways and roof trusses are brought in truck-size bundles, dumped where the front yards will be, separated and attached to the wall frames.

Thus far there is little indication of the styles that the completed houses will have, except perhaps for variations in roof shapes and window openings. At this stage it is the uniformity and standardisation which is most striking—the same methods and materials are used for all the houses, big or small, expensive or inexpensive, Tudor or Colonial.

But the style of each house is not a matter of chance or left to the whims of the construction manager. It has long ago been decided by the architects who have selected designs that will be commercially successful and then arranged them on a detailed site plan. In the conformist 1950s all the dwellings on a street might have been the same. Not so now. The architects of the developers create styles that are complete in every respect and will need no additions or modifications by the future homeowners; they also prepare streetscape drawings to ensure that a varied scene will be created and that no two identical houses will be adjacent.[3] In a development of several hundred houses there may be four or five basic styles. Colonial, Tudor and Mediterranean or Spanish are popular; ecostyles, with wood siding to give a natural or West-Coast look, have been recently introduced but are not usually mixed with other designs. All these styles are, in fact, no more than facings of brick, stucco, wood or whatever, applied to the standardised structures. Thus a mock-Tudor house will have imitation leading on the windows and boards nailed to the outside and painted black to resemble half-timbering, while a Colonial style has imitation sixteen pane windows, returned eaves and raised brickwork quoins (Figure 3.10).

With only a few basic styles variety is achieved by using a modular design approach. Each house comprises a number of modules—the garage, the windows, the roof, the porch, the door—which can be combined in many different ways. Furthermore, whole floor plans and facades are reversible, so a house may face its mirror image across the street. A Tudor-style house with a small porch, bay window, simple gable roof and a one-car garage on the left may elsewhere have no

Figure 3.10: Suburban house styles for the 1980s. Tudorbethan, with fake half-timbering and leaded panes; Colonial, with an inlaid-wood garage door installed by the owner; Ecological, or Organic, with dark bricks and stained wood-siding in the Californian manner. All in Brimley Forest, Toronto, 1980.

porch, a picture window, gablets on the roof and a two-car garage on the right (Figure 3.11).

By the time that the facades are being added to the houses, or even earlier, the sales office on site will have opened. This is usually a futuristic prefabricated building decorated with bunting and signs proclaiming the name of the developer and this particular development. Development names may be elaborations of existing place names—Malvern becomes 'Malvern Glen'; or they may simply be invented—

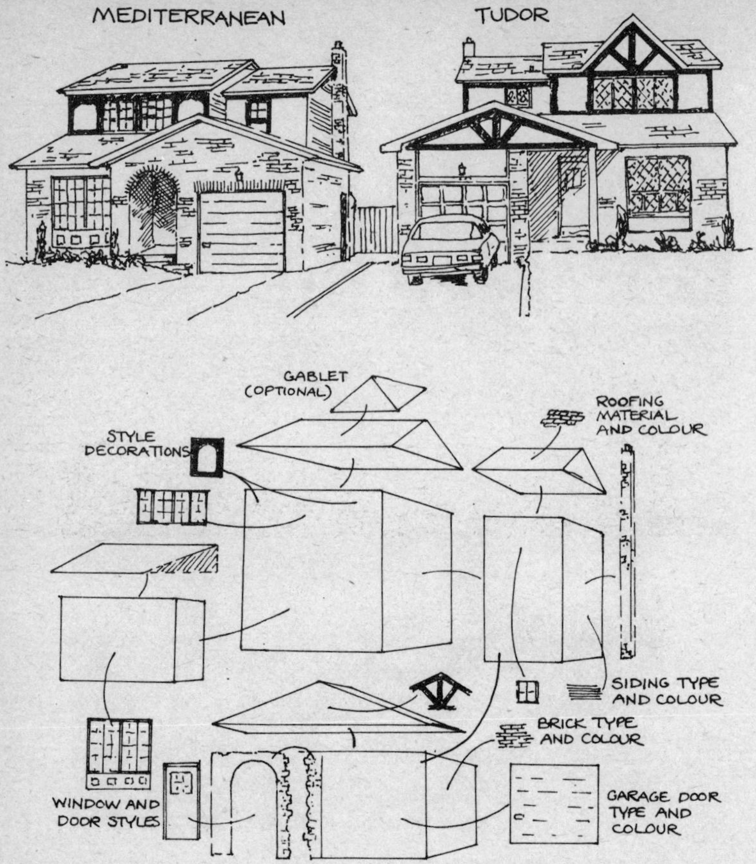

Figure 3.11: The modular principle of suburban house design. Each style consists of a number of parts which can be easily rearranged to make a different style or a variation on a single theme.

Bramble Tree Hamlet, Walden Spinney, Oakstone Mews, The Governor's Club, Rolling Hills, Middlefield on the Park, and so on (Figure 3.12). These names are sales gimmicks and mean nothing in spite of their intimations of nostalgia and rusticity. They come from trade journals and study tours which the designers make around North America. When the development is completed and fully occupied the names are usually forgotten.

The facings and interiors of the remaining houses are finished, roads and sidewalks laid, construction rubble cleaned away. Finally the

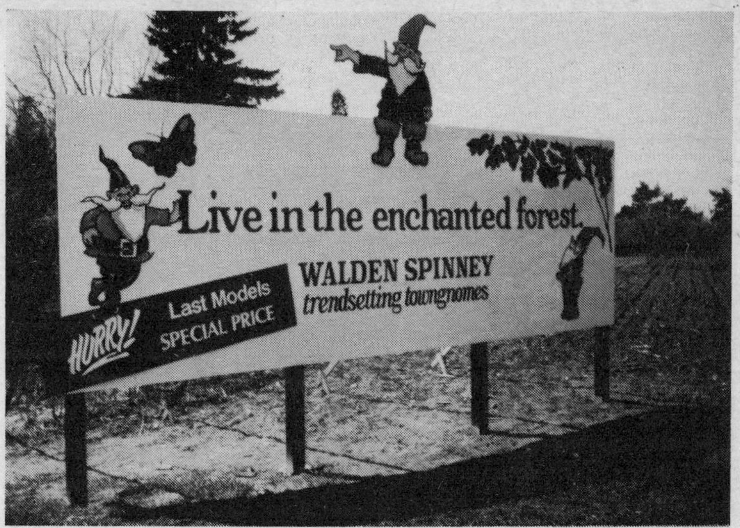

Figure 3.12: Live in the Enchanted Forest and own a gnome of your own – a billboard for suburban townhouse development at Walden Spinney, Mississauga, Ontario, 1979. (Photograph by D. Holdsworth)

properties are landscaped. The lawns are sodded so that the sight of machine-worked earth disappears suddenly, and the streets take on the trim and tidy appearance which they are always going to have.

The new homeowners put up fences around the backyards, plant a few trees and flowers. The construction teams take down their signs and flags and move to the next site. The entire transformation from fields to house-lined streets with children playing on the sidewalks and their fathers washing cars in the driveways has taken less than a year. The transformation has been complete, precise, premeditated, arbitrary and enduring. Complete because nothing remains of the farms. Precise and premeditated because the new landscape was wholly preconceived on blueprints and in design drawings. Arbitrary because the names and styles have been invented or borrowed and owe nothing to this place and time. Enduring because it allows for no more than incremental modifications such as garden ornaments (Figure 3.13) or a new garage door (inlaid wood doors are popular). The new suburban landscape has been conceived and made as a total package as though it will exist unchanged in this trim and tidy form for ever, except perhaps for the slow growth of trees, and the rhythmic coming and going of automobiles.

Figure 3.13: Snow White and her seven dwarfs waiting on a townhouse doorstep in Brimley Forest for her prince to come, 1977. An example of personal modification to a precisely designed landscape.

Hyperplanning

Suburban landscapes are not the creation of developers working alone. Certainly the developers decide on and manufacture house styles, lot sizes and street layout, but they are constrained in what they can do by a host of by-laws, building-codes, density guidelines, zoning regulations and planning concepts. These complexes of rules are the means by which planning is executed. They guarantee that certain construction and design qualities will be achieved, they protect the individual home-owner against unscrupulous builders, they make sure that fire engines and ambulances can get to all the dwellings, that there are adequate illumination levels at night and that there are sufficient schools and churches. They ensure, in effect, that the suburban environment is safe and secure, that it is orderly, pleasant to look at and capable of meeting the demands placed upon it.

But for all their beneficial qualities, these planning standards and by-laws constitute an intricate and extremely thorough set of constraints on what can be done in making suburban landscapes, constraints that are imposed uniformly and with little regard for local circumstances.

Peter Blake (1964, p. 17) writes scathingly of this in the United States:

> In our egalitarian democracy, we have achieved the ultimate in making certain that all men are created equal: we have just about empowered a branch of the government, the Federal Housing Administration, to specify the size and shape of the typical American master bedroom (in which all Americans are thus created equal); to specify the size and shape of the typical family room (in which all American tots crawl around equal); to specify the size, shape, and style of the suburban house (in which all American youngsters grow up equal); and we have just about empowered the FHA to specify the width, length, straightness-or-curvature, surface, presence or absence of trees, sidewalks, telephone poles, etc, etc, of most suburban streets (on which all American teenagers play equal—at their considerable peril).

Overstated perhaps, but not much overstated. It is this web of rules which gives the sense of uniformity to suburban developments regardless of where they are in the nation, and in spite of the varieties of building styles and layouts used by the developers.

Of course some building rules and regulations have existed for centuries. Rules relating building height to street width and governing building materials were introduced long ago to try to reduce the spread of fires. Regulations about door size, window openings and various public health requirements were instituted in the nineteenth century. But since the Second World War the number of planning standards and regulations has greatly increased and their character has changed. Community planning concepts, coupled with zoning, control the population density patterns and spatial designs of entire suburban regions. At the same time the smallest details of the landscape are subject to regulation—everything from nail spacing in the timber frames of houses, to the number of steps on the front path, to manhole size and spacing, to permissible weeds. And there is little in between the large spatial scale and the most detailed level which escapes the purview of some regulating agency or another (Figure 3.14).

The character of the planning and design regulations effected since about 1945 has changed because the earlier 'empirical and arbitrary' controls have been replaced by ones that are 'science-based' (Lyall Addleston, cited in Crosby, 1973, p. 188). In other words the earlier rules were a response to local experience, often based on trial and error until some suitable solution was found. The new regulations involve a

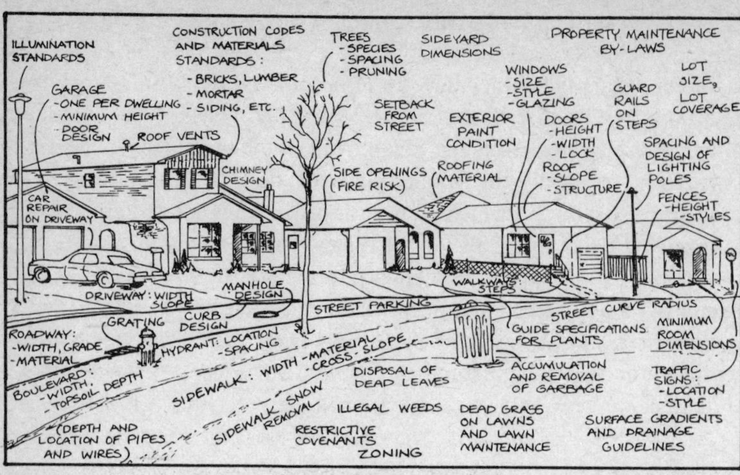

Figure 3.14: Suburban Hyperplanning. These are some of the rules and regulations which govern the appearance of the modern suburban landscape in the Borough of Scarborough, Metropolitan Toronto, Ontario, Canada. Four levels of government – municipal, metropolitan, provincial and federal – are here involved in regulation. There are, of course, national and local variations in the types of regulations, but their breadth and intensity seems everywhere to be similar.

rational and researched anticipation of problems, the development of experimental designs and materials which are tested and, if they are satisfactory, implemented or imposed uniformly. The consequence of this is that there is almost nothing in the making of modern suburban landscape which is not within the scope of planning and design regulations or standards.

In the 1830s the French nobleman Alexis de Tocqueville (1945, vol. II, p. 336) predicted that American democracy would become ‘a power that is absolute, minute, regular, provident and mild’. There can be no better description of the way in which planning functions in the suburbs. Everything is subject to bureaucratic control and direction, yet this is clearly beneficial and in everyone’s best interests. Indeed this is no longer merely planning. It has become ‘Hyperplanning’ – planning so thorough and all-embracing that it does not only serve to direct change in an orderly way, but also effectively determines the form and content of the entire landscape. Hyperplanning involves control over the largest patterns and the smallest details of development; it is based on meticulous research, model-building and analysis; it is the enemy of chance and serendipity. With hyperplanning all change is subject to standardised directives, and this means that in making suburban landscapes, when everything is being changed, that the entire form and pattern of the landscape is controlled. The only unauthorised alterations of the suburban environment that are possible are trivial ones, some flowers around the front lawn perhaps, a change in the colour of the house paint (and even that is sometimes restricted to a pre-selected range of colours). With hyperplanning the responsibility for making and changing environments has effectively passed from the people who live in them and use them to experts and properly trained professionals who devise and implement the regulations and standards which are necessary to ensure that nothing untoward ever happens. (Figure 3.15)

Figure 3.15: The detached and benevolently authoritarian approach of the professional and expert to urban design – magnifying glass, scale model and pen. (Source: promotional pamphlet for Meadowvale New Town, Ontario, by Markborough Properties, Toronto)

Commentary: Benevolent Environmental Authoritarianism

Modern residential suburbs are neat, easily maintained and comfortable environments, with a variety of carefully designed houses and streetscapes. This variety may not be the sort which someone accustomed to Victorian streets and downtown cityscapes can see readily, but it exists for those who are prepared to look for it. The styles and arrangements of 1980 are quite different from those of 1965 or 1950. Furthermore, the people who live in these houses have the pleasures and concerns of people everywhere, they are neither more nor less conformist and materialist than those who live in renovated houses near the city centre.

Yet if suburban landscapes are considered thoughtfully problems do begin to present themselves, problems not of appearance so much as of the ways in which appearance is achieved. And problems which are not only suburban but which can be found in most modern landscapes—they happen to be especially clear in the suburbs because there they are unadulterated by relics from former ages.

The radical beginning and rapid creation of a suburban landscape renders it virtually timeless. Evidence of the past is erased, within months the totally designed landscape is complete and will not change significantly in the foreseeable future. Except for the passage of the seasons and the growth of trees, which cannot yet be controlled, all is in an enduring present—a landscape which cannot evolve. However, the fact of a radical beginning is not a significant criticism in itself. There have been other times in North American history when an existing environment has been destroyed and replaced by one quite different. The fields that become subdivisions were once a forest that was cut and burned so that the land could be farmed. But in that encounter the pioneer farmers of the early nineteenth century were directly involved. It was they who cut and burned the trees, made the houses and barns and fences; they had assistance in this perhaps, but they were the agents of change and were necessarily deeply implicated in it. In the transformation from fields to suburbs there is no such involvement, the change is accomplished by machines and construction teams. The house purchaser moves into a completed landscape and can have no clear sense of what once was here.

This too is not an entirely new process, for ready-made houses in tract developments have been built by developers and sold to whoever wanted them since at least the beginning of this century. Indeed the famous crescents and squares of Bath and of other Georgian urban developments were speculative housing. What has happened since then, and especially since the Second World War, is that the scale of this process has increased—there is now more speculative housing than any other kind—and the alternative of making one's own dwelling has been all but eliminated. Ivan Illich (1973, p. 40) has reported that as recently as 1945 in Massachusetts 32 per cent of all dwellings were self-made either by the owners from foundation to roof or under the full responsibility of the owner. By 1970 this figure had dropped to eleven per cent. Many of the immediately post-war suburbs were made by the owners, who lived in basements or garages while they literally put a roof over their heads. But now the combination of readily available and complete houses built by developers, higher incomes to enable people to buy these, and the daunting maze of construction regulations, make self-made housing an unattractive option appropriate only for whole-earth cultists and squatters in the barriadas of Third World cities. In fact the elimination of effective participation in landscape-making has been so complete, with total house and streetscape designs and the breadth and minuteness of hyperplanning controls, that the suburban house owner cannot modify his place in anything other than trivial cosmetic ways. If someone wants their environment to be arranged differently they have to move elsewhere.

In modern suburban landscapes a small but important freedom is therefore denied. This is the freedom to demonstrate a commitment and responsibility to a place by engaging in the making and maintenance of its landscape in something other than a cosmetic fashion. The process by which this is denied can be called 'benevolent environmental authoritarianism'.

It is benevolent because the careful designs of the developers and the regulations of the planners are intended to be in everyone's best interests. Poor house designs will not sell and the developers are seriously concerned with providing buildings that look attractive and work well; the planning regulations are to guarantee that nobody is short-changed and that larger social and amenity considerations are met. Since these designs and regulations contribute to the maintenance of property-values and to comfort and convenience the homeowners are quite willing to give up the responsibility for making their own place. In fact they are not even there when it is being made so there is really no means by which they could take such responsibility even if they wanted it.

It is an environmental process simply because it is directed primarily at the relationship between people and their built-environments. Other relationships, for instance social and political involvement, may well be involved, but of these I am not qualified to comment. All I can say with certainty is that in the suburban built-environment the small freedom of an individual to be involved in making, or to be responsible for, a fragment of landscape has been denied.

It is an authoritarian process because all the decisions about design, layout, appearance, population sizes, social mixes, types of housing, park and school facilities, access to stores, and everything else, are made by the designers and planners – the professionally trained authorities who possess the necessary expertise for making such decisions. Relatively inexpert citizens and homeowners can contribute little to the making of suburban environments since they lack the necessary training to understand the jargon, the concepts and the techniques that are being used. Even the politicians may be at a loss to grasp many of the details of planning procedure.[4] In other words authority for making landscapes has been arrogated to a small group of professionals who act on behalf of the present and future residents of suburbia. Even if they act benevolently the situation is clearly authoritarian. Lewis Mumford (1961, p. 513) uses an even stronger term to describe it – he considers it to be 'totalitarian'. He argues that mass production of housing and the rise of 'automatic forces which encourage the use of automobiles and which concentrate channels of communication' have led to the construction of suburban landscapes in which there are few facilities for meeting and debate and which foster a habit of conformity rather than protest and debate. This habit, Mumford suggests, has worked its way back into the city in 'every manner of totalitarian compulsion and corruption'. He sees a new kind of absolutism at work, 'invisible but all-powerful'. With the new means of communication and benevolent regulation a population can thus be kept compliant and under control.

I hesitate to describe these processes of total design and hyperplanning in the suburbs as 'totalitarian' – they are not yet sufficiently absolute to warrant such a description, nor are they as deliberate as this term implies. That there has been a steady erosion of small freedoms is, I believe, indisputable, but this has occurred not because of some cunning totalitarian conspiracy but because of the growing dependence on benevolent expertise which unintentionally takes away responsibilities even as it provides environments of comfort and convenience. In modern suburban environments individual autonomy and the freedom to participate in making one's own place and community has been quietly and unwittingly sacrificed to social and environmental manageability.

Are Modern Landscapes Dehumanised or Too Humanised?

The material benefits that are so obvious in the built forms of modern landscapes have been achieved through the development and application of technical procedures which ignore and even deny, in a subtle and non-obvious way, ethical and political rights and freedoms. In the case of the landscapes of fast-food, convenience has been attained by reducing animals to organic machines; in suburban landscapes, individual and community involvements have been given up for social manageability and material comforts. In neither instance has there been any deliberate conspiracy or connivance; instead the erosion of rights and freedoms seems to have happened as an almost accidental consequence of the use of rational techniques for the organisation of human activities. Accidental or not, this erosion is discernible, albeit in many different forms, in almost every type of modern landscape.

Shopping malls and climate-controlled shopping centres are entirely post-war creations. In the hot humid summers and cold winters of north-eastern North America they have obvious advantages over their out-of-doors predecessors, though they are often promoted as meeting places and public thoroughfares similar to the main streets of small towns. This comparison is false, for only in the trivial sense that both malls and main streets have lines of stores accessible to pedestrians is there a similarity. Streets are public territory but shopping malls are private property, small totalitarian states with their own security forces moving swiftly to eject undesirables, whether vagrants or students taking photographs.[5] Shopping malls are sophisticated profit machines with vast parking lots and blank walls on the outside, and on the inside, not public amenities, but a complex array of devices to promote sales. These include advertisements and window displays, and also carefully manipulated light intensities, muzak, insufficient seats and countless mirrors so that we can compare our shabbiness with the studied elegance of the mannequins. In short, climatic constancy and the convenience of a concentration of stores have been gained at the expense of genuinely public streets and by subjecting ourselves to all sorts of seductions and inducements to consume.

International airports are also a creation of the last thirty years bearing a certain topographical similarity to shopping malls – built islands in a sea of concrete and asphalt. Airports represent enormous expenditures of time, expertise and money and are as much symbols of the modern age as the glass and steel high-rise offices of downtown. Their visual and other qualities are both ahuman and anti-nature – they

(a)

(b)

Figure 3.16: More modern hyperdesigned landscapes. (a) The shopping centre as private property – the sign says 'For use only while shopping or on business at Scarborough Town Centre'. Presumably the photograph was illegally taken. (b) The machine spaces of the utterly modern environment of Toronto International Airport, 1979.

are machine landscapes of vast expanses of windswept, sun-baked concrete, filled with ear-shattering noises, multi-storey parking lots covered in grime and automobiles, chain-link fences and buildings, scaled to machines rather than people, all undergoing ceaseless reconstruction. In airports we submit more or less passively to being questioned, searched, crowded, herded, delayed and harassed in surroundings which have no redeeming features. John Ruskin (cited in Herbert, 1964, p. 164) wrote of rail travel in the nineteenth century that: 'The whole system . . . is addressed to people who, being in a hurry, are for the time-being miserable . . . it transmutes a traveller from a man into a parcel.' Railway builders may have invented parcel people, but airport designers made the system scientific and have somehow persuaded us to accept these not inconsiderable indignities for the sake of faster and more efficient travel.

And so it is in virtually all modern landscapes. Whether we consider expressways, downtown office buildings, theme parks or oil terminals, it seems that all the benefits that accrue from improved efficiency have been achieved only by some loss of qualities or a denial of human sensibilities and freedoms. Perhaps this is inevitable, for efficiency requires some standard (often profits) that is measurable and capable of evaluation and of improvement by controlling all or part of the environment. In other words, efficiency is an analytic device that can be applied to no more than a fragment of human life, namely its material and economic conditions. The philosopher Patrick Corbett has written (1972, p. 236) that: 'The things that really make life valuable – love, friendship, strength, dexterity, imagination and peace of mind – owe little to analytic intelligence and are often undermined by excessive cultivation of it.' In modern landscapes there is ample evidence of such undermining, and though it is not usually visible and on the surface of things it is readily accessible to anyone who is willing to make the effort to see it.

Paul Goodman, the social critic well-known for his arguments against a centralised and authoritarian society, has stated (1969, p. ix) that: 'It makes sense to say that the conditions of modern society are "dehumanising".' Clearly this 'dehumanising' does not mean the physical consequences of disease and malnutrition and personal and political brutality. Rather it refers to the fact that so much that is modern is concerned with a small range of human attributes and needs. It announces that much of the present-day built-environment has been made by machines for people in machines, and that the scale and character of its spaces and forms fill the machineless person with awe. Modern 'dehumanising' attacks human spirit and feeling, not the physical person. Precisely because of this it is easily dismissed, for the rational and analytic intelligence which is expressed in the forms and structures of modern landscape has already assumed that spirit and feeling are of no great importance. From the rationalist perspectives of scientific humanism the modern landscape represents a great human achievement.

They may be dehumanising but it is quite wrong to describe modern landscapes as 'dehumanised', or devoid of human content. On the contrary they are entirely the products of rational human intelligence doing its best to control uncertain environments, to guarantee a food supply or achieve orderly and efficient urban development and transportation systems. Such rationalism has developed in a direct line from the humanism of the eighteenth century which stressed the authority of human reason over the senses and over nature. It has been deeply influenced by paternalistic or philanthropic humanism which emerged in the nineteenth century, and which maintains that those people with special expertise can use it to improve the material living conditions of others. But only in the present century has rationalism bloomed and found its full and clear expression in the attitudes and methods of scientific humanism. These maintain that the quality of human existence can best be served by the precise analysis and technical resolution of all social and environmental problems by those who have had an appropriate scientific training. The success of scientific humanism in achieving these ends is demonstrated beyond all reasonable doubt in distinctive forms and patterns of modern landscapes. The philosophical position of humanism has had a long and mixed association with landscape, but its effects were always tempered by other beliefs, by religious attitudes and by craft traditions. In this century, as scientific humanism, it has become the supreme and rarely challenged master of landscape making, it has found an appropriate new aesthetic style and the technical means to express it. For these reasons modern landscapes are distinctively different from their predecessors.

The paradox of modern landscapes is that they are dehumanising because they are excessively humanised. There is almost nothing in them that has not been conceived and planned so that it will serve those human needs which can be assessed in terms of efficiency or improved material conditions. But there is also almost nothing in them that can happen spontaneously, autonomously or accidentally, or which expresses human emotions and feeling. If this absence diminishes the quality of our lives it does so sadly, quietly, unobtrusively, rather than with some overt and brutal denial. Paul Goodman (1969, p. ix) writes: 'As I walk the streets of the city it does not seem to me that people are less human than when I was an adolescent fifty years ago, only sadder and more harassed and more anxious.'

Figure 3.17: The architecture of eighteenth-century humanism meets the architecture of twentieth-century commercial, scientific humanism at Stamford, Lincolnshire, 1977; from grace, proportion and craftsmanship to function, line and machine.

Notes

1. This information comes from the district purchasing manager of Foodcorp, Toronto, May 1979. Swiss Chalet is part of this group of fast-food restaurants.

2. Such cloning may not be very far in the future. In the *Guardian Weekly*, (4 May 1980, p. 5) it was reported that Unilever had already succeeded in cloning the palm trees from which oil for margarine is produced. The chairman of Unilever announced enthusiastically 'I have seen them growing. They grow to identical heights and all put out the same new sprig, at the same time, on the same day. This is only the beginning of the whole story of biotechnology.'

3. Information on the practices of developers in designing suburban landscapes came from Wimpey, Costain and careful observation of the development of Milliken in Metropolitan Toronto from March 1979 to the summer of 1980.

4. This comment about politicians bowing before the expertise of planners I can support only by reference to a study of politicians in Gothenberg in Sweden which is mentioned by Christopher Alexander in *The Oregon Experiment* (1975, pp. 24-5). After the master plan for the city was adopted some sociologists interviewed the responsible legislators. It turned out that most of these simply did not understand the plan, and in some cases could not even read the maps.

5. I know of several students who have been prevented by security guards from taking photographs of the interiors of shopping malls. They were given no explanation why photographs were not permitted.

PART TWO

HUMANISM AND ITS DEFICIENCIES

When he was asked what worried him most Gandhi replied: 'The hardness of heart of the educated.' (cited in Hoffer, 1952, p. 43)

4 VARIETIES OF HUMANISM

Modern landscapes have been quietly slipped into a straitjacket. A smothering web of rules and regulations to promote safety and efficiency have served to control both natural and man-made environments. Yet even as a madman in a straitjacket has some parts of his body which are not confined and which take on a wild and unkempt look, so those parts of modern landscapes which are not subject to the full force of control, such as ribbon developments, ghettoes and urban fringes, are untidy and disorderly. The buildings in such areas are poorly maintained, even derelict, the land not well tended, the roads have potholes, garbage accumulates.

The landscapes in which many of us live and work thus take on two quite different appearances. They are demonstrations either of imposed order and control or of unregulated mess. The mess illustrates just how necessary the straitjacket of planning and development regulations is for our own well-being; it protects us from ourselves, from rampant and destructive self-interest, from exploitation and confusion and a world of tacky developments. It is not difficult to come to believe that without building codes and zoning by-laws most houses would be jerry-built, the traffic would get hopelessly clogged on inadequately designed highways, property values would be depressed and anarchy would reign.

The development of these controls and regulations, and the general acceptance of their necessity and worth has been very rapid. Before about 1930 there was little legislated urban, social and environmental planning; now almost everything is planned—parenthood and families, population, communities, production, economies, renovations, recreation, highways and transportation. As an illustration of this rapid growth of planning, in the Province of Ontario in Canada the first town planning legislation was passed in 1946, by 1950 there were still only six local planning departments and 49 professional planners, but by the late 1970s there were over 1500 planners, departments in all towns over 10,000 population, as well as regional planning departments. In less than forty years there has been a shift from no rational and coherent planning, apart from some controls over public works like sewers and water supply, to a situation in which planning is undertaken with a legislated force on all levels from that of the individual lot to urban regions of several million people. There are good reasons for this efflorescence of planning: rapid population growth and urban development, new means of transportation, new and powerful technologies capable of causing serious environmental and social side-effects. Without control and direction these might well have had disastrous consequences, though of that we can never be absolutely certain. What is clear is that in these forty years the standard of living has risen remarkably, even as individual and untrained responsibility for making places and environments has been restricted.

Malcolm Carder (cited in Crosby, 1973, p. 244) has written that: 'In our Western culture where freedom of expression of the individual is so highly prized, it seems curious that most of our environments are so carefully designed to imprison it.' This is the paradox of modern landscapes. Any enquiry into its sources soon discloses the belief that human reason and well-trained intelligence can be used to order the world so that it can better serve man's needs—in other words it reveals a philosophical position of humanism.

There is much in humanism that is undoubtedly commendable. It is an optimistic philosophy that seeks to improve the conditions of life and it has had a wide appeal in many different circumstances. But even a cursory examination of the growth of humanistic philosophies shows that it has been fragmented and contradictory. Since the beginning of the nineteenth century a variety of humanisms have developed which often have fundamental differences; there are, for instance, both Christian and atheistic humanisms, and both liberal-democratic and Marxist humanisms. Furthermore, the alliance of rationalism and humanism, which showed such promise in the eighteenth century, has in the last fifty years become its own orthodoxy, an orthodoxy which can be called 'scientific humanism'. Scientific methods now seem to be the only valid ways of investigating both social and physical issues. Yet the technological achievements that have come from these scientific methods have become so awful that some philosophers have begun to speculate about scientific totalitarianism, and the likelihood of societies run entirely according to scientific principles and in which individual and spontaneous actions are not merely not allowed, but inconceivable.

Possibly because they have had a similar vision of a perfectly ordered and controlled future, or possibly because they are reacting against some of the more crass, data-manipulating and quasi-scientific procedures of some of their colleagues, a number of psychologists, sociologists and geographers have begun to advocate and to adopt humanistic approaches to their respective disciplines. This seems ironic—rather like prescribing whisky to attempt to cure alcoholism. The confusion has arisen because humanism can mean so many different things; at one level it does seem entirely sensible to oppose the excesses of the sciences by attending to the lessons of the humanities, but at another level science is itself deeply humanistic for it is based on the achievement of human reason. However, by failing to recognise the contradictions and confusions within humanism many of these arguments for a humanistic approach in social science undermine their own case and become little more than nostalgic or idealistic accounts of hopes that have already waned. Above all they do not come to terms with the fact that the sentiments of humanism have not made people's behaviour more humane. There is no evidence that brutality and suffering and exploitation have grown any less in the world because of humanism, though they may have been disguised or moved from our own back-yards. Indeed through its association with science and, for instance, nuclear or chemical technology humanism may have made us more dispassionately, devastatingly and efficiently inhumane than our ancestors could ever have believed possible.

Difficulties in the History of Humanism

The word 'humanist' first came into use in the sixteenth century to describe a teacher of classical literature. Not until the nineteenth century was the term 'humanism' first employed to describe a philosophical position which was devoted to human interests and concerns. This means, for the Renaissance and Enlightenment at least, that 'humanism' is a term applied by interpreters of thoughts and deeds rather than one used by the thinkers and doers to describe themselves. In fact even since the beginning of the nineteenth century the conscious espousal by individuals of humanism as a philosophy to live by has been rare. Nevertheless humanism, understood in a general way as a belief in the unity of mankind and in man's potential to improve himself by his own efforts, has been an important and persistent theme in Western history since the Renaissance.[1]

The fact that humanism has such a long but vague history poses difficulties, for it means that this recently named but loosely defined perspective can be identified in some form in most phases of European and American philosophy and history. A comprehensive attempt to trace its development must therefore involve a characterisation of the humanism of very different cultures and ages. For such a task an almost impossible knowledge of the history of the Western world is needed. On the other hand it is essential to know something of the development and ramification of humanism, so that some of the confusions and simplicities which have been uttered in its name can be exposed and perhaps cast out. In this account the necessity of historical context takes precedence over intellectual caution, but I am aware that the following general descriptions subsume and may well distort the detailed arguments and qualifications of individuals who have proclaimed the virtues of humanism.

Renaissance Humanism

At the close of the Middle Ages there occurred what was described by the historian J. Huizinga (1949, p. 335) as a change in the 'tone of life'. There was no abrupt shift away from theological ways of thinking, but a slowly developing awareness of the merits of classical literature with its relative simplicity and its stress on man rather than God and angels. The artists and scholars began to paint and discuss subjects which were not inhibited by a theological context. The first secular paintings other than portraits depicted classical myths such as the birth of Venus, or events from the history of ancient Greece and Rome. The forms of Roman architecture were revived too, though many of the earliest buildings in this revived style were churches. The classical revival was in no way a rejection of Christian faith, but took place firmly within it. However, the new thinking was not dependent upon the authority of the church, and the artists and architects of the early Renaissance slowly broadened their interests to include secular subjects and buildings such as palaces and hospitals.

This rediscovery of classical Greece and Rome and their art and literature involved the learning of Latin and Greek, and the poetry and philosophy written in those languages. An education in the classics therefore became essential for anyone who wished to become familiar with and to emulate the achievements of the ancient world. Through this classical or, as it came to be called, humanist education, a view of man gradually emerged which stressed human reason and intelligence as the highest manifestations of existence, and maintained that these were to be achieved through the practice of virtue (Figure 4.1). Virtue was not merely goodness and temperance, but then meant the intrinsic capacity of an individual to realise his capabilities and especially to realise his humanity. Luxury, gluttony and sloth rendered man somehow less than human, for they were demonstrations that human qualities were not being fully achieved. Human potential was to be attained

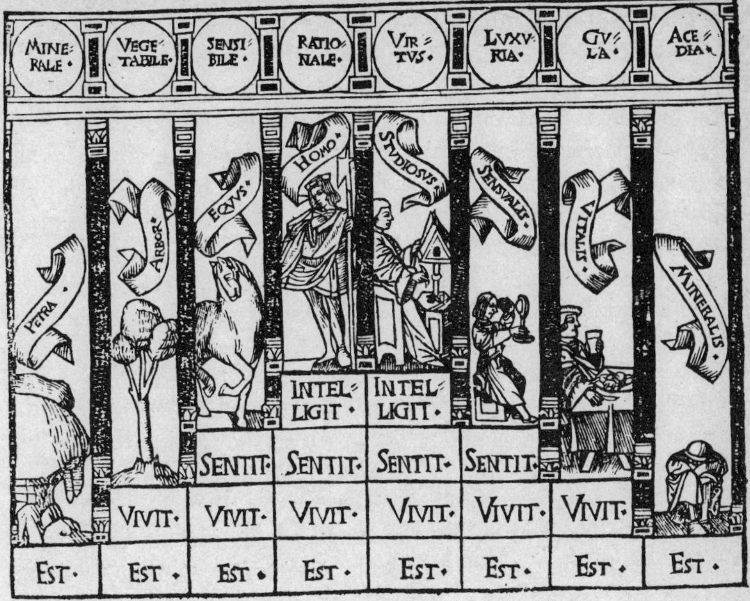

Figure 4.1: The hierarchy of being as it was understood in the Renaissance – an illustration from Bovillus' Liber de Intellectu, *1509. The hierarchy of earthly existence is shown twice. First, man's natural potential is greater than that of the other kingdoms of being because he has the power of reason. Secondly, by an act of intelligence he can choose to tread the path of virtue; luxury reduces man to the animal world of feeling, gluttony to the vegetable state and sloth to mere existence. (Source: Dresden, 1968, p. 67; original in Bodleian Library, Oxford)*

through reflection and contemplation and the full development of reason. Rational man was therefore at the pinnacle of being and was identified with the harmony and order of the world; he was both figuratively and literally the measure of all things.

This idea of man as a rational and responsible being was the source of humanism. It was a difficult and ambiguous idea. Erwin Panofsky (1940), an art historian whose special interest was the art of the Renaissance, traces its origins in the twin meanings of the word *humanitas.* This term had been used by the Romans to draw a distinction between man and what is less than man, for instance animals or even those barbarians who lacked respect for moral values. But in the Middle Ages *humanitas* had referred to the contrast between man and what is more than man – namely God, and in this sense it suggested some sort of limitation. The Renaissance notion of *humanitas* incorporated both of these meanings and it was out of this ambivalence that humanism developed. Humanism, Panofsky writes (p. 2) is 'an attitude which can be defined as the conviction of the dignity of man, based on both the insistence of human values (rationality and freedom) and the acceptance of human limitations (fallibility and frailty); from this two postulates result – responsibility and tolerance'. Although it is drawn from his knowledge of the Renaissance, Panofsky clearly intends this definition to be general and enduring. He sets it on the one hand against those attitudes which are authoritarian and deterministic and hence deny human values; and on the other hand he compares it with thosc attitudes which deny human constraints such as intuitionism and vitalism. The humanist, he declares (p. 3), rejects authority but respects the weight and reality of tradition.

It is this ambivalent but balanced and reasonable quality of Renaissance humanism that has been the continuing source of inspiration for humanists, even those of the present day. It is unquestionably an attractive quality and is an appealing attitude. But while Panofsky and many others quietly assume that this ideal has endured and is still appropriate, there is ample evidence that the character of humanism has changed in such a way that rationality has itself become authoritarian and now denies freedom even as it offers the promise of overcoming human limitations.

A major feature of Renaissance humanism was that it was a philosophical perspective that it had a clear aesthetic expression. In his famous study of *The Architecture of Humanism*, Geoffrey Scott (1914) argued that it is in fact only as an aesthetic that the idea of humanism has any real substance. Scott took issue with romantic and ethical theories of architecture developed by Ruskin and others – romanticism, he maintained, led to quaintness and picturesqueness, it was capricious and lacked any objective basis; ethical and moral arguments were false appeals to spirit and sentiment rather than to lucid reason, and were imposed on buildings rather than built into them. Mechanical approaches to architecture he also criticised on the grounds that they result in buildings which are merely structural demonstrations, recognise no law but the mechanical one, and represent a dehumanisation of thought. In romantic, ethical and mechanical architecture the aesthetic of human achievement is suppressed or denied. But the humanist architecture of the Renaissance made no romantic or ethical appeals, nor was it a servant of mechanical concerns. Humanist architecture, Scott argues, was a transcription of man, it was related to his proportions, his moods, his senses and his needs. This was not accidental but was done self-consciously and deliberately. 'The centre of that architecture was the human body; its method, to transcribe in stone the body's favourable states; and the moods of the spirit took visible shape along its borders, power and laughter, strength and terror and calm' (Scott, 1914, p. 239). The humanism of the Renaissance can therefore be seen precisely in the well-proportioned forms and spaces of the contemporary architecture.

In time the self-consciousness faded, and humanist styles and forms became a tradition in which designs which worked and looked well were copied or modified incrementally to suit local circumstances. Of course there were temporal and geographic variations in these styles—Mannerist, Baroque, Georgian, Colonial and so on—but the humanist aesthetic impulse was maintained in all of them, in their proportions and symmetry and classical lines.

Geoffrey Scott points out that all architecture is necessarily a human expression of some sort, but maintains that only the buildings of the Renaissance and their immediate successors warrant the description 'humanistic'. Only in that architecture was there a self-conscious effort to translate the values of humanism into built-environments. In other periods it may be possible *to interpret* the architecture and landscape as humanistic, but that is in spite of rather than because of the expressed beliefs of the architects and builders. In the period between 1400 and 1800, many of those who developed and wrote about humanist and classical ideals and philosophies were also artists and architects. There was no gap between the philosophy and its expression in buildings, gardens and townscapes.

Enlightenment Humanism and Rationalism

Throughout the seventeenth and eighteenth centuries the necessity of a classical or humanist education remained undiminished. At the same time there was a growing confidence in the possibility of original rather than just revived thinking. With scientific discoveries and the formulation of new philosophies the Renaissance was gradually transcended. Central in this was the argument for the effectiveness of systematic reflection into the nature of all things that was provided by Descartes in his *Discourse on Method* (1637). Although Descartes, a Jesuit and a mathematician, tried to erect a proof of the existence of

God, on the grounds that man is imperfect but has a sense of perfection and that this could only have come from God who is perfection, in effect what he did was cast God out of the world by making Him into a remote initiating force. This argument was developed by atheistic humanists of the eighteenth century–if God was remote why was He necassary at all, man could perfect himself through the exercise of human reason and without the assistance of supernatural powers. This atheistic turn was a logical progression from the original humanist questioning of the orthodoxy of Christianity; it is a connotation of humanism that has persisted up to the present day.

Towards the end of *Discourse on Method* Descartes wrote (1637, *Discourse* 6, p. 78) that he had devoted his life to the search for a practical and necessary science that would make us 'as it were, masters and possessors of nature. Which aim is not only to be desired for the invention of an infinity of devices by which we might enjoy, without any effort, the fruits of the earth and all its commodities, but also principally for the preservation of health.' In the eighteenth century Descartes' speculation became increasingly real. The scientific discoveries of Newton and other scientists suggested that it was possible that the achievements of the classical era of Rome and Greece might not merely be emulated, but could be exceeded. Science and scientific improvement were the bases of what an historian of the Enlightenment, Peter Gay (1970, p. 30), has called the 'recovery of nerve'. This was a mood characterised by a decline in mysticism and superstition, a growing hope for life, a commitment to enquiry and social reform, and a sense of progress through the development and application of human reason. Science was an irresistible force–the *philosophers* of the eighteenth century identified themselves with its method, poets extolled it, and educated people discussed the latest discoveries and theories as avidly as they discussed the poetry of Ovid and Livy.

The ancient world remained a source of inspiration and guidance, yet new questions were being raised which demanded new attitudes and approaches if they were to be resolved. Some of these new concerns had to do with the conditions of humanity and the rights of individual human beings. Voltaire, for example, mounted a public campaign against political torture in an effort to rehabilitate the name of a Huguenot, Jean Calas, who had been tortured to death by police authorities while they were attempting to extract a confession that he had murdered his own son. In 1795 the philosopher Immanuel Kant wrote a treatise in which he argued that perpetual peace among nations could be achieved if only men would make the appropriate political, social and psychological adjustments. Others campaigned against the slave trade, the treatment of the insane who were commonly regarded as little better than animals, the conditions in prisons and the death penalty; political and social inequalities were identified and solutions to them proposed; and vice, oppression and brutality in all their forms were widely condemned. In short the concern of the Enlightenment humanists for humanity was not some general sympathy for mankind's welfare, but a discriminating and active interest in the life-problems of the poor and the persecuted. They recognised, furthermore, that everyone is not capable of good and virtuous behaviour, and that moderation and benevolence would not simply spring into being but had to be worked for and firmly established. This was to be done above all through an education in which the reason of individuals would be awakened, and they would thus come to see the fundamental inhumanity of torture and exploitation even as they recognised the essential merits of reasonable attitudes and rational practices.

From the revival of classical thought in the fourteenth century reason had been held in high esteem. In the eighteenth century it came close to deification. There was nothing that seemed to be beyond its scope – science, letters, art, landscape gardening, architecture, manners, were all deeply influenced by the self-conscious espousal of reason. Of all these science seemed to be the best expression and highest achievement of human reason, for it was the discovery of laws of nature unknown in the classical era which demonstrated that this was not just a restoration of the old ways, but also an improvement upon them. In eighteenth-century thinking humanism was combined with a scientific outlook. This was made clear in the 'Sketch of the Progress of the Human Mind', a utopian manifesto written in 1794 by the Marquis de Condorcet while he was in hiding from the Revolutionary authorities in France. His essay summarises many of the hopes of the Enlightenment humanists that science, reason and education would rid the world of inequalities and sufferings. He wrote:

> We shall show how the discovery of the correct method of procedure in the sciences, the growth of scientific theories, their application to every part of the natural world, to the subject of every human need . . . ensure that no science will ever fall behind the point it has reached . . . Is the human race to better itself either by discoveries in the sciences and arts, and so in the means to individual welfare and general prosperity; or by progress in the principles of

> conduct or practical morality; or by a true perfection of the intellectual, moral or physical faculties of man?
>
> (cited in Gay, 1973, p. 804)

His answer was unequivocal. All three avenues would be followed; progress and the perfectibility of man would continue indefinitely; and with improvements and even perfection in preventive medicine, in food supply and in housing there would also be an increase in the human life span so that death would occur only by accident or decay of vital forces.

Paternalistic and Marxist Humanisms

The aims and hopes of Renaissance and Enlightenment humanism were to fulfil individual human potential through the exercise of reason. The specific means by which this was to be done was education, especially a classical education that would enable the universal awakening of reason and so lead to the eradication of inequalities and inhumanities. Social changes were therefore subsequent to and dependent upon changes in individual understanding and outlook.

Between about 1800 and the middle of the nineteenth century there was a remarkable change in humanist attitudes. The aesthetic styles and forms of humanist or classical art and architecture faded. Gothic styles were revived, Romantic poets and painters asserted the importance of feeling, and the development of steam technology and other industrial inventions gave rise to a new set of structures and landscapes. Furthermore, the rapid urban and industrial growth involved social and economic changes which were without precedent. These did not result, as Condorcet had hoped they would, in the improvement of individual welfare and general prosperity. For all but a few the conditions of life got worse rather than better. As the factories were built and the cities burgeoned there was no parallel development of drainage, schools, hospitals and adequate housing. The exploitation of the labour of men, women and children by men of business and wealth became a matter of course; crime, disease and extreme poverty abounded. In 1845 a Royal Commission on the state of 'Large Towns and Populous Districts in England' enquired into the quality of water supply of fifty cities, and found only six with a good and clean supply; thirteen had a supply of indifferent quality, and thirty-one had insufficient or impure water; in Newcastle eleven out of every twelve houses were without water (cited in Woodward, 1962, p. 463). In that same year Friedrich Engels (1845) published his account of working-class life with detailed descriptions of slum housing in Manchester, Leeds, Liverpool, Birmingham, Nottingham. Back-to-back rows of cottages, inadequate ventilation, countless thousands living in damp cellars, unpaved streets with piles of refuse and open drains, privies shared by many families and houses built with the cheapest possible construction methods.

There were two humanist responses to these horrendous conditions. One was the paternalistic or humanitarian reaction, and involved a complex blend of evangelism, professionalism and utopianism. The other was more direct and more radical: it was the response of Marxist humanism.

It was entirely consistent with the spirit of reform which developed in the early nineteenth century that there should be systematic enquiries into the many environmental and social problems that had been created by rapid urban and industrial growth, and attempts to resolve them. The motives of the reformers were mixed. Some were continuing the utopian and rationalist arguments that had been developed by their Enlightenment predecessors; others had religious and compassionate reasons for seeking to improve the circumstances of the poor and oppressed; yet others were adopting the utilitarian doctrine that the aim of society should be to provide the circumstances for the greatest happiness for the greatest number of people. At least one group of influential atheist and agnostic intellectuals, including J.S. Mill, George Eliot and Frederic Harrison, tried to formulate what they called a 'Religion of Humanity' which was based on 'the sentiments (1) of attachment, comradeship, fellowship, (2) of reverence for those who can teach us, guide us, elevate us, (3) of love which urges us to protect, help, and cherish those to whom we owe our lives and better natures' (Frederic Harrison, 1893, cited in Houghton, 1957, p. 347). These were values that were to be learned in the home and which would extend from there to all civilisation.

Whatever the motives and background of these reformers the humanism which they preached and practiced implicitly was undoubtedly paternalistic. They sought to act on behalf of, or at least to set an example for others. Their proposals for change were not to be acted on by those who were being exploited but were translated into reality by themselves or by benevolent professionals of their own class.

The development of the reform movements was one of the dramatic features of the early-nineteenth century. The simultaneous refinement and expansion of professionalism was much less obvious, although it was exactly this process which made possible the effective implementation of many of the reforms. Between about 1790 and 1830 civil engineering became a recognised profession with responsibility for the design of roads, bridges, aqueducts, docks, drainage and machinery. In the same period architecture, medicine and law were freed from much of the patronage, nepotism and corruption which had existed in them, allowing the establishment of high and consistent professional standards based on sound technical training. The new professionals were experts who could identify social problems, examine them systematically and then work to eliminate them by technical means such as improving drainage and hygiene, developing vaccination procedures and instituting better building methods. In *The Age of Reform* Sir Llewellyn Woodward (1962, pp. 447-8) writes of this new professional outlook: 'The expert, by definition, knew what could be done and what he had to do. He expected to be paid for his work, and in return maintained a relatively high standard of personal and professional conduct.' As the nineteenth century progressed the various public health and planning measures taken to clean up the mess created by the industrialists and slum-builders were increasingly policies and programmes devised by experts, appealing to experts and executed by experts (Kitson-Clark, 1962, p. 109). In short, the technically trained engineers and officials began quietly but systematically to impose their ideas about the rational organisation of the everyday affairs of society, for they believed that rational organisation was the necessary foundation for a secure, healthy and otherwise well-ordered existence.

That the methods of these experts were successful is undeniable; death rates fell, epidemics of typhus and cholera were drastically reduced in extent and frequency, standards of housing and urban development were greatly improved, child labour was stopped, systems of cheap transportation were created. Yet the motives of this professional middle-class were not entirely altruistic. Not only were they selling their services directly, but it was often the case that they stood to benefit indirectly by general improvements in the well-being of society, for their professional status would grow and astutely made investments would appreciate.

Friedrich Engels had nothing but contempt for these bourgeois experts. In *The Conditions of the Working Class in England* (1845, p. 301) he exclaimed of the bourgeoisie – 'I have never seen a class so deeply demoralised, so incurably debased by selfishness . . . For it nothing exists in this world except for the sake of money.' The bourgeoisie of middle-class professionals and businessmen was, he declared, charitable and benevolent out of self-interest, and he poured scorn on them all, addressing them directly: 'As though you rendered the proletarians a service in first sucking out their very life-blood and then practicing your self-complacent, Pharasaic philanthropy upon them, placing yourselves before the world as mighty benefactors of humanity when you give back to the plundered victims the hundredth part of what belongs to them.' (Engels, 1845, p. 303). Whatever the spirit with which they were given, the various charities, reforms and improvements were undertaken *for* the workers and the poor and destitute; they were not undertaken *by* them. Engels' concern was, of course, with winning for these exploited and powerless people the responsibility for their own lives which had been taken away first by the factory owners and then by the new class of experts.

Many of the criticisms and hopes which Engels expressed were the same as those of Karl Marx, with whom he was to write *The Communist Manifesto* in 1848. Marx was explicit in describing his philosophical position as a humanist one. In his essay 'Critique of the Hegelian Dialectic' (1844, p. 187) he wrote that 'atheism, being the supersession of God, is the advent of theoretic humanism, and communism, as the supersession of private property, is the vindication of real human life as man's possession and thus the advent of practical humanism.'

Marx apparently understood his philosophy in part as an extension of eighteenth-century humanism, at least in so far as it kept the aim of perfectibility through the exercise of reason and man's own actions. But he also understood it to be radically different; for Marx the notion of an individual striving for enlightenment through education and contemplation was hopelessly idealistic. In effect he reversed this concept of social changes accumulating from individual insight and argued that in practical and positive humanism it was necessary to study and understand society, history, politics and economics, and then to take collective social responsibility for the material conditions of life. In other words the life of the individual was dependent upon the circumstances of society.

In Marx's writings the interests, preferences and needs of human beings were always the primary concern. Yet these are, he argued, denied by capitalism with its abstractions of profit and commodity and exchange value, and with its oppression of workers by a wealthy clique. Practical humanism and the fulfilment of human possibilities had to be achieved by the working classes for they are uncorrupted by these abstractions and forms of exploitation. Furthermore, by virtue of the fact that workers have in common their labouring they possess a shared sense of humanity that transcends divisions of class, nation, race, age or sex. In his essay on 'Private Property and Communism' (Marx, 1844, p. 135) he claimed that communism, with the abolition of private property, is 'the real appropriation of human nature through and for man. It is, therefore, the return of man himself as a social (i.e. really human) being . . . This communism . . . equals humanism.'

So in the nineteenth century humanism branched into two quite different directions. Both branches came from the rationalism of the previous century, and both recognised that social improvements would come about not through individual enlightenment but in some way through direct social and community action. There the similarities end. The paternalistic or philanthropic humanism which grew out of the reform movements maintained that a few expertly trained professionals could use their technical knowledge to improve the circumstances of the many. In contrast, the humanism of Marxism and communism argued that truly human relationships can be achieved only when everyone can take responsibility for the conditions of their own lives and when there is freedom from the ideologies and actions of a bourgeois professional class which acts on behalf of others.

The Many Paths of Modern Humanism

The development of humanist thought from the early Renaissance to the late nineteenth century can be read as an orderly sequence: the revival of classical literature and philosophy, the questioning of religiosity, the emphasis on the power of reason, the possibilities of reason and education to overcome suffering and cruelty, the need for social action to achieve freedom from material constraints. However, the initial bifurcation into a paternalistic humanism and a Marxist humanism that occurred in mid-century suggests that humanism—never a very clearly formulated philosophical position—was losing its sense of direction, for these two political philosophies were radically opposed. This suggestion is amply confirmed by the way in which humanism has branched out into many different types in the twentieth century.

In part this ramification might be because the idea of humanism has become increasingly self-conscious in the last one hundred and fifty years; the word 'humanism' to describe a philosophy which stressed the needs and qualities of human beings did not exist before about 1830, but since then it has come to be so widely accepted as a commendable notion that it is espoused by virtually everyone regardless of their other philosophical or political inclinations. Indeed it is difficult to imagine anyone now denying outright that he is a humanist. So Marx's arguments for a truly human society are embodied in socialist humanism (Fromm, 1966); existentialists have formulated their own brand of humanism (Sartre, 1946); and the biologist Julian Huxley (1961) has tried to make a case for an evolutionary humanism. Perhaps reacting against the fact that humanism has come to be so closely associated with atheism, some theologians have made the case for a Christian humanism (Maritain, 1936). Meanwhile predominantly atheistic and scientifically inclined humanists have been writing manifestoes which embody elements of most of the other humanisms and continue the optimism for man's future through the exercise of reason that was first expressed in Enlightenment thought (Lamont, 1949; Kurtz and Wilson, 1973).

The case for Christian humanism has been made by Jacques Maritain in *Integral Humanism* (1936). He argues from Aristotle's suggestion that: 'To propose to man only the human is to betray man and to wish him misfortune, because by the principal part of him, which is the spirit, man is called to a better than purely human life.' Whether this is a humanist or anti-humanist statement depends on one's conception of man, and the religious conception holds that spiritual experience is as much part of human reality as reason or as material and social conditions. Maritain (1936, p. 52) directs his argument against the economic determinism and atheism of Marxism in which the highest social ideal is 'a monism of collective humanity'. But he does not want to see a return to some type of liberalism in which each individual is the source of right and truth; rather he hopes for an organic and plural social structure in which there is private property but in which this is used for the common good. This social structure is, however, subordinate to and imbued by ethical and spiritual considerations, for it is these that give us our sense of human dignity. In short, religious belief is the source of integral humanism.

In Maritain's humanism technical and economic matters are secondary to religious experience. Julian Huxley's evolutionary humanism (1961) is, in contrast, solidly scientific and technical. Huxley was concerned with the problem of desirable evolutionary directions for mankind, and maintained that evolution has proceeded from the inorganic, to the organic, to the psycho-social, and is now entering a consciously purposive phase. To cope with this new responsibility for selecting our own evolutionary course, Huxley proposes a humanism which is based on understanding man as an organism in relationship with natural environments. This understanding comes from 'the three great activities of man in which he transcends the material basis of making a living—Science, which increases the volume and depth of knowledge; Art, which increases the qualitative richness of human experience; and Religion, or applied spiritual ecology, which guides our relations to the rest of nature, to our internal nature and to other people' (Huxley, 1961, pp. 27ff). Properly used these three activities should manifest themselves in a humanism characterised by its concern for the continuity of human beings with the rest of life, by its recognition of the unity of the spiritual and material worlds, by its awareness of the oneness of mankind, by an improved knowledge of human behaviour and by a realisation of the possibilities of individuals—for the individual is 'in a strictly scientific sense the highest phenomenon of which we have any knowledge'. Evolution could then be directed self-consciously in a way that would enable the fulfilment of human potential.

Evolutionary humanism is a specific form of modern scientific humanism. Though the name is not always used, scientific humanism is a widely adopted philosophical position. It is characterised by an opposition to supernaturalism and a desire to build a society based on scientific methods. In *The Philosophy of Humanism*, Cortiss Lamont (1949) describes contemporary humanism as a synthesis of, among other things, Renaissance humanism, materialism, democracy, scientific methods and ethical ideals that embrace the worth of the individual and a concern for all mankind. He maintains that it is a philosophy based on the 'enjoyment, development and making available to everyone the abundant, material, cultural and spiritual goods of the world' (1949, p. 3). Humanism, he claims, requires a complete social implementation of scientific method, an unending questioning of basic assumptions, a faith in man, a freedom of creative choice. Lamont's humanism exudes optimism and altruism—he rejects the belief that human beings are moved by self-interest or inclined to violence, he ignores the fact that science is destructive as well as constructive and, in effect, blends together all the nice ideas he can identify in Western history and philosophy.

Lamont's humanism is hopelessly unrealistic, and I suspect that if it were expressed in some built form it would be a theme park dedicated to the achievements of science and American democracy. It is nevertheless significant because it represents the sort of simplistic reduction to which humanism is susceptible. Fortunately not all scientific humanism is this naive. For example a much stronger case is put by H.J. Blackham in *Objections to Humanism* (1965). He suggests that humanism comprises, first and foremost, free enquiry. Each must think for himself or herself, and nothing is exempt from question. This is a radical suggestion for it means that there can be no ultimate beliefs, and free enquiry must therefore be exercised with considerable discipline or it can lead to despair and a loss of faith in the importance of everything. Free enquiry is pre-eminently the method of science, though science can become dogmatic and that must be resisted. For Blackham humanism also involves social agreement since human beings are human by virtue of society and their shared customs, values and languages. Such social conventions are, of course, provisional and open to question. Humanist ethics recognise that 'there are many possibilities, better and worse, and ways of avoiding the worse and increasing the better. Thus there are many patterns of good living' (Blackham, 1965, p. 17). This ethical position requires an attitude of tolerance, being willing to accept differences of habit and opinion and to forgive mistakes. And finally scientific humanism requires a commitment, a guide to the conduct of human life and a basis for human action. The humanist is, Blackham suggests (1965, p. 26), more than ordinarily public-spirited, takes a shared responsibility for 'creating the conditions for all of a life worthy to be called human', and faces squarely the problems of mankind such as the classical evils of ignorance, poverty and disease.

The principle of free enquiry makes unacceptable any traditional religious beliefs, for these are based in faith. Modern humanism is instead tied closely to science and to the development of technology as an aid for human progress. That these have caused serious social and environmental problems is recognised by scientific humanists, and they propose that we must take our ideas and techniques in hand, make them more sophisticated and less damaging, and must then use them deliberately, beneficently and responsibly to design a 'secular society on a planetary scale' (Kurtz and Wilson, *Humanist Manifesto II*, 1973, p. 15).

An admiration and advocacy of science and technology runs through most modern humanisms. But in existential humanism these are brought into question – science and technology are interpreted as having reduced freedom and choice, as making life seem empty and pointless, as surrounding individuals with such dense systems of objective and mechanistic thought that the will is stifled (P. Mairet, in Sartre, 1946, pp. 6ff). The separation of feeling and thought and action that science has caused can be overcome, according to the existentialists, through approaching the realities of life as they are experienced by struggling and uncertain human beings. Instead of working out some rational scheme for explaining and even living life, life should be accepted as it happens with all its confusions and ambiguities. These ideas were expressed most clearly by Jean-Paul Sartre in his essay *Existentialism is a Humanism* (1946). From the existentialist assumption that each of us is always free to choose our own purposes and actions it is clear that the responsibility for existence lies firmly on one's own shoulders. And since all actions are made not only for oneself but also on behalf of all mankind, each individual has responsibility for everyone. In the Western world the very manner of our daily living has serious implications for the countless millions of malnourished and starving people in the underdeveloped countries or those who suffer and are deprived in the developed countries. I know this and can choose to ignore it or to send money to relief agencies or to act in some positive way to redress the burden of suffering. Whichever I choose, my life is inextricably tied to the lives of countless others. However, in choosing how to act I cannot rely on innate goodness or some theory of behaviour derived from scientific research. These are vague abstractions, and in existential humanism it is commitment to actual people in real situations that is paramount.

Existentialism as a humanism does not uphold man as an end in himself or a supreme value against which all other values are to be measured. Instead, individual men and women are understood as being continually determined by the situations of their lives, as changing, as filled with doubts and fears and hopes. Man and his works are not the pinnacle of everything, nor can we live in some sort of reflected glory by wallowing in the glorious achievements of science and art. Yet Sartre (1946, p. 55) writes that: 'There is no other universe except the human universe, the universe of human subjectivity.' This may seem paradoxical but what he means is that there is no knowledge of which we are aware other than human knowledge, and that individual human beings are the source of knowledge – someone else cannot know the world for me. In short existential humanism proposes that whatever we know, whether it is commonsense or scientific understanding, is known only from a subjective and human perspective. Because of this we must take full responsibility for our actions and decisions. Such responsibility must not involve an authoritarian or idealistic stance, but must be realistic and humble.

The Confusions and Contradictions of Humanism

It should now be clear that humanism does not refer to a single, coherently circumscribed set of ideas that has persisted over several centuries. On the contrary, it changed its meanings and branched out in so many different directions that it now has to be qualified by some adjective or another if it is to be more than a vacuous expression of nice ideas. Even with the adjectives there is still confusion, for there appears to be a humanism for every persuasion and every personality.

The history of explicitly humanist arguments reveals shifts from theistic humanism in the Renaissance, to atheistic humanism in the Enlightenment, to Christian humanism now. The foundation of humanism in the concept of human reason is questioned by the humanism of existentialism and its recognition of irrational man. An emphasis on individual enlightenment has been challenged by Marxist humanists who stress the necessity for social change. Modern scientific humanists do not deny this need, but argue that it is to be achieved through free enquiry and technical progress rather than through political upheaval. Existential humanists, however, reject modern science and technology as alienating forces, and throw the weight of responsibility for the world back to individuals.

Humanism is, in fact, its own contradiction in almost every way that can be imagined. It is for God and denies God, for science and against science, for mankind's condition in general and for a man's situation in particular, for change through humanistic education and for change through political action. If there is some essential philosophy or attitude in all these positions it is no longer easy to recognise. Probably the only credo that would be accepted by all the factions of humanism is the statement of the pre-Socratic philosopher Protagoras: 'Of all things the measure is Man' (cited in Freeman, 1962, p. 125). But while they are all certain that this is an important and central idea, there is no agreement about what it actually means.

Notes

1. Humanism is also a central and persistent theme in Chinese philosophy. Since the relevance of this Chinese tradition of humanism to modern Western philosophy and landscape is limited and my knowledge of it is superficial, I do not consider it here.

5 HUMANISTIC AND SCIENTISTIC GEOGRAPHIES

Out of the variety of modern perspectives that call themselves 'humanism' there has developed a humanistic approach that can be adopted in academic investigations. Just as there has been discussion of scientific methods in sociology, psychology, geography and other disciplines, so now there is talk of humanistic perspectives and procedures. The exact character of these is still far from clear, and it differs from discipline to discipline, but it is apparent that humanistic approaches are united at least in their distaste for scientism and the reduction of human beings to mere units of behaviour in deterministic theories and quantitative models. Furthermore, great stress is placed on the humanist spirit of free but tolerant enquiry and on the diversity, subtlety and meaning of human experiences.

Humanistic Sociology and Psychology

The case for humanistic sociology has been put by Peter Berger (1963) in his *Invitation to Sociology*. All of Berger's writings and research are phenomenological, which means that he attempts to understand the various aspects of societies not primarily in terms of institutions, structures or class interests, but as they are experienced by individuals. Phenomenology is implicit in his argument for humanistic sociology. He maintains that the basic questions of sociology are: What are people's relationships to each other here? How are these relationships organised in institutions? What are the collective ideas that move men and women? These questions become important to sociologists through a sort of passion to find out about societies. However, this is unlike the passion of the physicist or archaeologist, which can be segregated from the rest of life, for a sociologist not only studies but lives in society. Of course there is some segregation, yet his own life is necessarily part of his subject matter. This poses the problem of familiarity—everything seems so obvious that there is nothing worthwhile to be said about it. Berger suggests, however, that sociology is a form of consciousness that looks always for the levels of reality behind those which are immediately apparent.

Humanistic sociology is opposed to an unthinking dependence on method and it rejects 'humourless scientism', but it is not anti-science. On the contrary it stresses those human values which are endemic to scientific procedures in both the social and the natural sciences. Such values are 'humility before the immense richness of the world . . . an effacement of self in the search for understanding, honesty and precision in method, respect for findings honestly arrived at, patience and a willingness to be proven wrong' (Berger, 1963, p. 166). The scientific methods which embrace these values are, in sociology, applied to 'the human condition' itself (p. 167), and the motives for using them should have to do with human needs and not with grandiose political or academic programmes.

According to Berger (p. 162) humanistic sociology can contribute to a modern humanism that does not call attention to itself and which is suspicious of too much enthusiasm or certainty; a humanism that is 'an uneasy, uncertain, hesitant thing, aware of its own precariousness, circumspect in its moral assertions'. It can nevertheless enter into passionate commitments where its fundamental insights into human existence are touched upon and denied, for instance where there is discrimination because of race or sex, or where the counter-human practices of torture and capital punishment are employed.

The strong argument for humanistic psychology that has been made by Abraham Maslow (1968; 1971) shares Berger's concern for human values in scientific methods but differs in its specific directions and its practical rather than academic interest in the possibilities of individuals realising their potential. Maslow contrasts humanistic with behavioural and Freudian psychologies, though he maintains that it embraces rather than opposes these, and develops it as an orientation which is based on a sound respect for the worth of persons, their potentials and their differences. He examines the desirable traits of human beings—love, creativity, intelligence—and considers how these can be nurtured to the fullest degree of humanness. Reason is given no special status in this humanistic psychology, and is understood as one among many human traits.

In this attempt to examine the potential of individuals there is no crass utopianism, but a recognition of what is really achievable for those who exercise self-control and responsibility. Everyone cannot be a genius in a single area, nor can everyone be accomplished in many different aspects of living. Maslow was, however, convinced that each one of us has potential in some area, whether art or music or cooking or personal relationships, and that this potential can be encouraged by us to reach its highest possible level.

In his investigations of the ways in which individual potential can be attained Maslow adopted an approach that he maintained was soundly scientific, though not in a reductionist way that seeks predictions and external control. Maslow's procedures did not take a neutral perspective and they did not shut out part of the data of experience arbitrarily on the grounds that they were not 'objective'. Indeed he argued that the scientific study of life should not try to be value-free, but should quite deliberately include values, personal goals, plans and intentions. He also argued that instead of seeking generalisations and averages attention should be focused on the best individuals and their best traits: 'If we want to know the possibilities for spiritual growth, value growth or moral development in human beings, then I maintain we can learn most by studying our most moral, saintly or ethical people' (Maslow, 1968, p. 7).

These best people should be investigated systematically, rigorously, using experiments whenever appropriate, but not with a cold and manipulative objectivity. They should be studied with 'Taoistic' objectivity. 'Taoistic means asking rather than telling. It means nonintruding, noncontrolling. It stresses noninterfering observation rather than a controlling manipulation. It is receptive and passive rather than active and forceful' (Maslow, 1968, p. 15). Instead of being detached this objectivity has the quality of 'loving perception', the sort of perception with which a mother regards her baby; it is absorbed, meticulous and thorough. Such loving objectivity, unlike those value-free methods which are inclined to murder and dissect, is passive and receptive and will leave alone whatever is being studied. Maslow acknowledged that this is not the only method for attaining truth, but for the issues of life and being human he thought it to be unquestionably the preferred approach.

Maslow's humanistic psychology is an elaboration of the best qualities and most profound experiences of people through the use of this compassionate objectivity. His research emphasised always the possibilities that were open to individuals to improve the quality of their living (he called this self-actualisation) within a social context. He believed that by emphasising the best that has been done and that can be done to meet the wide range of needs of human beings, it should be possible to make better and more humane societies.

The Brief History of Humanistic Geography

Intellectual and philosophical trends come late to geography. Thus phenomenology, positivism and Marxism, though debated and employed since the 1930s by sociologists, anthropologists and psychologists, have been discussed by geographers only since about 1970. There can, of course, be great benefits in standing apart from the current enthusiasms, allowing the philosophical chatter to fade and then adopting the fragments of wisdom that endure. This does not, however, seem to have been the situation with geographers; to judge by the evidence of publications they have simply been slow to grasp the significance of intellectual changes, or inclined to ignore them.

The current wave of interest in humanistic perspectives in the social sciences began in the early 1960s, and both Peter Berger and Abraham Maslow were then in a position to develop their arguments for sociology and psychology on the basis of studies of substantive topics (including their own writing and research) which were, in their terms, clearly humanistic. In contrast, the first discussion of humanistic geography was in 1976 (Tuan, 1976a); since then there have been published only one paper (Entrikin, 1976), part of a small conference at the University of Michigan (Deskins, 1977), and one book of original essays (Ley and Samuels, 1979) which deal with humanism or humanistic approaches in the discipline. In all of these it seems to be tacitly assumed that there is a viable humanistic tradition in geography; Entrikin (p. 616n) relates it to the use of phenomenological procedures, and Andrew Clark (in Deskins, p. 5) understood it as being manifest in historical geography, Ley and Samuels recognise it in the work of many human geographers. The fact is, however, that these identifications are imposed. There are no geographers who have called themselves humanists and deliberately written about geographical topics from a humanist perspective. There is no explicit humanistic tradition in geography.

The lack of a clear tradition leaves open three options for giving an account of humanistic geography. First, I could continue the efforts to disclose humanism in the work of geographers who did not think of themselves as humanists. This could perhaps uncover an unselfconscious tradition of humanistic geography. But it does require a precise understanding of humanism as it applies to geography, otherwise, given the many types of modern humanism, it would be quite possible to consider as humanistic the work of any geographer one happens to admire. Thus discussions of the spatial distribution of hunger and poverty, of love of place, of geographical wisdom, or of the human personality of regions and landscapes could all equally well be considered humanistic geography.

The second option is to write a manifesto – or at least some statement declaring what humanistic geography ought to be and do. This is, in part, what Yi-fu Tuan (1976a) did when he argued for a humanistic geography that takes its insights and methods from the humanities. To be developed in depth such a manifesto would require not only a grasp of the complex character of humanism, but also an elaboration of the need for this new humanistic perspective. In other words it requires a criticism of non-humanistic approaches.

The third option is to review and assess the few programmatic statements that have been made about humanistic geography. This is the most straightforward route, and it is the one with which I will begin here. I will then identify and describe those approaches used by some geographers which cannot be considered humanistic, and the deficiencies of which are one of the primary reasons for the recent proposals for humanistic perspectives. These approaches I describe as 'scientistic'. The final chapters of this book comprise a statement about what I believe humanistic geography should be, but, as I hope to demonstrate, the weaknesses and confusions of humanism are so great it is better to abandon altogether the word 'humanistic' and to think instead in terms of 'geographical humility', or 'environmental humility'.

Humanistic Geography Reviewed

Recent and limited though it is, the literature of humanistic geography already reproduces many of the difficulties apparent in modern humanism. Thus Nicholas Entrikin (1976) in his paper on 'Contemporary Humanism in Geography' argues that the humanistic approach is one which stresses meanings and values and which derives its impetus from phenomenology. It has been developed as an alternative to scientific methods, though he concludes that it can offer little in the way of substantive contributions of its own because it lacks any clear methodology. Indeed it can be no more than a form of criticism of scientific studies.

Yi-fu Tuan (1976a), who has himself adopted a phenomenological perspective in his writing on experience of place and landscape, gives an account of humanistic geography from a quite different perspective. He emphasises the links between geography and the methods and philosophies of the humanities. Humanistic geography must, he suggests, be tolerant of ambiguity and paradox, philosophically inclined, and directed towards an understanding of the appreciation of landscape, of attachment to place, and of the range of environmental experience.

Furthermore, Tuan maintains that this type of geography does not deny science, but works beside it to seek a comprehensive view of things and an awareness of the nature of human existence. He argues that the humanistic geographer needs a training in the nuances of language and in systematic thought or philosophy. With these skills he or she can then address questions of geographic knowledge, sense of place, privacy and crowding, livelihood and religion. The usefulness of humanistic geography, he believes, lies in the degree to which it raises the level of awareness about the subtleties and complexities of environmental experience.

Though he does not consider the idea of humanistic geography beyond a brief mention, it seems that Andrew Clark (in Deskins, 1977) held a notion very like that of Yi-fu Tuan. He equated it with the established traditions of historical and cultural geography, and argued that its distinguishing characteristics were imaginative synthesis and the careful interpretation of information.

David Ley and Marwyn Samuels (1979), in their introduction to the book of essays they edited under the title *Humanistic Geography*, argue that humanism aims to repair the destructive effects of scientific rationalism by putting 'man back together again with all the pieces in place, including a heart and even a soul, with feelings as well as thoughts' (pp. 2-3). Humanistic geography for them is not merely a form of criticism, but an active and constructive approach offering research possibilities in which there can be a reconciliation of '*human* geography and social *science*' (p. 9). Humanistic geography is thus conceived as a reorganised and redirected social science, neither critical of science nor beside it—but part of it.

These are the only four explicit discussions of humanistic geography, and they are not particularly helpful in clarifying its nature. Entrikin dismisses it as a minor and peripheral perspective, a terrier yapping around the heels of the sacred cow of scientific geography; Clark seems to be doing little more than substituting the word 'humanistic' for the word 'human'; Tuan and Ley and Samuels are more constructive, but do not agree on its relationship to other approaches within the discipline nor on the ways in which humanism meshes with the distinctive perspectives of geography. In fact, humanistic geography as it has been presented to us thus far seems to lump together many of the modern humanisms—Marxist, Christian, scientific, existential, as well as the elements of Renaissance and Enlightenment humanism, and the paternalism which advises that we should use our special geographical knowledge to help others.

Ley and Samuels, as editors of *Humanistic Geography*, left it up to the individual contributors to the book to decide just what humanism is (1979, p. 10). The consequence was that the various authors followed their own inclinations and enthusiasms. Thus Marwyn Samuels addresses 'Existentialism and Human Geography', David Ley considers the role of humanism in a geography of social action, Iain Wallace argues that a humanised economic geography must involve accountability to God, Graham Rowles describes the experiential approach he has used to study the ways in which elderly people relate to places, and so on. Though Ley and Samuels express satisfaction that all these diverse approaches have the common theme of 'man's place in the reconciliation of art and science in geography' (p. 10) this theme does not come through strongly and clearly. Furthermore, it carries with it much of the vagueness that besets humanism in general – 'man's place' could mean almost anything one chooses.

It is unfortunate that the argument for humanistic geography has been opened almost simultaneously on several fronts, and with little concern for the difficulties inherent in modern humanism. If humanistic geography is to develop coherence and utility it must avoid descent into banalities about 'human needs' or the 'human condition' or similar vague sentiments. It also has to avoid being reduced to simple methodologies for research into socially relevant problems, for it is precisely such naive dependence on method and orthodoxy that humanism claims to challenge. And more books of essays by many authors who are united by little more than an imprecise and unexpressed hope for some better, humanistic way of doing geography can only add to the confusion. The example of Peter Berger (1963) and Abraham Maslow (1968), writing respectively of humanistic sociology and psychology, should be followed – each author arguing his case through in terms of subject matter and method and philosophy. One may disagree with their arguments, but at least there are arguments to dispute, to modify, to develop and to apply to specific situations.

Humanistic geography at present consists of little more than a few expressions of possibilities. I am sympathetic to some of these possibilities yet I find little in them to debate or to build upon other than a few hints about sense of place and environmental experience. A sound formulation of humanistic geography must go much further than these. It must identify the types of geographical approach which are not humanistic, for if any approach can be considered humanistic then humanism is an undiscriminating and empty concept: I will argue that the non-humanistic types of geography are those based on an unthinking adulation of scientific method. It must also recognise that humanism is not all benign and in the best interests of others; it has deep deficiencies. And finally it must attempt to relate the concepts of humanism to the distinctive perspectives of geography so that the product really is 'humanistic geography' and not just some vaguely humanistic approaches forced onto an unchanged geography.

Scientistic Geography

Humanism has such breadth of meaning and flexibility of interpretation that it can be identified with almost any philosophical position. Furthermore, it is so noble and virtuous, with its apparent concern for all that is truly human, that there is surely nobody who would reject the title of humanist. In consequence humanism is always close to banality; to declare that someone is a humanist scarcely differs from saying that they are human. To avoid this it is necessary to set humanism against attitudes and approaches which cannot be considered humanistic. And it is necessary to make such a contrast both for humanism in general and more specifically here for humanistic geography. The type of geography which I believe cannot be considered in any sense humanistic is that which takes its inspiration and methods uncritically from a simplistic conception of the procedures of natural science. This is scientistic geography.

Scientism

Scientism has been defined by F. von Hayek (1955, pp. 15-16) as an attitude which is 'decidedly unscientific since it involves a mechanical and uncritical application of methods of thought to fields different from those in which they have been formed'. Not only is scientism not disinterested but it is very prejudiced, for before it has considered its subject it claims to know the best way to study it. In other words, there are appropriate ways of thinking for particular disciplines and subject areas, and these are not necessarily interchangeable. It may be possible to use the approaches of physics in sociology, but this must be done with careful attention to the differences between the two disciplines. When methods and philosophies are used without care for context they will confuse rather than clarify – even if all the methodological rules are precisely followed.

Scientism is an easy term of criticism and needs to be used with some caution. I am certainly not condemning all science by using it, but

I am questioning the appropriateness of the methods of natural sciences for investigating geographical and social issues.

There are two related types of scientism. The first of these involves the misapplication of scientific method. This method as it is usually understood involves the use of an hypothesis-testing, deductive approach that develops generalisations in order to explain particular events. Thus explanation involves bringing phenomena under mathematically describable laws, or generalisations, and research consists of attempts to disclose such laws. Law-finding has become the chief aim of much social research, and an hypothetico-deductive approach, aided by numerical data collection and statistical analyses, is used on the basis of an *a priori* assumption that such methods are valid ones for investigating social matters.

The second form of scientism involves the extension of a set of ideas and methods that have been developed in a specific and limited situation to a far larger context. This is what has happened with the belief that scientific methods can be used to study all issues, including such things as determining the authorship of the books of the New Testament by counting word frequencies or assessing landscape quality by measuring the grey tones in photographs. But this second type of scientism has another form – the dilation of results obtained in a single discipline or fragment of a discipline to all of life and society. For example, behavioural research in psychology has demonstrated that some animal behaviour can be conditioned; on the basis of this B.F. Skinner (1971) has proposed that human freedom, dignity and morality can also be conditioned and thereby transcended.[1] Similarly the microbiologist Jacques Monod (1970, especially Chapter 9), having discovered that globular protein is ordered by principles of chance and necessity, proposes that social organisation can be similarly ordered, and that religion must be rejected in this ordering because only science can be truthful. Such extravagant claims may be unusual, but it is common for economists to see the root of all problems in economics, for sociologists to argue that everything has a social significance, and so on. In every case considerable distortions and a quite remarkable arrogance are involved.

Scientism in Human Geography

The origins of scientism in geography lie most obviously in a paper by Fred Schaefer published in 1953. In that he argued against what he called exceptionalism – the notion that geography has its own distinctive approaches – and for the use of scientific methods to study spatial relationships since 'Spatial relationships are the ones that matter in geography and no other.' By defining geography as a discipline concerned solely with geometric space Schaefer made it accessible to scientific methods alone.

Schaefer's lead has been followed by most of a generation of geographers who have convinced themselves that geography is indeed a science like any other, or specifically a science like physics from whence all models of scientific method are drawn. Though it is not possible to get all geographers to agree on a definition of their discipline a definition like that of Maurice Yeates (1974, p. 1) would certainly meet with popular approval: 'Geography can be regarded as a science concerned with the rational development and testing of theories that attempt to explain and predict the spatial distribution and location of the various characteristics of the surface of the earth.' Such a definition requires a rejection of much that was traditionally considered to be geographical, for instance the study of the personality of regions and landscapes. Kevin Cox (1972, p. 371) declares that the formulation of geographical models 'usually involves a discarding of the unique or irrelevant characteristics of phenomena and a focus on the characteristics which phenomena share'. So uniqueness is equated with irrelevance and we gather that scientific geography deals with subjects only at an aggregate and abstract level in which the distinctiveness of place has no part.

Of course, redefining geography's field so that it is amenable to scientific approaches is not necessarily scientistic, even if it does ignore much previous practice in the discipline. What is especially scientistic is that this shift in orientation has allowed the use of all sorts of simplistic procedures which masquerade as scientific methods. Not all scientifically inclined geographers are guilty of this and some do use scientific procedures thoughtfully and critically, but there are many cases of simple outlines of method being offered with the clear implication that if you follow all the steps you will be doing *Science.* For example, J.P. Cole and C.A.M. King (1968, pp. 18-19) outline the stages of scientific method as (1) Develop some objective or problem to solve; (2) Collect relevant information from field work or published sources; (3) Prepare and store the data on maps or punch cards; (4) Process the data using mathematical procedures and statistical inference; (5) Present the results in a comprehensive way 'in the accepted language of science'.

More recently Fitzgerald (1974, p. 2) has given an account of scientific geographical method which requires making hunches about the relationships between distributions, the selection of data and their analysis to discover order in relationships, the development of a hypothesis to reduce the problem to a relationship between two or more variables, testing for statistical significance and generalising to create theory or a more structured model. The final stage is simply 'Predict'. All this is quite magical and marvellous; each stage is connected to the next by little arrows. The idea seems to be that statistically significant relationships constitute theory and that theories predict something. Similarly L.J. King and R. Golledge (1978, pp. 6-7) offer what they admit is a grossly oversimplified outline of scientific method. It involves raising questions about spatial regularities, seeking explanations to these questions by constructing a theory that yields a number of predictions by virtue of its logic, matching predictions against observations and, if the match is poor, modifying or reformulating the theory.

There are serious problems with these sorts of descriptions of scientific method. Not only are they grossly oversimplified, but words like theory, model, hypothesis and explanation are used inconsistently and even interchangeably. Furthermore, these accounts are usually offered as a recipe for scientific geography: get the right ingredients, follow the steps faithfully and science will be the result. In fact not only is there no guarantee of this, but the recipes have not been tested by experience and seem to be little more than approximate formulations of the way in which some geographers would like research to be done. The imagination, creativity and insight that are so fundamental to science are simply omitted. To reduce scientific method to a few simple steps is to promulgate scientism, and to follow those steps is no more science than painting by numbers constitutes art.[2]

Geographism

That scientific approaches are a possible way to investigate spatial problems cannot be seriously questioned, though to maintain that they are the only valid way of doing geography is certainly wrong. Scientific approaches properly used (that is, used according to their own sets of conditions and with due regard to the differences between natural science and geography) should lead to the formulation of 'positive theory', or accounts of spatial organisation and relationships as they actually are. Some geographers, however, have attempted to go beyond this and to develop 'normative theory', or an account which proceeds by an abstract and logical reasoning from a set of *a priori* postulates to a statement of how things *ought to be* spatially arranged. Now in physical science speculations about how cells and sub-atomic particles may be arranged are useful when no direct means of observation is possible, and the question of rearranging cells and particles to fit the theoretical speculation does not arise. In social science, however, normative theory is almost always linked to application through policy and planning. Economies and communities are manipulated so that they accord more closely with the supposed ideal situation that is indicated by normative theory. Used in this manipulative way normative theory is a manifestation of the second type of scientism, the type in which a limited idea is presented as a principle for the large scale reordering of the world.

In geography this scientism usually involves proposals that spatial distributions should be arranged to accord more closely with spatial theories. I call the belief that this is possible and desirable 'geographism'. It is a form of determinism, but unlike environmental determinism, which maintains that we *are* products of our setting, this is theoretical determinism and maintains that we *should be* determined by our theories about the ideal spatial arrangements of cities, roads and industries. For instance, Abler, Adams and Gould (1971, p. 575), in their introductory textbook *Spatial Organisation*, declare that 'Geography must continue to be theoretical and geographers must produce better theories than they have to date . . . Once formulated and tested such theories will create new dimensions of reality.'

Geographism embodies the view that people should behave rationally in geographical, two-dimensional space, or, in other words, that cities and industries and transportation routes should be arranged in the most efficient way. Efficiency is generally measured in economic terms and manifests itself in straight roads and neat hexagonal patterns of settlement with large cities surrounded by smaller cities, surrounded by towns. By implication, where such rational distributions and behaviour are not found there must be inefficiency and the people's behaviour is presumably spatially deviant. In these cases they can be guided and manipulated towards efficiency. Abler, Adams and Gould (1971) understand geographers to be the social engineers of spatial systems and they suggest that, just as physicists provide us with new sources of energy to heat and cool our homes, so 'Geographers are expected to rectify spatial incongruities and to take action against spatial incompatibility in the future' (p. 28). I am not sure exactly what this means, but for social engineers tasks are clearly defined, the essential variables are controllable, and people are simply manipulable units who can be redistributed to maintain spatial efficiency. Indeed Abler, Adams and

Gould announce that 'Explanation and manipulation are the focus of our discipline today' (p. 88; see also p. 575).

The aim of all this is to make actual places as spatially efficient as the idealised normative theories. Hence Michael Chisholm (1975, pp. 146-7) has argued for the application of geographical theories through planning. He writes that:

> It is probably necessary to conceive of normative theory for the system of settlements as a guide for the planner who, through the operation of controls, can impose his view upon the real world. Failing this the main use of normative theory at this level is to provide a yardstick against which to judge the efficiency of the real world.

So in contradistinction to the conventions of scientific method, which require that theory be tested against observation and the theory modified if they fail to match, here reality is tested against theory and reality changed where necessary. This notion that the scientific theories of geography are somehow better than reality seems to be a commonplace. For example Chorley and Kennedy (1971, p. 298), in a book promoting systems approaches for geomorphological and environmental research, claim that we are entering a period when:

> man, organised in ever more effective decision-making groups, is increasingly able to exploit his growing knowledge of the nature and operation of natural process-response systems so as to be able to intervene in them to exert an influence which will modify their operation in a planned and predictable manner, beneficial to man in the widest sense.

In other words Chorley and Kennedy believe that research teams of physical geographers and equivalent experts are rapidly developing such accurate explanations of the natural processes of rivers, shoreline erosion and mass movement that it should soon be possible to control them for economic gain without fear of unexpected side effects.

Such confidence in geographical understanding, whether of city systems or process-response systems, I cannot share. Certainly the logic is neat – these improved scientific methods are generating theories which demonstrate clearly how we can reorganise our lives and environments to make them better and more efficient. And since these are geographical theories it follows that geographers will have a major role in directing the reorganisation. The weaknesses in this logic are, however, manifold. The assumptions and reasoning on which the theories are based are dubious: why should spatial organisation be taken as the fundamental principle for a system of settlements? Serious doubts arise too about the expected success of applied technical and scientific knowledge: dams built with the best techniques available can crack, and new towns based on the latest and most sophisticated research have serious social problems. Especially there are doubts about the implications of these geographistic claims; the intention may be to encourage further economic growth and prosperity but a society founded on organised spatial efficiency has to be authoritarian and centrally planned, effectively manipulated by a group of experts to prevent it slipping into inefficiency. I find no arguments which demonstrate that this specialist geographical knowledge cannot be used for devious and repressive ends, such as the justification of the arbitrary uprooting and decline of some communities and the aggrandisement of others.

If there is doubt about these implications of normative geographical theory, there is no doubt that their application to particular communities and places will diminish the distinctiveness and individuality of these communities and places. Geographism involves the imposition of generalisations onto specific landscapes; it breeds uniformity and placelessness.

Humanistic and Scientistic Geographies Have a Common Basis

The problems of scientism in geography are trivial when compared with the evidence of widespread political oppression and torture, with the fact of hundreds of millions of people suffering from chronic malnutrition and undernourishment, with the threat of global nuclear war. Yet they cannot be dismissed simply because they do constitute a danger to our physical survival. The increased application of scientific geographical expertise could have a considerable impact on the quality of the cities and landscapes in which we live, an impact which could well be detrimental and make our lives that much more difficult or sadder.

It is fashionable to adulate the use of scientific method in the social sciences and to look with contempt upon the old-fashioned methods of description. But the case is that for all their analysis and exactness the new ways repress subjective experience. Individuals are considered only as single units within systems and structures, or as units for aggregation and averaging. That an individual life is inexact, that pleasure can come from unpredictability and from the unmeasurable qualities of persons and places, seems to be quite overlooked. Of course, scientific geography is not wrong for failing to treat subjective matters—no method can be expected to do everything. But it is wrong in so far as it demeans approaches which do consider subjectivity to be important, and in so far as it actually denies the individuality and distinctiveness of communities and landscapes.

The promotion and application of normative geographical theory has another serious consequence, one which it shares with the use of all forms of specialised knowledge and expertise. This is the reduction of the freedom of laymen or non-experts to decide and act on matters which directly affect their lives because they are now judged insufficiently qualified to take reasonable and informed decisions. Geographical theory has its impact chiefly through the medium of planning, and laymen are consulted in public enquiries or whatever and their knowledge is taken to be impressionistic and of an inferior kind. Freedom, it seems, has become freedom to acquire a professional training and then to impose one's expertise on others and on environments.

Gunnar Olsson is a geographer who was once enthusiastic about spatial scientific geography. His enquiry into the limitations of the logic employed in such geography (Olsson, 1975) has made him deeply disillusioned with it. He now recognises that it adopts 'a simplified and dehumanising conception of man', that it can be used detrimentally and repressively as easily as it can be used to encourage spatial efficiencies, and that 'scientific methodology can be made the handmaiden of authoritarian ideology' (p. 500). The possible consequences of the continued uncritical use of this scientistic thinking are not attractive: 'At the end', he declares bitterly (p. 496), 'is a society of puppets with no dreams to dream and nothing to be sorry for.'

Humanistic geography, hesitant, fragmented and peripheral though it is, is at least opposed to crass scientism and the prospect of a society of puppets. In its emphasis on the subtlety and meaning of environmental experiences and on the distinctive character of places and landscapes humanistic geography seems to provide a counterbalance to scientific geography. As yet the proponents of humanistic geography have been unable to demonstrate agreement either on the direction or on the methods which they wish to adopt. So it would, I think, be a serious mistake to talk with confidence of the prospects for humanistic geography. Its record is too brief, too constrained and too confused to warrant optimism. Without a clear and accepted approach it can never become more than an eccentric part of geography, a part that will be remarkable because its practitioners share no method and dwell in idiosyncracy as they try to show that love of place and a thoughtful humility towards environments are worthwhile concerns for geographers.

Nevertheless, there is a real need for a humanistic geography that can challenge effectively the easy generalisations of scientistic geography and geographism. Superficially it appears that a confrontation between scientism and humanism could well lead to a more popular and practical humanistic geography and more sensitive and less arrogant scientific geography.

Unfortunately it is not that simple. By a deep paradox it seems that the shortcomings of scientism are extensions of weaknesses that lie within humanism itself. Scientistic geographers are merely the latest participants in the well-established humanist tradition that expertise can be used rationally to improve the quality of life for others. The problem is that with increasing scientific and technical sophistication this best of intentions has become an orthodoxy that is restrictive and manipulative rather than beneficient. So it scarcely makes sense to propose humanistic geography or any other humanism as a means of resolving deficiencies that are derived from humanism, and certainly not without first trying to understand the character of those deficiencies.

Notes

1. It is indicative of the confused character of humanism that B.F. Skinner is a signator of the Second Humanist Manifesto (Kurtz and Wilson, 1973), and I find myself here describing as non-humanist the work of someone who has explicitly considered himself a humanist.

2. In this context the observations of Paul Feyerabend, an outspoken philosopher of science, are relevant. He claims (1978, p. 98) that there is no single scientific method or set of rules underlying research which guarantees that it is scientific, and he emphasises, as have many scientists, the importance of imagination, insight and unconventional approaches.

6 DEFICIENCIES OF HUMANISM

Geoffrey Scott (1914, p. 191) writing specifically about the humanist architecture of the Renaissance defined humanism as 'the effort of men to think, to feel and to act for themselves'. The questioning of orthodoxy and accepted beliefs, and the stress on responsibility for one's own ideas and actions, to which this philosophical position leads, are perhaps the central merits of humanism. These principles have, however, been adopted by so many different and contradictory traditions—science, Marxism, even theology—that they have been obscured and confused. Furthermore, they have frequently been diluted into ethically uplifting slogans and sentiments about love for mankind or the brotherhood of man. These are difficulties enough, but no doubt the confusions could be systematically clarified, and sentimental love for one's fellows somehow given substance, were it not for still deeper and possibly intractable problems. These problems bring into very serious question the value of humanism as a philosophical position in geography, in social science, or at all.

A suggestion of these problems lies in the development of scientism as an outgrowth of the emphasis on reason that is made in humanism. The ideology of objective observation, free enquiry and rational argument was essential in liberating the science of the eighteenth and nineteenth centuries from theological dogma and mysticism. As recently as the 1920s fundamentalist accounts of human origins were being taught with official sanction in the state of Tennessee and it took the famous 'Monkey Trial' to allow the Darwinian version of evolution to be taught in schools there. Yet in 1977 *The Times* of London reported the case of a secondary school teacher in Rickmansworth who had been dismissed for teaching the literal Genesis account of creation instead of the officially approved evolutionary version (cited in Schumacher, 1977, p. 146; see also pp. 111-16). An individual case perhaps, but one which symbolises the way in which the results of scientific, objective, free enquiries have have quickly become accepted as beyond question. While scientific methods are promoted as and believed to be the best ways of grasping the true nature of things, they have, like the religious orthodoxies which they displaced, become restrictive and inflexible. This means that in so far as humanism is linked with science, and in so far as scientific method is considered to be the only valid way of understanding reality, humanism contradicts its own basic principle of free enquiry.

There is a second deep weakness in humanism which must be addressed. Since the eighteenth century humanism has been advanced by its more zealous advocates as a possible solution to many of the world's ills. Their argument has been that torture, brutality, war, poverty and hunger are the results of ignorance; a universal humanistic education will necessarily result in the disappearance or reduction of these because everyone will then know better than to perpetrate or allow these inhumanities, and will have the knowledge and skills to correct those that exist. In spite of almost universal schooling, at least in the developed world, this has not happened. Indeed the history of the twentieth century suggests that as more people have become better educated the means of inflicting suffering have become more widespread, sophisticated and callous: consider biological warfare, the Somme, Auschwitz, Dresden, frontal lobotomies, neutron bombs and Cambodia. And the problems of poverty and hunger have not been resolved, merely hidden or transferred to the Third World. A universal education does not, it appears, have anything to do with creating more humane and compassionate societies.

There is little in our late-twentieth century lives that has not been invented, manipulated, explained and produced by industrial engineers, social scientists or natural scientists using objective methods of investigation and design, all with the express intention of improving our well-being. Since these methods and motives are clearly humanistic, elements of humanism can be found in most aspects of our existence. In part I can argue this because humanism is a vague term and a fuzzy philosophical position. Given this lack of clarity it is quite possible to attribute to humanism the blame for most of the ills of modern society. For instance, D. Ehrenfeld in his book *The Arrogance of Humanism* (1978) chooses to identify humanism in all those approaches which stress the domination of things and beings through the use of human intelligence. Practically everything he finds disagreeable can therefore be traced back to humanism because he is using the term in its vaguest way and is defining it as the chief source of everything he finds disagreeable. I will try to avoid such tautology by considering only the two major deficiencies of humanism which I have already introduced – its association with science and scientism, and the failure to achieve its own aim of causing a significant change in human behaviour. In both cases the contribution of humanism has been explicit, and I can therefore be reasonably sure that I am not criticising some illusion of my own making.

Scientific Humanism

The bonds between science and humanism have always been close. The classical scholars or humanists of the Renaissance translated many classical works on science. In the eighteenth century their successors, stressing as they did free thinking and rigorous enquiry into the nature of all things, came to recognise that these attributes were well represented in the approaches being adopted by scientists. Furthermore, the achievements of scientists—especially Newton's discoveries about mechanics and optics—provided persuasive evidence of the value of these approaches. With subsequent discoveries in chemistry and physics and the evolutionary explanations of Darwin, science came to be regarded not merely as a successful manifestation of humanistic philosophy, but as the highest accomplishment of man and human civilisation. This attractive idea is still widely maintained. The philosopher Ernst Cassirer (1944, p. 229) has written that: 'Science is the last step in man's mental development and it may be regarded as the highest and most characteristic attainment of human culture.' Cassirer acknowledged fully the importance of myth, religion, art and language, and he was well aware of the inadequacy of scientific method alone to answer the question 'What is Man?'. Yet science was for him the foremost achievement to have resulted from the application of the principle of scepticism which is, he suggested, simply 'the counterpart of a resolute humanism' (p. 1).

The period between 1920 and 1950 was the heyday of arguments to promote scientific humanism as the philosophy of the future. Cortiss Lamont (1949) maintained that humanism depends on the unimpeded exercise of reason and that we are closest to the life of reason when we approximate most closely the methods of science in solving all human problems. Since he believed scientific method to be socially and ethically neutral he argued that a humanist ethic of 'happiness for all humanity' must be applied to science to ensure its goodness (p. 227). Almost two decades earlier the historian of science George Sarton (1931) had contrasted the old, narrow-minded anti-science of the humanities with the 'New Humanism'. 'The New Humanism will not exclude science,' he wrote (1931, p. 162), 'it will include it . . . science is the core of it . . . it will extol the human implications of science.'

A similar case for a new scientific humanism had been made by Lothrop Stoddard, a professor at Harvard, in 1926. A New Age (not just a new age) is at hand, he declared, one that will involve the freeing and opening of the mind through the scientific attitude of the working hypothesis and the coupling of modern science with Renaissance humanism. He concluded condescendingly that the 'common man' can be encouraged to understand that a 'Humanistic Age' could mean to him 'a richer, fuller, happier life' (p. 174).

The vision of these evangelists for scientific humanism was of a future in which scientific method would be used faultlessly by expert scientists for the good of the whole society. It was not a fanciful and idealised vision, but had immediate and practical applications. In 1933 Frederic Towndrow published a book titled *Architecture in the Balance: An Approach to the Art of Scientific Humanism.* In this he criticised all revived and aesthetic styles of building and made a case for the 'scientific architect' whose prime concerns are to reason or calculate scientifically according to the best of his ability, to design functionally in the logical manner of an engineer, and to serve aesthetic needs not by being concerned with beauty but by increasing the efficiency of well-being—that is by making buildings more ordered and better organised (p. 176). But what is really significant is that Towndrow was able to identify recently constructed buildings—houses, automobile showrooms, yacht clubs, restaurants—which matched his criteria for an architecture of scientific humanism. He was already writing in the 1930s not about a future age but about current practice.

Reason and Rationalism

It is no longer fashionable to write polemics praising scientific humanism. This does not mean that the attitudes which it encompasses are not important. On the contrary it is because many of the hopes of those who promoted scientific humanism half a century ago have been almost completely realised. Scientific method, the principle of efficiency and the unquestioned acceptance of science in the service of man are manifest in factory farms and fast-food chains, in urban and transportation planning, in micro-computers and video games, in the design of shopping centres and airports, in the format and content of countless research reports written for business and government, in the search for cures for cancer and new transplant techniques, and in television programmes and monthly magazines which examine enthusiastically the latest scientific advances. Because our lives are circumscribed by scientific method used for human benefit it is no longer necessary to promote and praise scientific humanism.

In scientific humanism science ceases to be just a way of wondering about the nature of the world, and is transformed into technical knowledge. Most scientific activity is now directed towards practical ends, even though these may not be immediate and obvious. Scientific knowledge has become knowledge that can be used to control natural processes or social conditions. It is precisely because of this that the philosopher Max Horkheimer (1947, p. vi) could declare wistfully that:

> It seems that even as technical knowledge expands the horizon of man's thought and activity, his autonomy as an individual, his ability to resist the growing apparatus of mass manipulation, his power of imagination, his independent judgement, appear to be reduced. Advance in technical facilities for enlightenment is accompanied by a process of dehumanization.

Horkheimer called his book *The Eclipse of Reason* because he thought that the excessive and unreasonable use of methods based on reason and free enquiry was rapidly overwhelming the validity of such methods. In short, the concept of rationality which is at the basis of modern industrial culture contains defects which vitiate itself. Reason, the committed but disinterested intelligence reflecting on things, has become rationalism, the belief that truth can be ascertained only by objective analysis.

This vitiation has occurred in part because the method of scepticism has been applied with such ruthlessness that nothing has been able to stand before it and nothing has been permitted to have value merely by virtue of existence. Opinions, feelings, beauty, personal relations, love, have all been subjected to the cold gaze of scientific method. To be 'real' something must be observed objectively and verified by controlled experiment or logic. Without such formal verification only trivial statements can be made about something, and therefore nothing meaningful can be said about beauty, goodness, love or faith because they all have to do with subjective and unverifiable feelings. This attitude was justifiably ridiculed by C.S. Lewis in *Screwtape Letters* (1968, p. 232); an older devil is giving advice to a junior devil currently on active missionary duty on Earth:

> The general rule is that in all the experiences which can make them happier or better, only the physical facts are 'Real', while the spiritual elements are subjective . . . Your patient, properly handled, will have no trouble in regarding his emotion at the sight of human entrails as a revelation of Reality, and his emotion at the sight of

happy children or fair weather as mere sentiment.

The obvious callousness in the methods which scientific humanists have advocated as the basis for the full flowering of the human spirit is, E.P. Schumacher has argued (1977, pp. 15-25), a manifestation of a drastic reorganisation in conceptions of the way in which matter, life and thought are ordered. The understanding of Renaissance humanists was that man is the pinnacle of creation; above him was the supernatural, beneath him were the animal world of feeling, the plant world of life and the world of matter (Figure 4.1). Schumacher points out that these four levels are discontinuous; there is nothing in the world of matter to suggest properties of life, nothing in plants that anticipate the consciousness of animals. Conversely each level includes all the levels beneath it so that:

Man comprises Intelligence, Feeling, Life, Matter
Animal comprises Feeling, Life, Matter
Plant comprises Life, Matter
Matter is irreducible

Scientific humanism has wrought havoc with this hierarchical conception of things. Physics, the study of matter, has become the model discipline for scientific method and the most sophisticated in terms of its formulation of scientific laws. Biology, the study of life forms, has yet to formulate laws and theories of equivalent sophistication and universality as those in physics, but descriptions of life properties have become highly refined. Ethology, the study of animal behaviour, is as yet quite rudimentary. Psychology and sociology, the studies of man as an individual and in groups, have gained scientific respectability largely by reducing human properties to numbers or to animal qualities (hence behavioural psychologists study rats, pigeons and fish). The humanities, including philosophy, may have something to say about man, about self-awareness and thinking, but since it is all non-verifiable it is, for the scientific humanist, inconsequential.

In short the hierarchy of being that was part of Renaissance humanism has been exactly inverted in scientific humanism. Material reality is what is best known, and life properties, feelings and self-awareness are respectively less well explained. In the new chain of being 'reality' has come to mean the world of inanimate matter and process, and all experiences, moods, feelings, opinions, imaginations and beliefs are real only in so far as they can be measured and tested scientifically. But our commonsense shows this to be ridiculous. Schumacher (1977, p. 24) wrote that 'The most "real" world we live in is that of our fellow human beings. Without them we should experience a sense of enormous emptiness; we could hardly be human ourselves, for we are made or barred by our relations with other people.'

Scientific Expertise and Contempt for Ordinary Knowledge

The view that scientific methods are neutral and objective and therefore the best methods for explaining reality is by implication contemptuous of other forms of knowledge. Noam Chomsky (1967, p. 25), in the course of a discussion which brings into question this supposed objectivity and demonstrates how many scientists sell their skills regardless of the ends, gives a frightening example of such contempt; he cites a statement by Harold Agnew, who was then the director of the Weapons Division at Los Alamos: 'The basis of advanced technology is innovation and nothing is more stifling to innovation than seeing one's product not used or ruled out of consideration on flimsy premises involving public world opinion.'

Though its eventual implications could be all too close, weapons technology is remote from most of us. The development of similarly contemptuous attitudes in medicine can have much more immediate consequences for our day-to-day lives. P. Feyerabend (1978, pp. 136-7, 205ff), a philosopher of science who argues that scientific methodology has become a narrow ideology, maintains that medical science limits its scope to surgical and pharmaceutical cures; traditional herbal remedies, acupuncture and cures which are not demonstrably scientific are either professionally outlawed or dismissed scornfully—even if they are known to be successful. This criticism is developed further by Ivan Illich in *Limits to Medicine* (1976). He argues that because of its dependence on scientific expertise modern medicine has become elitist and has expropriated the power of an individual to heal himself or herself. The doctor or specialist is now rarely an artisan exercising a skill on a personally known patient, but is a technician applying scientific rules to classes of patients.

This sort of alienation, or scientific detachment, can result in quite appalling indifference. Consider the case, carefully reported by the parents in *The Atlantic*, of a premature baby who was kept alive for six months against the parent's wishes, largely, it appears, because the doctors thought he had 'interesting problems' (Stinson, 1979). The baby was fifteen weeks premature, weighed less than two pounds, but was declared 'salvageable' and put in a respirator. He subsequently suffered a host of iatrogenic (caused by medicine) inflictions including respirator lung syndrome, cyanosis, cessation of brain growth, demineralised and fractured bones and numerous infections. The parents had signed the normal consent form so the responsibility for the baby rested with the specialists who for several months tried one approach after another to keep him alive, as no doubt they felt professionally obligated to do. Perhaps some future premature baby will survive unharmed because of the information gathered from this case, but it does seem that Andrew Stinson was little more than an object of medical and scientific curiosity and was used for testing new technologies. Eventually the respirator tube became detached, the parents' protests were respected, the tube was not replaced, and the baby was allowed to die.

The problem apparent in this case is a widespread one. It is that technical knowledge has so outdistanced ethical understanding that what is beneficial or detrimental, and even what is life and what is death, are determined first and foremost on technical grounds. These technical grounds are not fully comprehensible to anyone other than technicians who must therefore take value decisions even though their knowledge is supposed to be ethically neutral. In the instance of Andrew Stinson, as in many others, this invariably means placing the acquisition of knowledge for the public and future good above the damage or destruction of the particular and present circumstance. Commonsense knowledge is now worthless opinion and compassion is irrational sentiment.

Scientific and technical expertise is absolutely necessary for maintaining many aspects of modern life, and ours is a society dependent upon experts. There are no grounds for thinking that such experts, merely by virtue of professional training, will be benign in their actions; indeed if their training has been rigorously scientific it will have been quite neutral with respect to such matters. Furthermore, this dependence on scientific expertise is fundamentally non-democratic—the person without specialist training cannot participate equally or effectively. Indeed, even scientific experts have authority only in their limited specialist areas. This hardly fits with the vision that the scientific humanists of the 1920s and 1930s had of a society run according to the principles of scientific method and promoting happiness, health and freedom. In fact one philosopher, A.R. Louch (1966, p. 239) sees a quite different prospect:

> Totalitarianism is too weak a word and too inefficient an instrument

> to describe the perfect scientific society . . . In the engineer's society, perhaps unwittingly promoted by psychologists and sociologists bent on being scientists, we should have to give up the idea of an open or civil society which, however inefficiently, serves as the prop for a social order based on respect for men as persons or autonomous beings.

Scientific Humanism and the Fallacy of Environmental Control

Humanism stresses that each of us is responsible for our own thoughts and actions. Scientific and technical knowledge offer the possibility of translating that responsibility into the control of environments and social circumstances. In the perfect scientific society both human and non-human nature are precisely controllable and predictable; the Brave New World has neither free-will nor natural disasters.

David Ehrenfeld is a biologist and conservationist who has levelled an attack at scientific humanism on the grounds that it is an attempt to use rationalistic human intelligence to dominate human and natural environments (Ehrenfeld, 1978). From the perspective of scientific humanism the world has been designed for man to manipulate to his own ends; through the effective use of engineering structures, chemicals and planning techniques, resources can be harnessed, rivers tamed, yields increased and pests eliminated. Ehrenfeld argues that humanism is arrogant because of its conviction that all problems are solvable, most of them by technical means, and that human destiny can be controlled. This conviction has led to persistent attempts at control, and indeed many extremes of climate and hydrology have been reduced, resources systematically exploited and environments everywhere managed successfully for human benefit.

Ehrenfeld maintains that many of these benefits are illusory, and that confidence in the powers of rational analysis and technology to resolve environmental problems is a form of self-deception. Of course much environmental manipulation and management does benefit us and has enabled us to achieve a high material standard of living. But at what price? Ehrenfeld lists the destructive impacts of scientific humanism as the loss of wilderness, the elimination of plant and animal species and communities, the erosion of cultured landscapes by uniformly efficient modern developments, the disappearance of human skills and craftsmanship, the profligate use of resources for dubious ends and the increase in man-made threats to health. He has no faith in the powers of science and technology to put these right, but suggests rather that they will make things worse. Indeed he proposes (p. 97) two laws of human experience which are, first, that most scientific discoveries can be developed in such a way that they are capable of doing great damage to people, their cultures and environments; and second, if a discovery or technology can be used for evil or mischievous purposes it will be so used.

These criticisms are not easily dismissed for we are surrounded by evidence that supports them. Newspapers and television documentaries provide an impressive list of new technologies to dam, mine, drill, calculate, irrigate, shoot into space and destroy; and there is a parallel litany of unintended side effects and misapplications of these new technologies. The cases of DDT, mercury, PCB, 245-T, thalidomide and their effects on wildlife and human health are well known: they are but a few of thousands of hazardous chemicals and processes which have been invented in the last fifty years. Then there are the instances of forgotten chemical dumps, missing uranium and plutonium, meltdowns and near meltdowns, chemical explosions, silted reservoirs, oil tanker sinkings, extermination of whales, destruction of tropical forests and possible radiation damage from micro-wave transmitters. Plutonium has been taken from peaceful nuclear power stations in order to make atomic weapons, anthrax is cultivated for biological warfare, computers are used to compile complete records on suspect citizens, even solar technology is being adapted for possible military uses (satellites which concentrate solar energy onto targets by means of laser beams). The list of side-effects and misapplications is as long as the list of new technologies. Even legislation can provide no safeguard: there are reputed to be botanists and biologists employed by construction companies to rid potential sites of rare and endangered species and thus prevent the chance of a development being stopped because of its threat to those species.

Ehrenfeld's polemic against scientific humanism and this familiar list of environmental mistakes demonstrate the fallacy of attempts at perfect control of environments. In this there is some small cheer for it reduces the likelihood of a society based on scientific totalitarianism. In its place we are left with what George Steiner (1971, p. 58) calls 'a truth that mocks us'—the material progress that comes with technical achievement is implicated in a dialectic of damage that destroys irreplaceable equilibria between nature and society.

This is the generous view. I believe that it was Noam Chomsky (1967) who reflected on the mandarism of scientists of all kinds and their remarkable ability to generate ever more potent and destructive technologies, and then he concluded that: 'As the scientists are busy engineering the world's annihilation, the social scientists have been entrusted with the smaller mission of engineering the world's consent.' Of course this is not their intention. There is no great scientific conspiracy against our lives and liberties. On the contrary the motives of scientific humanists and humanistic scientists are utterly benevolent. They wish to preserve peace and to increase prosperity. The final demise will be in spite of their intentions but because of their rationalistic methods and the humanism and scientism which underlie these.

The Failure of Humanism to Teach Humane Behaviour

It has been the hope of humanists from the Renaissance to the present day that a universal humanistic education would be instrumental in ridding the world of folly, cruelty and suffering. These are, they believed, the products of ignorance, and the cultivation and dissemination of humanist wisdom, reason and scientific training would result in the development of rational and beneficial behaviour and the creation of gentle and humane societies in which man's inhumanity to man had all but disappeared. This has not happened, even though for a century now there have been public education systems founded on a sound versing in the humanities and sciences.

In a book called *Humanism and Terror* the phenomenological philosopher Maurice Merleau-Ponty (1947) argued that any philosophical position, if it is to be honest and realistic, must acknowledge the necessity of violence to overcome greater violence. Appeals to reason and brotherly love are simply not enough and by retreating from violence and terror these may well be prolonged. Merleau-Ponty (p. 176) identifies what he terms 'a humanism of comprehension' which has been based, in the eyes of its members, on a love of humanity and on guarding the achievements of Western civilisation. Man's highest accomplishments in art, architecture, music and science are the concern of those who hold to this sort of humanism, and for them wars, political torture and mass starvation seem to belong to another world. Merleau-Ponty points out that this love for humanity and the refined products of Western culture proved to be a fragile barrier against the bestiality of the First World War, against the Holocaust, against the development and use of nuclear weapons. Indeed many of those who were deeply involved in these atrocities and wars were cultured and civilised individuals. Concentration camp commandants organised string-quartets of prisoners to play Beethoven to the Jews on their way to the gas chambers.

This condemnation of humanism has been reaffirmed by George Steiner, a scholar of literature and language. He states simply (1971, p. 64) that there has been 'no carry-over from humanism to the humane' and that we must recognise clearly the inhuman potentialities of cultivated men and women. 'A theory of culture', he writes (pp. 31-2), 'an analysis of our present circumstance, which do not have at their pivot a consideration of the modes of terror that brought on the death, through war, starvation and deliberate massacre of some seventy million human beings in Europe and Russia [between 1914 and 1946] seem to me irresponsible.' Humanistic models and traditions did not only fail to prevent this slaughter but may even, through their ingenuous faith in reason and human goodness, have helped to solicit authoritarianism and cruelty. George Steiner (1971, p. 69) again:

> What good did high humanism do for the oppressed mass of the community? What use was it when barbarism came? Do those for whom a great poem or theorem are the supreme values not help the throwers of napalm by cultivating 'objective sadness'?

The Death of Man and the Ontological Triviality of Humanism

The death of Man is proclaimed by Michel Foucault in *The Order of Things* (1970, p. 355). Foucault, an historian of culture and thought, maintains that man is no longer at the centre of Western thinking. Since the Dark Ages the grand paradigms which have conditioned Western thought were Theism in the medieval period, Humanism in the Renaissance and now Naturalism. From God to Man to Nature. Man is now merely one object among many to be explained by the methods of natural science.

If Foucault's observation is right it becomes anachronistic to argue for humanism. Its time is past. We can, he suggests, either join in the race of rationalistic science with its delusions of control and prediction, or despair at human arrogance and brutality, or be fascinated by the fact that we are alive at the time of such issues.

Fortunately such cynicism and hopelessness is not the only course open. Martin Heidegger, one of the most important and influential philosophers of the present century, was no less critical than Foucault of humanism, but he also sought to suggest other possibilities for thinking about humanity. In a 'Letter on Humanism' written in 1947 in part to address the question 'How can we restore meaning to the word "humanism"?', and partly to address the arguments defending existentialism as a humanism that had recently been made by Jean-Paul Sartre (1946), Heidegger formulated both a profound ontological criticism of humanism and provided other grounds for thinking about man's humanity.

Sartre had argued that 'existence precedes essence' or that subjectivity is the point of departure for all understanding and action; thus a man is defined by what he does and how he acts and not by some abstract principle such as reason or rationality. In response Heidegger questioned first whether there is much point in retaining the word 'humanism'; it is just another -ism, a category or label which like all labels suggests the end of responsible thinking (Heidegger, 1947, p. 195). To describe an idea as humanistic or to call someone a humanist is to pigeonhole them without seriously considering what those terms mean. The second question Heidegger raised had to do with subjectivity. Placing man at the centre and making human existence the source of values, as both existentialism and humanism do, is to commit a serious and distorting anthropocentrism. Man does not decide whether and how beings exist, or how the gods and history and nature have presented themselves. These have their own being, their own existence which cannot be reduced to or encapsulated in the humanist belief that man is the measure of all things.

Heidegger did not, however, reject entirely as false humanistic interpretations of man as a rational being—rather he said that they did not set the humanity of man high enough. By this he meant that as human beings we have a responsibility to all things that exist to acknowledge the simple fact that they are, and then to care for them. In the determination of the humanity of man what is essential is not man but Being: 'Being is It itself . . . Being is farther than all beings and yet is nearer to man than every being, be it a rock, a beast, a work of art, a machine, be it an angel or god' (Heidegger, 1947, p. 210). So things have value and meaning in themselves, and not just because of their utility for humans. As human beings our task is to respect the fact of existence, for we have no special status as beings except that by virtue of thinking and language we can acknowledge and care for Being.

This is a difficult but profound argument. It rejects humanism for its self-centredness, yet stands for all that is humane and reasonable. Heidegger asks (p. 255): 'Should we still keep the name "humanism" for a "humanism" that contradicts all previous humanism—although it in no way advocates the inhuman?' His answer is an unequivocal 'No'. 'Humanism' is best abandoned.

Humanism Rejected

The ideal of humanism – the exercise of free thinking for the benefit of all mankind – was once a laudable ideal. In the Renaissance perhaps, and in the Enlightenment, it made sense to attach great hopes to the exercise of human reason, it offered a new and non-dogmatic way of thinking and doing that stood to bring great improvements in the conditions of life for everyone. And indeed it did – our lives are more comfortable, healthier, longer, and less restricted geographically than those of any of our ancestors: these achievements were all guided by the usually implicit, and, until the mid-nineteenth century, unnamed philosophy of scientific humanism.

But the ideal has become tarnished. It is no longer something that seems worthy of aspiration. In the twentieth century humanism has become an easy label, an orthodoxy which circles around itself, impedes thinking with its sentimental slogans, encourages a dependence on spurious expertise, manifests itself in the striving to dominate nature, and has done nothing to prevent or reduce man's inhumanity. Humanism is a confused cause characterised by empty sentiments and high-sounding phrases from another age.

There is no choice but to reject humanism. I reject it in general because it does not, perhaps cannot, address the philosophical, political and social circumstances of the late-twentieth century. I reject it furthermore because under the guise of material beneficence it has helped to undermine ethics and the validity of subjective experiences, and it has contributed to a reduction in the freedom of individuals to make their own lives and places by arrogating such responsibility to technically-trained experts. And I reject humanism specifically as a philosophical perspective appropriate for geography, because it is naively anthropocentric and can give little direction for understanding non-human nature except as something to be dominated and controlled for human ends.

PART THREE

ENVIRONMENTAL HUMILITY

'Man is not the Lord of beings; he is the shepherd of Being.' (Martin Heidegger, 1947, p. 221)

7 FROM HUMANISM TO ENVIRONMENTAL HUMILITY

No matter how serious the deficiencies of humanism may be, it is impossible to dismiss everything written and done in its name. The humanist principles of reason, tolerance and responsibility for one's own actions lie deep within Western culture. They have proven to be peculiarly stubborn and enduring and it is not possible to undo them with a few paragraphs of criticism.

As an explicitly named and categorised philosophical position, however, humanism has a history that goes back only to the first half of the nineteenth century. It is this comparatively brief explicit tradition of humanism that has run its course. It seems that the very act of putting valuable principles and ideas into a distinct category robbed them of their vitality and made them prey to confusion. These weaknesses have subsequently been so compounded that it would be an extremely difficult and probably impossible task to reclaim the insights of the humanist thinking of the Enlightenment or Renaissance. Science is now confused by scientism, reason by rationalism, individual responsibility has been reduced to self-interest, and social responsibility has become authoritarian. Furthermore, since the original concepts and their distorted progeny are all part of a single, continuous tradition it is impossible to separate them neatly, rejecting the confusions and retaining the insights intact.

There is, I believe, a more constructive approach than that of attempting to clarify weary humanist concepts, an approach that keeps some of the vital features of humanism yet reformulates them and brings them into a new light. This involves, on the one hand, going back to the very roots of humanism, which leads directly to the idea of 'humility'; and, on the other hand, using this idea to transcend the deficiencies of humanism, to leave it behind as an obsolete and narrow philosophical perspective.

Environmental Humility

The sources of humanism lie not in the authority of man but, quite literally, in humility. The root of 'human' is the Latin *humanus*, which derives from *homo*, meaning man. Similarly the word 'humility' comes from the Latin *humilis*, also derived from *homo*. And *homo* is in turn a derivation of *humus*, earth, for man is the earth-born who will return to the earth (Partridge, 1958, p. 292).

The stale slogans and confused arguments of humanism have come to advocate ever greater control of both men and nature by human beings for their own furtherance. I reject these arguments and return to the notion of humility. Specifically I wish to make a case for 'geographical' or 'environmental humility', for this preserves and stresses the original sense of human-beings as earth-bound and as implicated in rather than as overlords of the world around them. But 'environment' does not simply mean 'nature'; as I understand and use the term here it embraces without distinction both man-made and natural settings.

Yi-fu Tuan (1976b, p. 5) has written that humanistic geographers must sacrifice the single vision of Newton and the capacity to act. This can equally well be said of those who practice environmental humility, but there are compensations for the loss of focus and practicality. There is a gain in the breadth of vision, and no narrow or proscribed method to be followed; and there is the inestimable benefit of restraint, the willingness to leave places alone and to allow them to be maintained and modified by the people who live in them. These gains are not merely academic—environmental humility has to do with the way in which life is lived. If it is not to be hypocritical and trivial it cannot be taken up and put down as personal whim or convenience dictate, but must contribute to every thought and action no matter whether those are abstruse and academic, such as writing a book on sense of place, or practical and mundane, like planting a vegetable garden. In short, environmental humility cannot be reduced to a single, simple method of definition. In that respect, even its name is misleading, for it suggests a distinct category of thought and behaviour, whereas I intend it to embrace loosely a multitude of ways of treating the world. These have in common only an inclination to work with environments and circumstances rather than trying to manipulate and dominate them.

Since they have a common source it is to be expected that environmental humility and humanism will share some principles, even if these are not understood in exactly the same way. Thus they both accept the importance of individuality and acknowledge that individuals must take responsibility for their circumstances and for the consequences of their actions. Merleau-Ponty (1947, p. 176) wrote that in every person there is a power more precious than their productive capacity, namely their individuality and the fact that they are capable of self-determination.

To grasp this fully requires that we develop the imaginative capacity to transpose ourselves into the lives of others, such as novelists do, so that we can see matters from their point of view and realise the effects of our actions for them. This is the ability needed too if we are to treat others as we would wish to be treated ourselves.

In addition to individuality environmental humility takes and extends the humanist principle of tolerance so that it becomes a willingness to be tolerant not only of different beliefs but also of things and places as they now are, a willingness in other words to leave them alone. Abraham Maslow, a humanistic psychologist, called this 'Taoistic objectivity' and characterised it in this way (1971, p. 18):

> We are content to leave it alone. We make no demands on it. We do not wish it to be other than it is. We are passive and receptive before it . . . Approving of its existence, approving of the way it is, as it is, permits us to be non-intrusive, non-manipulating, non-abstracting, non-interfering perceivers.

Whether we choose to call this attitude Taoistic objectivity or tolerance it is marked by the belief that knowledge and technique do not have to be used merely because they are available. And furthermore it resists what William James called 'vicious intellectualism' and A.N. Whitehead described as 'the fallacy of misplaced concreteness', namely the use of theories and abstractions as though they are real and have substance.

If some ideas are shared by humanism and environmental humility at least one is not—anthropocentrism. In environmental or geographical humility man is not at the centre, but understood to be a part of a continuum of nature and culture in which human beings both influence and are influenced by their settings. Human activities must therefore always be seen in their larger social and environmental contexts. This is perhaps the major insight of geography; it informs us that there are no clear boundaries to either human or natural processes, that nothing happens with absolute certainty and in isolation, that no systems are closed, that relationships rarely work in one direction only. Confronted with the recognition that a landscape is comprised of countless elements—such as houses, trees, soil particles, clouds, cars, advertisements and mountains—and involves countless processes, most of which are far more complex and intractable than anything encountered in a physics laboratory, the only sensible option for a geographer is to be humble, confess that none of it can be adequately explained and confine all efforts of understanding to description.

This may seem unduly contrite. However, environmental humility does not mean that we have to adopt a self-effacing subservience to nature. That would require returning to a life of bare subsistence which would be neither comfortable nor desirable even if the world's population could be convinced that it was necessary for their spiritual well-being. Throughout history men and women have struggled to escape the life of meagre survival, and the achievements of this struggle should not be lightly forsaken.

The philosopher Martin Heidegger, having condemned humanism, then wrote (1966, p. 278) that: 'The world cannot be what it is, or the way that it is, through man, but neither can it be without man.' In other words everything cannot be assessed solely in human terms because the existence of rivers, animals and clouds owes nothing to human beings; equally it is impossible to pretend that we are only a part of nature like ants or ostriches. We are implicated in nature, yet separated from it by virtue of our language and our thinking which make us self-conscious. Heidegger argued that this conditioned separation and self-awareness gives human beings a profound responsibility for the guardianship and protection of all things. In other words we have an obligation to look after people, creatures, plants, landscapes and everything else as they exist, simply because they exist. In the acceptance of this responsibility there is a humanity that is broader and deeper than is possible in any anthropocentric humanism. It is the responsibility for protecting and guarding environments as they are in themselves, and with neither domination nor subservience, that is the foundation of environmental humility.

Deeds and Actions: Social Change or Individual Insight?

The principles of guardianship, tolerance and individuality are easily written and easily borrowed in words. The real difficulty is to translate them into consistent deeds and actions, to behave in such a way that we do not treat others as mere elements in some abstract theory, or as ciphers in city systems, or as manipulable units in planned economies. There can be no rules or guides for doing this, and there is no ideology or political system that can provide unerring direction. Indeed any attempt to make environmental humility the basis of practice in environmental management and urban planning poses serious problems. Do we try to implement it by personal example and insight transmitted from individual to individual? Or is it better applied by direct social and political actions on behalf of others? And, in either case, is it not bound to be ineffectual against technical methods for control and planning, an intellectual version of lying down in the road to stop tanks?

These problems have been formulated and addressed in a rather different yet nevertheless appropriate context by Merleau-Ponty. In his examination of *Humanism and Terror* (1947) he argued that any philosophical position which does not acknowledge violence is deluding itself, and offered two alternative and apparently incompatible approaches for dealing with violence and terror. By violence he meant especially physical brutality, but his argument loses little of its validity if violence is taken to include all forms of authoritarianism exercised on the basis of some assumed special knowledge or privilege.

The first possibility is to be a 'commissar', working for men and women against violence yet necessarily treating them as instruments in so doing. Merleau-Ponty (1947, p. xxxviii) cites Montaigne: 'the public good demands that one betrays, lies, massacres.' In the extreme conditions of war this may literally be so; in more moderate conditions the public good may require only limited deceptions, expropriations and insensitivity to the lives of others. The commissar recognises a human tendency to violence and self-interest and seeks to minimise these by a selective use of further violence or control. In fact he has to choose between different kinds of violence; one can either have the freedom and chaos of rampant self-interest, leading no doubt to brutal dictatorship, or one can have the moderation of controls imposed in the public interest. Clearly this latter approach is that of the 'benevolent authoritarianism' of planned environments, societies and economies. It could equally well be the approach of a minority group striving for self-determination and recognising that though this may involve upheaval and suffering in the short-term, the long-term gain in freedom makes this worthwhile. The attitude of the commissar therefore involves acting vigorously on behalf of others who, it is assumed, will eventually benefit from these actions.

Alternatively, Merleau-Ponty suggests, one can be a 'yogi', calling men and women to inner reform, encouraging them to be sensitive to the needs of others. Such an attitude is passive and pacifist – it allows violence to occur and waits expectantly for a change to a less violent and more compassionate world. By advocating reason and compassion, by setting an example of non-violence, it is hoped, as Gandhi hoped, that others will also become reasonable and compassionate. This view is summarised by the Indian sage J. Krishnamurti (1973, p. 35) in his arguments against violence: 'change in society is of secondary importance, that will come about naturally, inevitably when you as a human being bring about a change in yourself.' Such a change he calls an 'inward revolution'. It does not mean a silent acceptance of violence and repression, but an active arguing for a different way of living that is based on a faith in the humanity and common-sense of one's fellow human-beings. It involves a questioning of any state of affairs which permits violence and encourages authoritarianism. It demands passive but outspoken resistance. It does not endorse violence used to suppress violence, nor does it expect others to act on one's behalf. Lewis Mumford (1964, p. 433), who deeply distrusts the system of centralised authority and powerful technology which dominates much of modern Western society, has written this of such an attitude:

> Each one of us, as long as life stirs in him, may play a part in extricating himself from the power system by asserting his primacy as a person in quiet acts of physical or mental withdrawal – in gestures of non-conformity, in abstentions, restrictions, inhibitions, which will liberate him from the pentagon of power.

The differences between the way of social change and the way of individual insight are perhaps not as dramatic in reality as this distinction between the commissar and the yogi would suggest. There are undoubtedly politicians and planners who work for social improvements only out of a deep conviction and concern for the welfare of others, and who suffer deep moral turmoil because they are obliged to manipulate others for the overall social good. Conversely, individual insight and non-violence do not mean that events have to be allowed to happen regardless; passive resistance and non-co-operation are always possible, as are argument and persuasion.

Yet while the edges of the two approaches are blurred and may even overlap, their basic assumptions are quite different and apparently irreconcilable. There are those who believe that the lives of individuals can only be improved by first changing the conditions of society. Since those holding such beliefs presumably have knowledge about the best way to make such changes they can work on behalf of others who are more ignorant or reticent than themselves. On the other hand, there are those who are convinced that the conditions of society follow from the shared beliefs of individuals; it is of course possible to manipulate these beliefs by propaganda but genuine and worthwhile change can come only through individual insights and direct communication. Which of the two paths we accept as our own does not seem to be a matter of self-conscious, rational choice. Instead, it appears to derive from a deep inclination or conviction which precedes choice.

In the way of individual insight environmental humility clearly has a central role, for they both emphasise non-violence and non-manipulation. In the way of social change environmental humility has a less obvious status. In working for modifications in the organisation of society it can perhaps temper tendencies to increased control and regulation, and it might provide a type of ethical touchstone by always drawing attention to individual circumstances and away from the abstract glories of great plans and programmes.

Environmental humility may serve as an ethical guideline but the questions 'How can I use this approach for research?' and 'How can this perspective be used in planning?' cannot be sensibly asked of it. These are questions of technique and scientific humanism. By its very character environmental humility is a perspective that can be imposed on neither a subject matter nor a setting. It offers no neatly packaged methods and can provide no convenient solutions to planning problems. This does not mean that it has no consistency and can have no effectiveness, only that its method is not narrowly constrained in advance and that its effects may not be obvious and immediate. Environmental humility has little value as a research tool but it can be taught as a way of seeing and thinking which is always responsive to what is seen and thought about. 'The teacher', wrote Heidegger (1954, p. 15), 'is far less assured of his ground than those who learn are of theirs. If the relation between the teacher and the taught is genuine, therefore, there is never a place in it for the know-it-all or the authoritative sway of the official.'

In the following chapters I attempt to give substance to what I mean by environmental humility by arguing that it is a perspective which looks always for the individuality in places and communities, which exercises a compassionate way of seeing and understanding landscapes, and which wonders at the essential fact of the being of things. The implications of this perspective for modifying and making places are unclear, but probably involve a recognition of the ethical character of all environmental actions and a greater sensitivity in planning and managing environments both natural and man-made. Such sensitivity will require, if environmental humility is to be genuinely pursued and adopted, the transcendence of planning and environmental design as they are now practiced so that the responsibility for places and landscapes would come to lie with those who live and work in them, and therefore know them best.

8 THE INDIVIDUALITY OF PLACES

Reason has been the central principle of every humanism. Only through the exercise of his capacity for reason could a man attain virtue; only by the awakening of reason through education could the world hope to be rid of man's inhumanities; only by the powers of reason can man tame nature's uncertainties and ensure progress. Yet it is now scarcely possible to sustain such a faith. The evidence of 'rationally planned' modern landscapes, the hedging of our lives with 'reasonable' regulations and restrictions, and the writings of many philosophers all suggest that reason is deeply flawed. Max Horkheimer (1947), for instance, has argued that reason suffers from a disease which causes it to deny its own principles; it tends inexorably to a reduction to mere method so that justice, equality, happiness and tolerance, all at one time inherent in reason, have been uprooted and brought into doubt. Since they cannot be rationally analysed and verified they must be suspect. Similarly William Barrett (1978, p. xiv) writes that because of the unrestrained use of rationalistic techniques 'the human mind is to be ensnared in a prison of its own devising'. Systematic enquiry and the development of technical knowledge have, he believes, led to the dissection and domination of both human and non-human nature. All life is increasingly subject to rationalisation and planning for the limited goals of profit, productivity and bureaucratic efficiency.

There is no easy way out of this, no philosophical or other formula that can be applied to cure reason of its deficiencies. Horkheimer proposes an effort of independent thought coupled with critical awareness. Barrett suggests that we attend carefully to those things and situations, perhaps quite ordinary, which give meaning to individual lives. They both caution explicitly against a search for simple answers and direct routes to some new understanding. It seems that what has to be done is to undertake a radical yet cautious rethinking of reason, free enquiry and the other tenets of scientific humanism. There are some philosophers, architects and even geographers who have begun to do this, but they have also shown that it is far from being a simple task. It is therefore with considerable temerity that I attempt here to explore some of these directions in so far as they relate to environmental humility.

Individuality and Generality

Modern landscapes are in no small measure the product of rational procedures for greater efficiency in planning being applied gently but relentlessly to built-environments. In a straightforward technical sense this process has been made possible by the development of what E.F. Schumacher (1977, p. 53) called 'science for manipulation', science which seeks to bring natural environments and then people under control. It has guaranteed water supply, spanned rivers with bridges, regulated traffic, improved health, controlled birth and made our lives better in countless ways.

The material achievements of science for manipulation are undeniable. What is truly remarkable, however, is that these are based on what Schumacher (1977, p. 52) describes as the observations of 'a single, colour-blind eye'. Only the simplest observations of primary qualities, those to which a number can be attached, are needed to build up explanations of natural and social processes which are sufficiently accurate to permit their controlled modification. Most of us perceive the world with three-dimensional colour vision, and with hearing, smell, touch, movement, memory and imagination. Science for manipulation takes only the most outward, most superficial and most easily shared of these senses, but it does so with such logic and precision that it has made possible the development of our technological civilisation.

The observations of a single, colour-blind eye have a great capacity for generalisation. By excluding the welter of immediate personal perceptions and experiences, it becomes possible to identify those characteristics and processes which are general to many situations rather than unique, and perhaps then to formulate universal laws which govern these shared features. There can be little criticism of this when it is done for scientific understanding, and with a full appreciation of all that is being omitted. But it spills easily into science used for manipulation, and when generalised knowledge is used to change specific situations and places the consequences are likely to be deleterious.

A single, colour-blind eye confronts the crowds, the traffic noises, the confusion of buildings and signs and activities, of a busy city street. It observes land uses, estimates property values, counts the people and the vehicles, then aggregates these measurements, compares them with observations from other streets, and makes generalisations about the forms and processes of cities. Through the medium of urban planning these generalisations are then conveyed back to and imposed onto particular streets in order to achieve more rational patterns of land use and traffic flow. Thus is the individuality of places systematically eroded. The next sequence of observations is made of places which have already been partially made to correspond with generalisations, and so on, until reality itself will have been generalised.

The obvious result of this generalising process is standardised, placeless environments, in which the same sorts of designs are used to meet the same needs of similar people. Of course some traits of landscape have always been shared, for instance the building of houses that provide shelter, but these were usually differentiated by local tradition and circumstances. With the development of science for manipulation this process of differentiation by locality has been sharply reduced and commitment to place has been deposed by an abstract admiration for efficiency and order. It is difficult to maintain that this is entirely reprehensible, but it does involve a deprivation of sense of place. To develop a strong sense of place in the precisely planned landscapes of a new town or suburban tract is possible, yet is somehow unnatural and incomplete – rather like falling in love with a mannequin in a store window.

The attitude of environmental humility takes issue with this technical and manipulative approach to places, and turns towards an understanding by all the senses of the individual realities of places. Such a concern for *individuality* has nothing to do with *individualism.* Individualism is the belief that personal growth, freedom and gratification take priority over everything else. It is self-serving and pays no heed to the costs incurred by others. Such individualism, or narcissism, is, Christopher Lasch (1978) has argued, merely the counterpoint to the paternalism of highly-trained technicians and administrators acting to improve everyone's material standard of living. Narcissism sustains the self-indulgent demand for more and better goods, paternalism works through the science of manipulation to ensure the supply.

An attitude which respects individuality is in opposition not only to individualism but to all approaches which treat individual people and places as no more than units for aggregation, as examples of some general process, or as specimens for analysis. It recognises above all that individuality is an indisputable and indivisible feature of all the entities of the world. C.S. Lewis (1968, p. 201) described this fact thus:

> In space and time . . . there are no 'trees', except beeches, elms, oaks and the rest. There is even no such thing as 'an elm'. There is only

> *this* elm, in such a year of its age, at such an hour of the day, thus lighted, thus moved, thus acted on by all the past and all the present, and affording such and such experiences to me and my dog and to the insect on its trunk.

In short, abstractions and generalisations are made from individual realities and are not the reality themselves (except perhaps where someone has been both silly and powerful enough to make the real world correspond to abstract models). Even the words 'place' and 'landscape' are misleading abstractions and have meaning only to the extent that we can relate them to specific scenes and situations.

The Individuality of Person and Place

Hans Jonas (1974, pp. 186ff) identifies two chains of thought about individuality. One emphasises numerical singularity, or the uniqueness of an individual in space and time; the other maintains that individuality is held within the entity itself and is inseparable from it. The first of these Jonas finds too external, it applies to everything no matter how standardised for no two things can occupy the same location at the same moment. The second he considers too self-contained and isolated. He argues that individuality is an attribute of all organisms and is simultaneously recognisable from the outside and created from within; every amoeba, every plant and every person possess individuality in some degree. Moreover, it is the case that the more complex biologically an organism is, then the more marked its individuality.

In her remarkable book on *The Ecology of Imagination in Childhood*, Edith Cobb (1977, p. 18) followed a similar line of argument but suggested that human beings are distinguished by a far greater capacity for individualisation than other species. In humans the processes of growing and maturing require the development of abilities to think, create meaning and act for oneself. It is not enough to copy others or rely on habit. To be human is to be a distinctive individual responsible for one's own thoughts and actions.

The individuality of places and landscapes differs in one fundamental aspect from that of people. It is accorded rather than self-created. A landscape is always an aggregation of objects and organisms arranged in a singular pattern which is the product of the interaction of physical, ecological, historical, economic and random processes. There is no single inner force directing and co-ordinating all of these. Yet it *seems* as though there is an individuality which lies behind the forms and appearances and maintains a coherent identity. We know that the spirit of a place can persist through countless changes in detail and structure. For instance, in a village which has existed for centuries it is quite possible that every building will have been reconstructed at least once, and they all will have been repeatedly changed in the course of maintenance and repair. There may also have been drastic changes to the fabric of the village – new churches, roads and housing estates being added to the existing ones. However, there can be little question that this is the same essential place that it has always been – grown and changed perhaps, yet as much itself as an old man is the same person as the boy of seventy years ago. In contrast a reconstruction of a village as it was at some point in the past, even if undertaken with every possible attention to detail, is none the less a new place bearing no genuine relationship to the original and lacking historical continuity and the signs of change.

The individual distinctiveness of a place therefore lies not so much in its exact physical forms and arrangements as in the meanings accorded to it by a community of concerned people, and the continuity of these meanings from generation to generation. Much as a craftsman imparts something of his personality to the things he makes, so a community can transfer its character to a landscape. The process by which this happens is difficult to identify. It appears to involve a combination of local responsibility with local traditions of building and doing. These then qualify repairs, replacements and additions to the fabric of the landscape so that it maintains a continuity and consistency of expression. These responsibilities and traditions are preserved in the shared memories of the inhabitants and are conveyed from one generation to the next through example and action rather than education. Furthermore, they are sufficiently flexible to allow changes and adaptations; they do not demand that everything must for ever be done in the same old fashion. Particularity in a place may not be self-generated but it is in a sense inherent, for it exists in the blend of a concern for the continuity of traditions and obligations with a willingness to respond carefully to changing circumstances.

Individuality, Continuity and Indeterminacy

An emphasis on individuality suggests egocentrism and fragmentation. Thus Hans Jonas (1974, p. 204) writes that: 'To be an individual means not-to-be-integrated in the world . . . Individuality implies discontinuity.' The implications of this, at first glance, seem to be destructive—a retreat to individualism and a myopic parochialism that looks only for the unique in places and can see no further than here. This would be no better than excessive generalisation.

Parochialism is a possible but not a necessary outcome of a stress on the particularity of places. Edith Cobb, having spent a lifetime studying the ways in which children come to develop their sense of personal identity, argued (1977, p. 37) that individuality depends on 'a sense of both discontinuity and continuity with nature and history'. Through a mixture of wonder and immediate sensory experience a child is implicated in the world, yet simultaneously and paradoxically recognises that he or she is different from other people and other beings. Cobb maintained that there is no clear break between human consciousness and ecological process—even imagination is in part ecological. She wrote (p. 65): 'Intellectual content is certainly more than biological, but the materials with which the mind works are nature's materials . . . The action patterns of the intellect follow biological action patterns, but the forms these actions produce are more than natural, for they have evolved from the minds of individual human beings interacting with their total environment.' There is nothing obscure in this idea of distinctiveness within continuity; though it is not easy to express, we know it from our own experiences. Cobb was simply recognising that there is a continuum of nature-body-mind-society in which no part of the continuum can be reduced to or cleanly separated from any other part.

The disclosure and recognition of individuality-within-continuity has obvious implications for understanding the distinctiveness of places. A particular place is clearly not isolated, it is a focus within a galaxy of other places with which it is conjoined through shared fashions, styles and meanings. This is quite apparent and needs no elaboration. More difficult is the recognition that places merge imperceptibly with the communities who occupy and maintain them, and with the minds of the individual people in those communities. As human individuality involves both something separate and something shared, so part of what is shared is a place and a sense of place. Thus there is a continuity both between each of us and our environments, and between us and other people because they too live in places. This sharing involves no aggregation or generalisation. It is based on a direct apprehension of of meaning; the continuity of sense of place transcends the discontinuity of particular places. This is possible because every place is an unselfconscious and uncontrived symbol of other places. The strivings, failures and achievements of a community are in part recorded in the settings it creates for itself. It follows that anyone who has been directly involved in making and maintaining landscapes, whether by gardening, building, house-painting or whatever, and anyone who also looks carefully, cannot fail to see evidence of human accomplishments in places other than their own. This is not a matter of deliberate reflection. Like recognising and participating in someone else's grief or happiness it is a largely unselfconscious act of noticing and reacting. Unique places share the fact of having been made by more or less committed individuals, and they therefore always reflect in some measure human abilities and concerns similar to one's own.

It seems to be impossible to specify the nature of the shared particularity of places. The simplest sense of individuality is that of singular objects with clear limits—a building, a person, an island. A landscape or a place is rarely such a singular thing. It is more likely to comprise a cluster of buildings with their foregrounds and backgrounds, a street, a village, a sweeping panorama, all of which consist of multiple, overlapping forms without clear boundaries. 'Landscape is the texture of intricacy' wrote Annie Dillard (1974, p. 133), and this is an exact description. William James (1901, p. xxiv) wrote less poetically but no less accurately that the world is a 'turbid, muddled, gothic sort of affair, without a sweeping outline and with little pictorial mobility'.

It just is not possible to draw boundaries around landscapes or to define and analyse systematically the individuality of a particular place. If someone insists on attempting these worthless pursuits it is utterly predictable that the very individuality they wish to measure will vanish beneath their methods. And if this is so, then there is even less likelihood of formulating the elusive relationships between continuity and particularity in places. These are matters which we know through our experiences and have to accept without subjecting them to analysis and verification. They are too fragile to withstand reduction into simple frameworks. The best we can hope to achieve is a clear description of the distinctiveness of a place, and even that is far from easy.

There is a principle of indeterminacy at work in the character of places. Generalisation and abstraction of their primary features can be achieved only at the expense of their distinctive and unique qualities. On the other hand it appears to be possible to do no more than describe the individuality of a place, for the sources of individuality cannot be disclosed without destroying them. It is undoubtedly the case that

London, New York, Paris and Toronto have their own personalities, and that within London the City, Fleet Street, the Inns of Court, the West End, each has its own distinctive appearance and mood. Yet we cannot say exactly wherein these places and landscapes the spirit lies. 'Individuality', as William James (1912, p. 48) put it simply and concisely, 'outruns all classification.'

9 WAYS OF SEEING LANDSCAPES

The technical methods of scientific humanism make designers and planners into disinterested parasitic outgrowths who have the gall to propose changes to what can be explained and reorganised but is not fully understood. In contrast, environmental humility acknowledges that individuality is the essential quality of a place, it is what sets place apart, makes it itself, a reflection of ecological diversity and human variety, and an expression of people's efforts and accomplishments. It is also a quality that is ineffable and easily destroyed. To recognise and respond to the individuality of places therefore requires a way of seeing that is not confined to the observations of a single colour-blind eye but which is thoughtful and compassionate.

On a superficial level seeing is simply a form of sense perception. It is, however, also far more than this. John Ruskin (1856, vol. I, p. 44) claimed that there is a 'great mistake people make in supposing that they must *see* a thing if it is before their eyes'. Though vision is continuous while we are awake it often involves little more than recognising things by glancing at their superficial qualities. Ruskin noted metaphorically (p. 59) that while we can know a book by its binding the true and essential characteristics lie inside. If seeing is to go beyond the trivial stage of recognition, imagination and creative effort are needed. Seeing can then become synonymous with understanding and insight.

Seeing Clearly

In *Modern Painters* Ruskin (1856, vol. III, p. 174) distinguished three ranks of men according to their ability to see. First, there is the man who perceives rightly because he neither feels nor cares for what he observes. Secondly, there is the man who perceives wrongly because he imposes his feelings and sentiments onto whatever he looks at. Thirdly, is the man who perceives rightly *in spite of* his feelings, and for whom a building or a landscape is never anything but itself.

The first of these men has the attitude of the engineer, detached, calculating and manipulating, making observations which are correct but truncated. The second man is the romantic or sentimentalist for whom everything must have a human emotive meaning. Ruskin referred to this attitude as embracing a 'pathetic fallacy' which transfers a human purpose or anthropomorphism to all of nature; hence valleys are cheerful, mountains are malevolent, foam in waves is cruel and crawling. Another version of this, not apparent to Ruskin but clear enough now, is the 'theoretical fallacy' in which the world is observed through a haze of abstractions and theories; thus real small towns become central places, city districts become examples of 'urban blight' and 'density decline functions', and the women who work or can work as secretaries in downtown offices become a 'female labour resource'. Of the tendency to impose human sentiment Ruskin (p. 173) wrote that it is admitted by a temperament too weak to deal with what it confronts. The same can be said of the tendency to impose abstract order. In both cases the result is false seeing which corrupts and distorts, and is therefore worse than blindness just as lying is worse than silence.

The third way of seeing is the one Ruskin sought to encourage. It is the unpretentious way of seeing that strives to omit nothing yet imposes nothing. It takes the world whole and as it is given, and attends carefully to the particularity of places and situations. It is the attempt to see clearly what there is.

Clear seeing is more easily written about than practiced. The reasons for this are twofold. First, vision is imperfect, for we can never see the whole of a thing—'place an object as close to the eye as you like', Ruskin suggested (1856, vol. I, p. 204), 'there is always something in it which you cannot see.' Conversely if you take it far away from the eye it becomes a mere dot. So the indeterminacy which marks the individuality of places and landscapes is further compounded by an imperfection in the primary means by which we can apprehend that individuality.

The second difficulty in practising clear seeing arises from the prejudice and habit that enters into the ways in which we look at landscapes. Landscape prejudices act like blinkers. For instance, some people notice only the works of nature and skillfully exclude the works of man from their view of the world; countless coffee-table books and television documentaries on wilderness and the beauties of nature are clear evidence of this. There is also an historical prejudice which manifests itself in a glorification of the old and a denigration of the new. This is apparent, for instance, in the claim by W.G. Hoskins (1955, p. 298) that anything built since 1914 has either destroyed or uglified the English landscape, and in countless heritage projects which preserve old buildings from the changes in the landscape around them. And there are the prejudices of architects who seem to notice only the buildings of reputable fellow architects; of engineers who see landscapes only in terms of their capacity for absorbing waste or generating power; of property developers who consider only property values; and countless others.

These prejudices are undoubtedly an impediment to clear seeing, but they cannot be put aside so that our vision can be like a *tabula rasa* or polaroid film continually recording images yet continually being swept clean or replaced by an unexposed frame. Prejudices or biases in the way in which we see the world are unavoidable and indeed necessary to direct our attention. What has to be attempted is not to eradicate these visual prejudices but to become aware of them and to grasp their limitations. It is when this is not done that serious misconceptions arise, as when someone with specialised knowledge derived from narrow observations proposes that their view has general validity or is the only right one. Clear seeing requires, as Ruskin suggested, that we teach ourselves to see in spite of our feelings and habits of mind.

To see clearly is to see with insight. It means to penetrate beneath the surface forms without destroying them, to understand the essential features of what one is looking at. Such penetrating vision must be known to almost everyone through those occasions, however infrequent, when they have studied something—a tree, a view, or a person's face—and suddenly seen it with an unexpected clarity and force. For many of us these insights are brief and we pass on to our chores or immediate business even though the memory of the insight lingers. But sometimes, for some individuals, such insights can be powerful visions. William James (1901, p. 71), for instance, wrote that:

> I have on a number of occasions felt that I had enjoyed a period of intimate communion with the divine . . . Once it was when from a summit of a high mountain I looked over a gashed and corrugated landscape extending to a long convex of ocean that ascended to the horizon; and again from the same point when I could see nothing beneath me but a boundless expanse of white cloud . . . What I felt on these occasions was a temporary loss of any identity, accompanied by an illumination which revealed to me a deeper significance than I had been wont to attach to life.

Moments of vision and insight such as this cannot be produced to order. It is, however, possible for them to be prevented by the sort of studied blindness that imposes feeling, prejudices and theories on what is seen. It is in part the task of clear seeing to make us open to such moments of insight, but it is also and more mundanely its aim to develop the capacity to look carefully and to understand the qualities and character of particular landscapes. In short, it demands that we try to see for ourselves.

Searching

There are no simple guidelines for seeing clearly, but there are examples from which we can learn something about suitable ways to proceed. Goethe provides one of these in the diary he kept of the journey to Italy which he made from 1786 to 1788. At the beginning of his diary he declared that he would take this opportunity to try to revitalise his mind and his senses, dulled by long years in the court at Weimar. He wrote (1970, p. 38): 'At present I am preoccupied with sense impressions to which no book or picture can do justice. The truth is that, in putting my powers of observation to the test, I have formed a new interest in life . . . Can I learn to look at things with clear fresh eyes? How much can I take in at a single glance? Can the grooves of old mental habits be effaced?' His journal demonstrates that nothing was too grand or too commonplace for his vision; he described the mountains and the faces of people he saw on the street, he wrote of rock formations, plants, Palladian villas, ancient sculptures and the ordure in the porticos of the grand houses of Verona. He was delighted with the results of this precise yet unbiased way of seeing. Later in his journal he wrote (p. 109): 'I have spent the day looking and looking. It is the same in art as in life. The deeper one penetrates the broader grows the view.' And later still, after a day carefully investigating Rome (p. 136): 'I am now in a state of clarity and calm such as I have not known for a long time. My habit of looking at and accepting things as they are without pretension is standing me in good stead and makes me secretly very happy.'

Goethe's account of his journey to Italy is a powerful testimonial for an unpretentious way of seeing, but it is remote from our age and its appropriateness can be questioned. He travelled in coaches or on foot, could afford to spend weeks wandering between cities, months exploring Rome, and was altogether two years on his pilgrimage. In comparison our lives are time-poor and detached from the geographies around us, and there are many things which preclude leisurely and contemplative travel. In fact only seventy years after Goethe made his journey to Italy Ruskin was able to feel the numbing effects of the benefits of the industrial revolution: 'Going by railroad', he declared (1856, vol. III, p. 321), 'I do not consider as travelling at all; it is merely "being sent" to a place, very little different from becoming a parcel.' Automobiles, expressways and air travel have made us into ever more rapidly and blindly transmitted parcels, sending us unseeing but swiftly over and across landscapes which have become no more than a distant blur. We are likely to take a 'package' tour, fly to Rome and spend a few days there looking at the thin, resilient gloss of monuments and entertainments apparently provided especially for tourists.

Clear and careful seeing now takes an effort that has to be even more deliberate than that of Goethe's because there is much in modern life-styles that militates against it. Many authors and artists have recognised this and have offered possible directions for us to pursue. For instance, the American novelist Walker Percy has written of what he calls 'a search' – the development of a curiosity that treats the everyday world as unfamiliar yet at the same time full of clues and hints about the meaning of life. This 'searching' takes the form not of an aggressive and energetic enquiry but of openness and receptiveness and wonder, of trying to see without judgement the styles of suburban gardens, the colours of shadows, the forms of skyscrapers and automobiles and fire hydrants, and attending to the details and qualities of whatever is encountered.

No modern artist has demonstrated this procedure of searching as it applies to landscapes more clearly than the Swiss painter Paul Klee. Between 1910 and 1940 Klee painted hundreds of pictures in which he tried either to represent the essential character of a landscape in itself or to show the complex relationships between seeing and landscapes. Unlike conventional artists who have tried to reproduce the forms or perhaps the light of a landscape, and so convey its character, Klee tried to show places from many perspectives, or to depict himself experiencing a landscape, or to represent the sheer vitality and force of what he saw. 'In earlier days', he wrote in his diary (1964, p. 122), 'the beauty of landscapes was quite clear to me. A background for the soul's moods. Now dangerous moments occur when Nature tries to devour me; at such times I am annihilated, but at peace.'

Klee tried to paint experiences that went beyond the possibilities of representational art. Just before the First World War he wrote (1964, p. 290) in his diary of seeing a moonrise at Tunis: 'The evening is deep within me forever. Many a bland northern moonrise, like a muted reflection, will softly remind me, and remind me again and again. It will be my bride, my alter ego. An incentive to find myself.' A moonrise motif occurs repeatedly in Klee's paintings and drawings (Figure 9.1), and he seems to have been striving to represent his experience at Tunis. He also attempted to illustrate the continuities of person and place, body and landscape. His notes to 'Landscapely-Physiognomic' (Figure 9.2) refer to 'the pure function of vision' and 'connection with the cerebral functions of feeling'. The painting suggests an integration of bodily features such as lips and eyes with landscape features such as trees and a moon, an interpenetration of body, space and landscape.

Perhaps Klee's paintings appear strange and unreal, full of spiky objects, suggestions of forms, familiar colours but unexpected arrangements. That may be, but they are certainly not nonsense. Klee observed precisely and reflected carefully before committing what he had seen and experienced to a painting. He may not always have been successful in communicating those experiences but he was successful in demonstrating that a radical effort has to be made to see through the prejudices and conventions that cloud vision. He showed also that seeing does not have to attend only to the surface forms of landscapes; it can penetrate beneath them to their essential qualities and so reveal a whole new world of individuality, colour, motion and meaning. Klee would surely have agreed with Ruskin's observation (1856, vol. IV, p. 321) that: 'Every advance in our acuteness of perception will show us something new, but the old and first discerned thing will still be there, not falsified, only modified and enriched by the new perception.'

Compassionate Intelligence

In her study of *The Ecology of Imagination in Childhood*, Edith Cobb (1977, p. 27) quoted with approval a statement made by Paul Klee in his notebook *The Thinking Eye*: 'Love of nature as process and love of knowledge as process are here combined as a unitary action, the mind as body interacting with the universe.' Klee sought this unitary action through his restless artistic vision; Cobb hoped to find it through the exercise of what she called 'compassionate intelligence'. This is, she believed, the mark of true humanity, the intelligence that sees clearly and carefully and wonders without interfering.

Compassionate intelligence is both a cause and a consequence of clear seeing. It is a cause because it makes it possible to see what is extraordinary in the commonplace things of the world and to care about what happens to them. It is a consequence because clear seeing

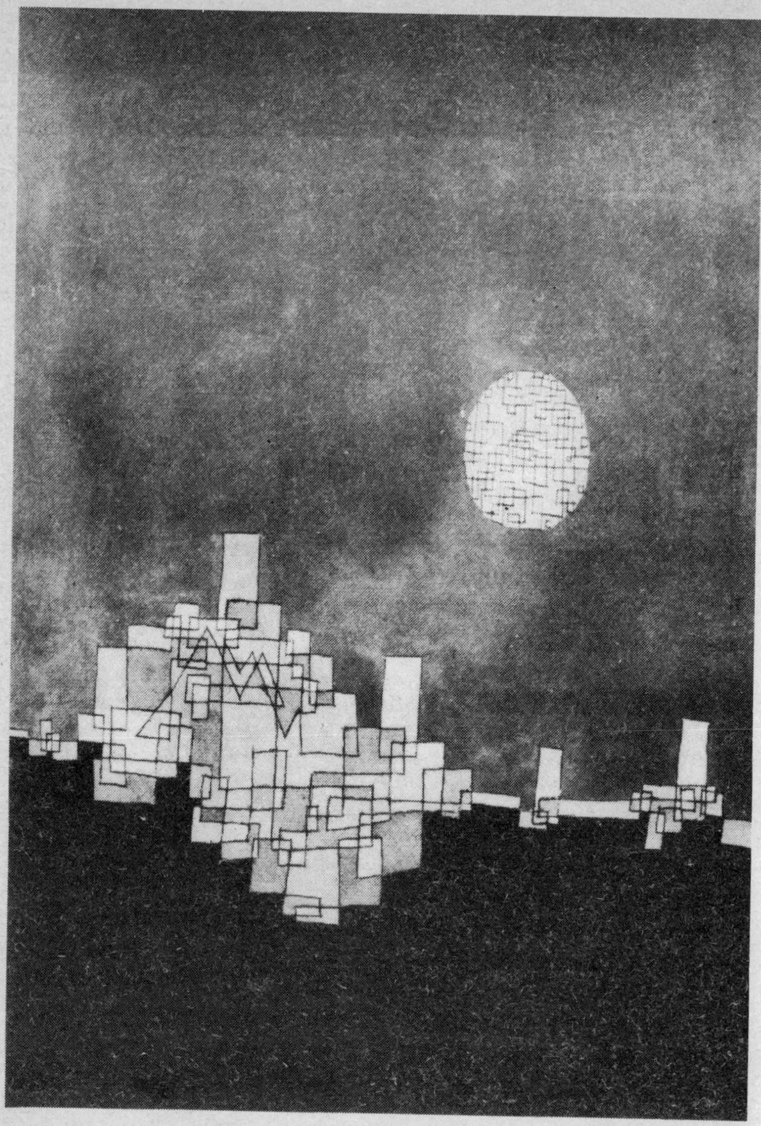

Figure 9.1: Elected Site, *1927, by Paul Klee. In this painting Klee seems to have been attempting to paint his experience of a moonrise in Tunisia about fourteen years earlier. For him landscape was not to be seen simply in terms of forms and colours but as implicated in the act of vision. (Source: Paul Klee,* The Thinking Eye, *Lund Humphries, London, 1961, p. 302)*

Figure 9.2: Landscapely-Physiognomic, *1923, by Paul Klee. A complex interpenetration of body, space and landscape which suggests that for Klee landscape was not an object or set of forms which could be observed with detachment. It was an all-embracing context for living, a part of us, but to discover this we have to learn to see through the surface forms. (Source: Paul Klee,* The Thinking Eye, *Lund Humphries, London, 1961, p. 128)*

is unpretentious and humble, and does not aim to dominate or manipulate places but to understand and identify with them. Indeed anyone who studies carefully and sees clearly the landscapes in which they live (and perhaps also those which they visit, though that is made more difficult by the brevity of experience), must develop a sympathetic and compassionate intelligence. There is nothing magical or marvellous in this—just a quiet and unassuming recognition that this is how things are and an understanding of the best ways to act so what now exists is disrupted as little as possible.

Clear seeing is manifest in those moments of insight when we grasp the identity and individuality of landscapes and places. Academically we can gather from this that the truth of landscapes does not lie in measurement and verification so much as in understanding their unique character. This character we can convey only through careful description. There is nothing easy or trivial in making such a description. Indeed it constitutes one of the hardest yet potentially most rewarding tasks we can set ourselves. This was explicitly acknowledged by John Ruskin, who may just as well have the last word on clear seeing since he has had so many of the earlier ones. 'The greatest thing a human soul ever does in this world', he wrote in *Modern Painters* (vol. III, p. 278), 'is to *see* something, and to tell what it *saw* in a plain way . . . To see clearly is poetry, prophecy and religion,—all in one.'

10 APPROPRIATION

The exercise of compassionate intelligence leads, in a direct sense, to description and tending rather than to explanation and manipulation. The attitude of concern and care that is the hallmark of compassionate intelligence must translate into a willingness not to use all one's knowledge and not to impose techniques simply because they are available, but instead to allow communities and places to be themselves. Such an argument for leaving alone, for guardianship, has been developed with great insight and depth by the philosopher Martin Heidegger in the context of what he called 'appropriation'. Appropriation is, he maintained, fundamental both to the character of our relationships with everything that exists, and to truth. It is a profound and difficult concept that lies at the heart of environmental humility.

Heidegger's philosophy is, in the literal sense of the word, original. He brought into question many of the concepts and methods that have been central to Western philosophy since the time of Aristotle, and he revived the ancient, pre-Socratic concern for Being—that is for the fact and nature of existence of things, creatures and people. This led him to a radical rethinking of ideas of truth and reality which are generally taken for granted. It also makes his philosophy very difficult to grasp and to express because so much of our language is grounded in ways of thinking which Heidegger found misleading and unacceptable. The following account of appropriation I have tried to make straightforward without rendering it trite or doing it serious damage.[1]

Being and Appropriation

At the superficial level of material convenience, rationalism and technical methods appear to be the servants of freedom. However, Heidegger argued that at a deeper level of understanding they have served chiefly to confuse our relations with nature and have led to 'homelessness'—the sense of being adrift in an uncaring world. The increasingly sophisticated and potent technologies of the last three hundred years have made man strive to be the master of all beings, to direct and control them so that they serve only human ends. This rise in technological mastery Heidegger understood not as something entirely new, but as the most recent phase in a development he traced back almost to the sources of Western thought, and specifically to the concept of truth formulated by Plato and Aristotle. In this formulation truth is based on a correspondence of perception and account, or a conformity of observation with idea. The world is treated as a picture which can be studied, and ideas developed independently can be compared with the real situation in the picture; if the ideas or accounts correspond with perceptions of reality they are correct, if not they are false. This is obviously a concept of truth which is basic to modern science with its concern for accurate and replicable observation and empirical testing. Heidegger believed this to be an inadequate concept. He revived in its stead the more ancient sense of truth as disclosure and openness.

Truth, as disclosure, lies in the moment of uncovering and insight in which some thing or some individual reality becomes evident and reveals itself to us. It becomes, in Heidegger's language, free to be itself for it has been liberated from obscurity. Truth is therefore a freedom and a non-concealment in which the being of an individual existence is manifest. In this event of non-concealment Being (with a capital) is also manifest. Such Being can be understood as the elemental and universally shared fact that things and people are, whereas being (in the lower-case) refers to the existence of something particular. Truth, freedom and Being are thus inseparably linked. They are constantly liable to concealment and obfuscation by familiarity, forgetfulness, the narrowness of science and the comforts and seductions of materialistic life. Truth as disclosure or illumination is always accompanied by darkness, into which it tends to retreat; it does not persist but has to be continually sought and reasserted.

Appropriation lies in that moment of insight that reveals beings for themselves, the moment in which we know that *this is.* In such understanding the truth becomes one's own even as one becomes part of that truth. Such a process must be known in a small way to anyone who has puzzled over a mathematical or similar problem which, though the procedures have been explained and can perhaps be followed to produce a correct result, make no sense; then comes a flash of insight, the process and its logic become clear, they are now yours for they have been appropriated. Mechanically or technically nothing has changed, yet everything is understood differently and stands in a new light. This is a trivial example of the event of appropriation though sufficient perhaps to convey the importance of disclosure and insight. In the context of Being and beings with which Heidegger was concerned it becomes far more difficult and paradoxical. For example, one of Heidegger's interpreters, Albert Hofstadter (1970, p. 252) attempts to clarify the complex bilateral relationships that are involved by suggesting that: 'Man's fitting relationship to things is the one in which, by appropriating them to himself and himself to them, he finally reaches the appropriate, what is appropriate both to him and to them. In such appropriateness lies the truth of his being, his freedom.' Obscure and difficult though this statement is, it does summarise the essence of appropriation – the taking over of some being by allowing oneself to be taken over by it.

There is, needless to say, no systematic method of obtaining insights and disclosing what is appropriate and true, only the slow and uncertain phenomenological process of 'letting things manifest themselves' (Heidegger, in Richardson, 1967, p. xiv). It is in the event of appropriation that we grasp the nature of things in themselves and our relationship to Being. This event cannot be forced. It has to be allowed to happen.

Appropriation is the source of all Heidegger's later writings and philosophy. It brought him to reject humanism and anthropocentric viewpoints. He came to recognise a world in which there are not principally men, but principally Being (Richardson, 1967, pp. 530ff). One can presumably go no further in transcending a bias towards the human, for Being encompasses everything that exists.

Man as the Shepherd of Being

For Heidegger the function of thinking was to help Being realise itself. In this it is necessary to recognise that while man 'is immeasurably more than a rational animal' (Richardson, 1967, p. 531) he is nevertheless only one being among many and is not master of all he surveys. 'Man is not the Lord of beings', Heidegger wrote in his 'Letter on Humanism' (1947, p. 221), 'he is the shepherd of Being.' This constitutes an appeal against attempts to control the individual bits and pieces of environment, against efforts to arrogate man into some dominant and authoritarian position with respect to nature, and against manipulation of other people. It is an appeal *for* guardianship, for taking care of things merely because they exist, for tending and protecting them. In this there is neither mastery nor subservience, but there is responsibility and commitment.

In an attempt to elucidate the character of this responsibility Karsten

Harris (1978, p. 71) gives the example of a fruit tree in someone's back-yard. It is, he suggests, a quiet presence that only occasionally attracts attention, and then not so much for detached contemplation as in a caring that involves pruning, picking the fruit, clearing away the dead leaves. It is in such care that the tree reveals itself and is appropriated. What is involved in this is neither a complete passivity, just letting the tree grow in any way it happens to, nor complete mastery which reduces the tree to a fruit-producing machine, ruthlessly pruned and sprayed with toxic chemicals with the single aim of maximising production. Instead there is a working together, so that the tree flourishes because it has been well tended.

The idea of caring for Being was usually illustrated by Heidegger by rather vague references to peasants' houses or Greek temples which seem to fit their settings and to meet all the social and spiritual needs of their users. However, in a somewhat more specific example Heidegger wrote (1977, p. 355) that the learning of a cabinet-maker's apprentice is not mere practice, nor the accumulation of knowledge about the things he is likely to make, but 'if he is to become a true cabinet-maker, he makes himself answer and respond above all to the different kinds of wood and to the shapes slumbering within the wood'. Without this essential relatedness to the being of wood the craft of cabinet-making is reduced to trivial busy-work. It is precisely this response to the different and particular characteristics of beings and situations that is demanded by guardianship and care for Being.

Being is not the same as environment or nature; it is the active and palpable fact of existence rather than non-existence. Every person, every plant, every stone, machine and building has its own being—it is what it is without necessary reference to human enterprises. The problem which especially concerned Heidegger is that of the quality of human being in its relation to the being of what is non-human. The humanistic attitude, he argued in the 'Letter on Humanism' (1947), has increasingly come to promote domination and technicity; it denies the truth of all forms of being other than those of value to humans (and through nuclear weapons and germ warfare it may even come to deny human being). By not allowing things to disclose themselves as they are, and by forcing them to meet exclusively human ends, it also conceals truth. William Barret, a sympathetic interpreter of Heidegger's writings, has written (1978, p. 342) that: 'Trees and rocks do not indulge in the impertinence of foisting lessons upon us. Their method of instruction is more circuitous and indirect, but perhaps all the more potent for that. Their first lesson is to draw us outside the narrow and presumptuous horizons of our humanism.' This does not mean that we have to descend to the level of the inhuman, nor that we should try to behave like ecologically-adapted animals. Rather it means, as Heidegger (1947, pp. 199-200) put it, that other vistas are opened, especially that of fulfilling the responsibility that is given to us by virtue of our awareness of Being. We must let ourselves be claimed by Being, he wrote, and in this claim there is already care for humanity.

Appropriation and Environmental Humility

Heidegger's philosophy points to a way of thinking and acting that is quite different from that of present-day material satiation and technical manipulation. Perhaps more clearly than any other modern philosopher, Heidegger has revealed the sources of uncertainty and tension that beset those affluent regions of the world where there should be satisfaction and a sense of accomplishment. We have, he argued, inherited a two-thousand-year-old tradition of anthropocentrism and truth which has devised ways to imprison itself. To escape from these long-established and deep-seated habits of thought it is necessary to return to the very foundations of thinking, to learn again how to let the things, situations and events of the world be themselves.

The principles of appropriation, guardianship and care for Being are implicated in the attitudes of environmental humility. The concern for individuality is no less a concern for the being of things and places. The development of a way of seeing that is based in compassionate intelligence opens the path for guardianship. Environmental humility requires a deep wondering at and respect for landscapes both natural and man-made. This does not, however, involve a slavish obeisance to the whims of nature, nor an adulation of the widely acclaimed products of human artistic genius. It simply means caring for, protecting and appropriating places.

The practical consequences of Heidegger's philosophy of appropriation and guardianship are not clear. In his writings there is a tendency to nostalgia and his examples are invariably of cabinet-makers, peasants' houses or other types of traditional craftsmanship, for these apparently illustrated most clearly his ideas about caring and appropriation. It is difficult to avoid drawing the obvious conclusion from these types of examples that they represent the life-style that might be expected in a world characterised by a care for Being. This might not necessarily be a return to some previous technological level, but it would certainly be a harmonious, organic type of culture in which the being of the earth, the gods and men are equally respected and held in balance.

Heidegger was insistent that all such thoughts of real or practical consequences stemming from his philosophy and his thinking should be dispelled. In his 'Letter on Humanism' (1947, p. 236) he wrote unequivocally that his thinking was 'a recollection of Being and nothing else. It has no result.' There are no directives from it that can apply to our active lives. He offered no promises for changing the world because, he claimed, all proposals for change rest on thought-foundations that his own thinking had found questionable. This seems to suggest that we can do little more than strive to think with clarity, and then despair if technicity continues to proliferate, or rejoice if appropriation should become the dominant way. In an interview for *Der Spiegel* (Heidegger, 1966, p. 277) he elaborated on this.

> Philosophy will not be able to effect an immediate transformation of the present condition of the world. This is true not only of philosophy, but of all merely human thought and endeavour. Only a god can save us. The sole possibility is to prepare a sort of readiness, through thinking and poetising, for the appearance of the god or the absence of the god.

Perhaps Heidegger was being thoroughly consistent in maintaining that we can attempt no more than lucid thinking and that all suggestions for action depend on a flawed reasoning. Perhaps, however, he was only trying to protect the sanctity of his own insights, concerned that they would be borrowed and distorted, for he wrote in the preface to an interpretation of his philosophy that 'every formulation is open to misunderstanding' (Heidegger, in Richardson, 1967, p. xxii). Whichever is the case, Heidegger could not help playing an active role simply by teaching and writing. If he really wanted to effect no changes he should not have uttered his thoughts; conversely, if he was genuinely committed to awakening a concern for Being it is difficult to grasp how he could not have expected this to have had consequences at least in the active lives of individuals. There can be no clear split between our thinking and our practical lives; to be convinced of the truth of appropriation and not to live one's life in the light of this truth would require deep cynicism and profound hypocrisy.

Whatever reservations Heidegger had about the roles of appropriation and guardianship in our active lives, I want to suggest, albeit with considerable trepidation, that there is no need to transfer these to environmental humility. His doubts none the less serve as an important caution, a reminder that these are not technical methods but ways of thinking that have to be continually reasserted and clarified. Heidegger's philosophy was a form of contemplation; environmental humility may have foundations in such contemplation of care for Being but it must also seek to translate this into a manifest guardianship for the individuality of places and landscapes. It has to be concerned with encouraging what is already distinctive in environments, and with re-establishing identities where they have been eroded. Environmental humility cannot merely allow events to occur and the identities of places to vanish into placelessness, for that leads to despair. Nor can it allow itself to become a technique which offers clear and complete solutions to environmental design problems, for that leads to complacency. It must instead find means of directing events and circumstances gently and appropriately, and it must encourage the making and maintenance of places by the people who understand them and live in them. This will involve neither pessimism and passivity nor arrogant attempts to impose authority. It is perhaps the only sensible direction open to us.

Note

1. This chapter is based on a number of sources, especially Heidegger, 1947, 1966, 1971, 1977; Richardson, 1967; Barrett, 1978; Versenyi, 1965; Hofstadter, 1970; and Murray, 1978.

11 ETHICS AND SENSITIVITY IN ENVIRONMENTAL PLANNING

It is not enough to suggest that environmental humility is better than technical planning, and to wait for it to prevail. That is far too vague and passive. On the other hand, it is not possible to provide a methodology for practicing guardianship because appropriation requires that each place and each community must be allowed to realise its own identity and being. What can be done, perhaps, is to follow Heidegger's proposal and to prepare a readiness for change. Initially this must mean thinking carefully about the possible manifestations of guardianship in environments. These would not necessarily be very obvious. Even in the somewhat remote likelihood of the exercise of compassionate intelligence and appropriation becoming prevalent, the visible consequences of this would have to flow from the actions of many individuals in the context of already existing landscapes. Any changes would be slow and incremental. Such planning as remained would cease to be a means of directing development through regulation, and would become instead a demonstration of environmental humility concerned with the ethical implications of change and with sensitivity and subtlety in the forms and patterns of landscape. Those entrusted with these new responsibilities would have to recognise that in all planning one is, in effect, planning oneself; the planner, too, is part of the environment that he guards or controls.

Environmental Ethics

Traditional ethics are either irrelevant or inappropriate for directing human behaviour towards the non-human world. Ethics conventionally have had to do with the relationships between human beings, and offer a guide to what is good and bad in those relationships. Furthermore, goodness and badness are usually taken to lie within a specific action or in its immediate consequences, to be within the act of charity or of violence. The ethical principle adopted to judge behaviour in such immediate situations is one of enlightened self-interest: do not act towards others in a way that you would not wish them to adopt in acting towards you.

'All this', Hans Jonas (1974, p. 8) declares, 'has decisively changed. Modern technology has introduced actions of such novel scale, objects and consequences that the framework of former ethics can no longer contain them.' Jonas questions the humanist argument that man is the source of all values, and extends Heidegger's reflections on Being as the grounds for an 'environmental ethics' in which there is respect for the existence of everything, be it human, natural, living or inorganic. From this radical and non-anthropocentric perspective it begins to appear that even responsibility for environment and guardianship may not be human inventions; they are discoveries made in the course of the development of language and thinking.

This idea of discovering obligation towards nature is a difficult one and requires clarification. In the context of Being humans are merely part of the living world, subject to the exigencies of mortality and circumstance. Nature is not just material for human purposes but has its own independent existence. Nevertheless Jonas asserts (1966, p. 282) that nature, and indeed everything that is not a human being, is none the less a human responsibility. This is so not because natural environments are useful or give people pleasure, but because the development of self-conscious thought and language has made human-beings aware of the existence of non-human things and capable of communicating this awareness. Other beings may also have such awareness and hence obligation, though of this we cannot be certain. We do know that through self-consciousness and language men and women find themselves to be executors of a trust which they did not create and may not even like, but which only they can understand and express. To ignore or neglect this trust is an act of weak irresponsibility, while to treat it as if it exists for the sole benefit of the executors is to commit a flagrant abuse of responsibility.

Since Being is universal and everything has value in itself by virtue of its existence, then every human action which affects the non-human world must have value-significance. There is no part of environment, whether human or natural, which is worthless, nor can human actions towards environments be neutral. Everything we do is therefore ethical and has ethical consequences. As executors of a trust we must acknowledge the ethical character of all our behaviour and act appropriately, in Heidegger's sense of appropriation.

Jonas argues (1974, pp. 6-19) that a code of environmental ethics has become increasingly necessary over the last four hundred years. The scale of the technologies developed in this period, and the remoteness of their impacts both in space and time, have meant that technical knowledge has outrun persistently the understanding of its consequences. To some degree this must always have been the case, but technology now occupies a central place in our lives; it has become essential to engineering, architecture, administration, communications and even medicine. Technology has invaded the realm of human existence and human values, so morality must now invade the realm of making.

Having identified the character of modern technology and the human obligations to nature and to Being, Jonas proposes this ethical guideline: 'Act so that the effects of your actions are compatible with the permanence of genuine human life.' At first reading this may seem anthropocentric, but by 'genuine human life' he means the life that is based in appropriation and accepts responsibility for Being both now and in the future. This is therefore an ethical standard of foresight and obligation that must, in its specific applications, always be as new and as particular as the situations to which it refers.

All this may seem very obscure and abstract, remote from the practical matters of landscapes and planning. And indeed it is remote from most current practices in which appropriation and ethics are subservient to economics and engineering, or not considered at all. Furthermore, it has to be accepted that ethics offer only guidelines and that people do not behave ethically just because such guidelines exist. Ethics cannot be forcefully imposed. Nevertheless, they are not irrelevant to the ways in which places are made and environments managed. Where they exist they serve as generally acknowledged criteria for judging actions even if they are widely ignored; where they are absent, and the pretence of neutrality in observation and explanation and action is adopted, the floodgates are opened for insensitivity and even destruction. If the substance of the world is just neutral stuff, and creatures are machines for producing food for humans, and humans are manipulable units in some vast economic system, then there are no values, no freedoms and no real dignities left.

Exactly how Jonas' environmental ethics can translate into built forms and environmental management it is impossible to say, for that would be to commit the same error of over-neat formulation that characterises rationalistic planning. However, one possible direction can be tentatively suggested. Instead of asking how a development can be carried out at least cost or highest productivity, the first question asked would have to be – 'How can this change be made with minimal impacts to environments and societies both now and in the future, and to enhance existence in all its aspects – material, mental and spiritual?' The answers to this must be conditioned by individual situations, and might be arrived at by attending to the details of the localities and to the needs of the sensitive members of communities, especially children and the elderly. Of course, every concern is not embraced by these criteria but they do provide a beginning for making landscapes that demonstrate appropriation and environmental humility.

Small and Local Pleasures

'It is no use telling us', J.B. Jackson (1953, pp. 28-9) has written, 'that the world is our home and we should learn to love it, unless we have learned to love our own corner of it, and until we have learned what that corner possesses in the way of beauty and potential for human happiness.' In other words, it is necessary to teach ourselves to look at what is local and often commonplace before allowing ourselves to become infatuated with exceptional landscapes and grand proposals for their reconstruction. We need to be able to see in detail what people have made of their lives *here*, and how this has been claimed as a distinctive place. Virginia Woolf (cited in Barrett, 1972, pp. 134-5) once observed that the small occasions of life may harbour as much or more significance than the larger ones. Similarly I believe that the environmental and landscape experiences that give pleasure and meaning can as often derive from the details of places and everyday tasks as from remarkable scenery and moments of joy.

If landscape details are important, and if they are being eroded by insensitive design and planning practices, then there is a case for overhauling these practices so that they become more responsive to detail. This cannot be done, however, by adding more to the already overburdened portfolio of planners, since that can lead only to more restrictions and regulations. It has to be done in the opposite way, by reducing controls and allowing landscapes to be changed and controlled by the people who live and work in them. The small pleasures of gardening, of looking at other people's gardens, of doing and making something for oneself, of appreciating the care someone has exercised in maintaining their house, of living in an attractive street or village, of knowing and being known in a place—none of these can be planned for, but they can all be denied by planning.

In hyperplanned, professionally-designed environments, conceived in the unornamented traditions of the twentieth century, the newness coupled with the eradication of details leaves little scope for the expression of individuality. Thus the well-furrowed, well-sprayed, geometric fields of machine agriculture, or the well-ordered variety of suburban streetscapes, or the empty angles and spaces of the modern developments around St Paul's Cathedral in London, have little which can easily inspire imagination or affection. Such affection has nothing to do with productivity or organising the world more efficiently, or promoting material consumption, or attaining a higher standard of living. That is precisely why it is so important. It is part of an attitude which looks upon the landscapes of the world, no matter how trivial or unassuming, and appreciates them as they are.

Landscapes for Children

Modern landscapes seem to be designed for forty-year old healthy males driving cars. These are the modern modules who relate to environments as much through machines as through their senses. The forty-year old male is the most adaptable, mobile member of society. He is also the least sensitive, capable of coping equably with heavy traffic on expressways, steep stairways, escalators, crowds, digital displays, the mysteries of the new international hieroglyphic signs and the countless confusions of modern city life. There are entire built-environments which seem to have been designed for him alone, and make no concessions for the elderly or for children. Office skyscrapers are filled with tens-of-thousands of executives and their secretaries—not a child to be found. Suburban developments are meant to be for families, but in fact make few allowances for the very young or the old, or even for those housewives who spend their days at home. The spatial scale of the suburbs is determined by automobiles, especially those driven by men to get to work, so there are great distances to walk and wide arterial roads to be crossed by any pedestrians. Zoning controls guarantee that there are no local shops, no public buildings except schools, few undesigned spaces for children to escape to and explore. If you are not in an automobile—an eight-year old boy perhaps, or a young mother with pre-school-age children, an old man with arthritis—the asphalt distances and the wind-swept spaces make you a virtual prisoner.

Existentially, and from the perspectives of environmental humility, all landscapes should accommodate most of the phases of life. With exact planning and total design, settings have been created which do not change and which cannot cope well with the realities of human aging. They are instead zoned for age groups—schools for children, apartments and colleges for young adults, suburbs supposedly for families, institutions and retirement communities for the elderly. As we grow older we are increasingly obliged to move to the relevant, unchanging setting for our age group, or to live our life in tension with the designed environment.

In his excellent study of *The Child in the City* Colin Ward (1978) sees children as helpless victims of modern city planning. Of course most children do now survive to become adults, whereas in the nineteenth century or before many did not, but this improvement in the chances of survival has been accompanied by a reduction in novelty and responsibility in the lives of children. They have, Ward argues, systematically been made the victims of the decisions of others—politicians, planners, educationists—whose values today they do not necessarily share and who do not take into consideration 'the psychic damage they inflict' (p. 34). Though their intentions may be benevolent these decision-makers have worked to create environments which keep children out of trouble by restricting their activities, out of sight by compulsory schooling, or which simply ignore children's needs. Thus it is not uncommon to find playgrounds comprising a few items of fixed equipment made from left-over pipes on a hard asphalt surface guaranteed to cause injury; or more spectacularly there are public housing projects intended for families but with no play facilities except the door-bells and elevators, or a sand-box storeys below.

This denial of children's needs is of no small importance if, as Edith Cobb (1969, p. 123) and others have argued, the environment in which one lives between the ages of about six and twelve deeply influences the development of personality. Just what this influence is may not be clear, and of course there are always those who transcend the circumstances of their childhood; but it seems likely that growing up in a materially comfortable but hyperplanned landscape will blunt sensitivity to environment and lead to an easy acceptance of imposed order. Paul Goodman suggests (1969, p. 90) that: 'The ideal of city planning is for the children to be able to see the city, for no city is governable if it does not grow citizens who feel it to be theirs.' If he is right then the alienation of children by modern landscapes could have serious consequences indeed.

Colin Ward declares (1978, p. 204): 'I want a city where children live in the same world as I do.' This requires that all settings have to be shaped with their needs in mind. It is not, however a *carte blanche* for a Disney World solution, in which fun and games are superbly organised for a permanently puerile population and everything is intended to satisfy child-like desires. Nor does it mean building countless adventure playgrounds; special facilities set aside for children have their importance but they are not enough. To make a city where children live in the same world as adults requires first a radical rethinking of the role of traffic and roads, for machines and young children do not mix; the sensible answer involves not the restriction of children, which is the practice now, but subduing traffic. A city for children requires that there are unorganised spaces for children to explore and hide in; it requires sufficiently high densities of housing to encourage supervision by 'eyes-on-the-street', that is parents and adults watching from a distance but not continually interfering; it requires safe and easy access to public areas, to shopping streets, libraries, parks and schools; it requires circumstances in which children can at least watch adults at work, and perhaps even work alongside them.

All of this would mean the creation of an urban environment which promotes the integration of children into society not as inferior and separate beings, nor as equals, but with respect for their special abilities and needs. If this seems unreasonable then that is an indication of just how constrained and divisive modern built-environments have become. Most of these requirements were met not long ago in rural areas, in small towns and in city districts away from the main centres. They have been displaced and forgotten in the course of a few generations.

Every move and measure to make cities, and indeed all man-made environments, more accessible to children will make them more accessible to everyone. A child of seven and a woman of seventy have equal difficulty coping with an environment designed for mature, healthy adults who drive almost everywhere, but both the seventy-year old woman and the adults will be able to manage well in a place made with the needs of the seven-year old child in mind. Ronald Blythe has examined thoughtfully the life of the elderly in Britain, the way in which they have become increasingly isolated in 'villages of the old' or alienated by urban redevelopments which have destroyed the old familiar streets. He concludes (1979, p. 248) with the observation that a city which is accessible to everyone is important both for them—'To walk in the streets themselves puts them back into the story'—and for us—'as with the glimpse of a child naturally and unaffectedly demonstrating his childhood in the multifarious scene, so the glimpse of an aged man or woman simply living his or her life at the centre of things is part of the enriching process.' (1979, p. 208)

A Comment on the Likelihood of Sensitive Design

J.B. Jackson is a traveller, sometime amateur geographer and essayist who has observed carefully, wondered at and written about American landscapes in all their moods and styles. Perhaps better than any observer of landscape, he has expressed the compassionate intelligence that is the mark of environmental humility. Every landscape he regards from the perspective of its inhabitants and their relationships to a physical setting, and he sees it as living, being lived in and always changing. If landscapes must be planned and organised, he believes that both abstract models and attempts at beautification are inadequate for this because they offer the wrong means to spurious goals. He has written (1970, p. 160):

> environmental design can take its place among the humanities . . . not by the diligent use of computers nor by concentrating on aesthetics . . . The primary task is to design environments where it will be possible to lead the lives of free and responsible citizens.

I do not doubt that it is possible to rethink planning and environmental design so that they become concerned with freedom, responsibility and guardianship for landscapes. The principles of environmental ethics, attention to details and sensitivity in design, or equivalent principles of smallness and conservation, have been carefully developed and widely advocated. All that is required is their adaptation to specific economic and environmental circumstances. Then it should be quite feasible to begin to create landscapes of a fine texture which are accessible to everyone, by means that are socially and environmentally as non-violent as possible. The basic thinking for this exists already. It is the will to apply it that is lacking.

It is children, the elderly, the poor and disadvantaged who have the most to gain from redesigned environments. Since they have little authority and expertise they cannot easily promote their own case. It is unlikely that planners and designers will do it for them because the consequence of practicing sensitivity in design may well be a reduction in their own authority. But this is probably ascribing too much responsibility and blame to planners and architects who are, after all, participants in a social and economic system based on assumptions of rationalism and efficiency which are deeply and widely accepted. These assumptions are in turn based in anthropocentric humanism. Though S.R.L. Clark (1977, p. 185) was writing specifically of the moral status of animals in the context of factory farming and laboratory experiments, at least one of his comments is relevant to all planning and management when considered from the perspective of environmental humility: 'The wholly decent man would garden and guard the world . . . We are not decent men.'

12 ENVIRONMENTAL DESIGN AND THE MINIMAL STATE

There are many matters which, though specialised in their character, are too public in their implications to be left entirely to the responsibility of experts. Nuclear power stations, the transportation and disposal of toxic chemicals, and genetic engineering could, in the event of carelessness or accident, kill *us* – hence they outrun the realm of the scientists who develop and manage them and become our concern. The potential consequences of totally planned built-environments may be rather less final, but they are not unimportant. The way the streets are laid out is the way in which we must drive or walk; geometric office blocks and neat suburban streets are the enduring contexts of the real lives of people who had no say in the design of these environments, and who must try to make the best of a place that has been built not for them but for statistical abstractions with their sorts of behaviour patterns and incomes.

Implicit in environmental humility is the transcendence of planning and management by technically trained experts. This does not mean that all planning would cease; some controls against undue exploitation and to encourage a just and equitable distribution of resources will always be advisable. However, places and communities would increasingly become the responsibility of those who live and work in them instead of being objects of professional disinterest. I am, of course, aware that it is heretical to suggest any reduction in planning. Rationalistic and technical approaches for the organisation of life and landscape have become so much part of the modern scene that they now seem to be the only ways of managing and surviving. Proposals to correct urban and environmental problems inevitably call for more and better planning. Yet the fact is that until recently almost all man-made landscapes were created without the benefit of detailed analyses of requirements, and without a plenitude of planning restrictions. Furthermore, it is precisely these 'unplanned' landscapes to which many people go when they have the money and opportunity – that is, when they are on holiday or retire.

In the age of scientific humanism much has been achieved and discovered but a great deal has been forgotten or buried. A major task of environmental humility is to recover what has been lost and to demonstrate its continuing relevance. It is patently impossible to do this by a simple retreat to the old ways because modern technologies cannot be brushed aside as thought they had never existed. What I am suggesting here is this: scientific humanism has provided the means of achieving a healthy and materially comfortable life, and some of us live such a life already. We must now attend to ways in which these benefits can be equitably distributed and to the recovery of the recovery of the qualities that have been lost in achieving them; in these tasks scientific humanism has little or no relevance. What has to be done is to develop technologies which are compatible with natural processes and social values, and to discover ways that continue the best aspects yet avoid the weaknesses of both the old and new ways of making and managing enviroı ments. These ways must then be given a political context that will allow them to flourish. Where such design approaches and political circumstance exist it is almost certain that their inspiration and consequence will be the compassionate intelligence and appropriation that are the hallmarks of environmental humility.

Making Places with a Nameless and Timeless Quality

J.M. Richards has both written about and, as a teacher, played a significant role in the development of modern architectural design. Yet when he encountered the old, unplanned and chaotic areas of Japanese cities he admitted that 'the city can be . . . a place that derives its interest and vitality from the fact of its *not* being consciously designed' (Richards, 1972, p. 590). The maze of streets and confusions of buildings and activities comprised a kind of 'anti-architecture' that demonstrated for him excitement, spontaneity and freedom.

There is in these fragments of Japanese cities, as in remnants of medieval towns and villages that we have inherited, a quality that is missing from modern landscapes. It is a quality that cannot be consciously designed or copied because doing so will lead only to the over-neatness of pioneer villages and restored buildings which are not quite real, and suitable only for purposes of education and tourism. Though we can see and feel this quality in individual buildings and in townscapes it is elusive and subtle and evades analysis. Christopher Alexander (1979, pp. 25ff) describes it poetically and accurately as 'the quality without a name', and understands it to be the essential expression of 'the timeless way of building'.

The quality without a name can be described, Alexander suggests, but no description fits it perfectly. It has to do with the life of place, with individuality, with wholeness, with feelings of being comfortable and free in a place. It seems to involve exactness, for everything appears to be right just as it is; it is ageless, for a place that has the quality without a name is always unpretentious; it is eternal and timeless, for though it is specific in time and place it nevertheless transcends these. Yet none of these terms of description is satisfactory, and Alexander can only offer a circumscript account of this quality. It is, he suggests (pp. 7, 10), manifest in all those buildings and places 'where you feel yourself, where you feel alive', in the traditional villages of Africa, the mosques of Islam, the temples of Japan, the country towns of England. It is an expression of an order that has grown directly from the inner nature of the people, animals, plants and materials which are in a place. In the language of geographical humility it is the manifestation of appropriation in landscape.

The fact that the quality without a name eludes simple description and analysis is perhaps a strength, because it renders it unsusceptible to any formulation in a simple reçipe for environmental design. It is also a weakness, for this quality is so complex and subtle that it has simply been ignored in rational approaches to design and planning. These approaches strive to create efficient environments which are, in Alexander's terms (p. 237), less than whole, or merciless and inhuman. No amount of abstract reasoning and drawing-board design can create places and qualities that have this quality without a name for it simply cannot be thought out and created systematically.

If this fundamental and nameless quality cannot be precisely described and designed how can anything be done to revive it? It is the case, Alexander proposes (p. 151), that: 'This quality in buildings and in towns cannot be made, but only generated indirectly, by the ordinary actions of the people, just as a flower cannot be made but only generated from the seed.' In other words an autonomous process of building must be allowed, encouraged and nurtured, because only in this way can places achieve individuality and express the concerns and hopes of the people who live in them.

This seems to be hopelessly idealistic. Such a return of responsibility to people for the environments they live in is all very well in principle, but without guidance it will surely create chaos. The old ways of doing and making have been forgotten or destroyed by the new ways of scientific humanism, and the self-confidence necessary for such tasks has been shattered by dependence on expertise. Alexander's argument against such doubts is this. Behind the forms and processes of all environments lies a 'pattern-language'; this is a sort of grammar or genetic code which directs the relationships that comprise those environments. It says nothing about the parts or objects in an environment, but only the manner in which they relate to each other. At one time these pattern-languages were largely unselfconscious, and having evolved through experience and tradition they became implicated in the way of life and were implemented by people who lived in and used the places which they made. The result was a shared language of expression in architecture and landscape, a visual language in which each building and each town possessed individuality yet at the same time shared their styles and symbols with all the other buildings and towns in the region. This sort of pattern-language is perhaps most easily seen in vernacular architecture. For instance in the borderland of Wales and England there is a distinctive style of farmhouse construction with dressed-sandstone walls, large chimneys, small windows and steep roofs; every farmhouse is none the less uniquely adapted to the particular requirements of its site and its users.

There is modern pattern-language that is used by architects, planners and developers now, but this is insensitive, based on catalogues, abstract principles and generally applicable regulations. It is not anchored in the reality of particular situations. It bears as little resemblance to the pattern-languages of vernacular building as a computer-programming language bears to spoken English; it works, but only in a very restricted way. The result is hyperplanning and placelessness.

To redress the deficiencies of modern planning and design, Alexander proposes that patterns in buildings and places should be sought out and described accurately and carefully. These patterns are not invented or imposed. They are in the world, and they can be disclosed so that they can be used to direct our efforts in making places and buildings. Alexander and his colleagues claim to have identified two-hundred-and-fifty patterns which refer to every aspect of environment from 'local transport areas' to 'sacred sites' to 'small public squares' to 'network of paths and cars' to 'entrance transition' to 'window place'. These cover environments from the scale of a city-region to part of a room, and they have been carefully described and articulated. There is nothing inviolate or fixed in them, they are continuously evolving and changing and there are certainly other patterns as yet undisclosed. By identifying and selecting the relevant patterns for a particular design or planning situation, and then combining them, a pattern-language can be developed to guide the process of making or modifying a place.

'The central task of "architecture" is', Alexander suggests (p. 241), 'the creation of a single, shared, evolving pattern-language which everyone contributes to and everyone can use.' If this pattern-language is properly described it should be capable of being used by anyone not only to design buildings but also, with many people working together, to redesign towns. These may not immediately manifest the quality without a name, but in time and with experience the pattern-languages should become unselfconscious and the landscapes that are created should merge into the tradition of the timeless way of building.

The pattern-language approach to rediscovering ways of making places that have the quality without a name is not simple and technical. Indeed it must seem rather obscure and mystical to anyone versed in models and systems. It is expressed in a language that owes much to Zen Buddhism yet it is based on a mixture of mathematical logic and careful observation. It is difficult to summarise without making it appear like a caricature, for summary denies its subtlety and complexity. What Alexander does is to address directly the inadequacies of modern architecture and planning and then to point to a way of building and designing that should resolve these. It is a way that enables laymen to be involved in making their own places, and it has been successfully employed in at least one instance – the replanning of the campus at the University of Oregon (Alexander, 1975). How it would work in other and larger situations it is impossible to say. Nor is it clear what the role of planners and architects would be, though there would surely be a need for individuals with skill and experience in identifying patterns and in realising appropriate combinations of patterns in particular situations. What is clear is that Alexander has shown that it is possible to conceive of a way of making and tending landscapes which is quite different from that of rationalistic analysis administered through regulation. He has also demonstrated that it is not always necessary to propose more planning to cope with urban or environmental problems. And he has proposed a means by which it should be possible to create once again places with all the qualities of those inherited and admirable landscapes which we have otherwise forgotten how to build.

The Minimal State

The way of building which Christopher Alexander is trying to recover has deep and wide-ranging social, political and economic implications. By assuming that responsibility for environments can reside in the communities which live in and use those environments, he is arguing implicitly against both expertise and centralisation. This does not mean that every person has to design the place he or she lives in: Alexander

(1979, p. 164) maintains that:

> It simply means that the care and patience needed to bring every part into adjustment with the forces acting on it can only exist when each detailed part is cared for, and shaped, by someone who has the time and patience and knowledge to understand the forces acting on it. It is not essential that each person design or shape the place where he is going to live or work. Obviously people move, are happy in old houses, and so on.
>
> It is essential only that the people of a society, together, all the millions of them, not just professional architects, design all the millions of places. There is no other way that human variety, and the reality of specific human lives, can find their way into the structure of the places.

This all sounds very fine but questions must arise about the sort of society and economy in which this widespread involvement in making places could happen. Certainly it is inconceivable in any situation where the principles of scientific humanism are exercised and well-trained technicians direct the affairs of society. Equally it is not possible in a centralised society, for that requires standardised and simplified solutions to problems and imposes them from afar with scant concern for local circumstances. Nor can it happen in a society in which some invisible hand is thought to be at work, managing supply and demand, directing business and trade and preserving economic and social distinctions. Such faith in unseen mechanisms absolves individuals of responsibility for the state of things and provides a thin justification for the wealth and authority of a few while the majority remain poor and impotent.

It is, the philosopher Robert Nozick (1974, pp. 333-4) has written, only the 'minimal state' which treats us as inviolate individuals: 'Treating us with respect by respecting our rights, it allows us, individually or with whom we choose, to choose our life and to realise our ends and our conception of ourselves, insofar as we can, aided by the voluntary cooperation of other individuals possessed of the same dignity.' It is in the minimal state that people can make and take responsibility for maintaining the places in which they live and work.

Peter Kropotkin was a Russian geographer who was one of the first and strongest advocates of the minimal state. Although he had a strong reputation and deep interest in geography, in the autumn of 1871 he rejected the offer of the position of secretary to the Russian Geographical

Society. His reasons he explained some thirty years later in his autobiography. 'Science is a wonderful thing', he wrote (1902, pp. 156-7), 'I knew its joys and valued them. But what right had I to these highest joys when all around me was nothing but misery and struggle for a moldy piece of bread . . . Knowledge is an immense power. Man must know. But we already know much! What if that knowledge . . . should become the possession of all.'

Kropotkin devoted much of the rest of his life to working towards a society in which knowledge and wealth were indeed shared by all. He rejected arguments that self-interest and greed must inevitably breed division and discontent, and in particular he disputed Darwinist accounts of the 'struggle for existence' between competing individuals and groups by pointing to a wealth of evidence, both in nature and in human societies, of 'mutual aid' or co-operation. Progress, he maintained, occurs not through competition, for that is necessarily destructive, but by people working together. He was able to document hundreds of examples, both historical and contemporary, of the success of co-operation, and he had no doubt that people could make something worthwhile of their own lives, their own communities and their own places, without the assistance of outside specialists.

In *Fields, Factories and Workshops Tomorrow* (1898), Kropotkin argued for local economies which are as nearly self-sufficient as possible, and for an integrated urban and rural society with decentralised industries which produced for the locality rather than for some remote city. This is an argument for regional autonomy and distinctiveness, and for a society in which the responsibility for production and management is widely distributed. Furthermore, Kropotkin maintained that by using then existing knowledge and machines for decentralised production, it should be possible to reduce the time individuals spend working without reducing productivity and standards of living. He concluded (1898, p. 198) that these changes 'cannot guarantee happiness, because happiness depends as much, or even more, upon the individual as upon his surroundings. But they guarantee at least the happiness that can be found in the full and varied exercise of the different capacities of the human being; in work that need not be overwork, and in the consciousness that one is not endeavouring to base his own happiness on the misery of others.'

The society of co-operating yet autonomous localities and groups which was described and advocated by Kropotkin is, I believe, the type of society in which responsibility for making and maintaining a place can lie with those who live and work there. Such a society requires only a minimal state to oversee its operations, because the responsibility for regulating and directing development and change resides locally. It is, however, a very idealistic conception of a society, probably even more remote now than when Kropotkin was alive for there has been a considerable move towards centralisation and dependence on expertise since 1900. This does not mean that its possibility has been entirely extinguished, and Ivan Illich, for instance, is still writing ardently and hopefully in its support. In *Tools for Conviviality* (1973) he argues that societies must be reconstructed to encourage the contribution of autonomous individuals and primary groups, and to reduce the servitude of people to machines and bureaucracies. Such a society would be 'convivial', based on free and creative interrelationships among persons, and between persons and their environments. The tools of such a society would themselves be convivial rather than manipulative—they would be capable of use by anyone and as often or as seldom as required. Such tools are particularly hand tools, but also include telephones and bicycles and all equipment which brings people together, and people and natural environments together, rather than forcing them apart. To achieve a convivial society Illich (1973, p. 47) argues that it is necessary, first, to demythologise science and technology—to rid them of their magical aura as the saviours of the world; secondly, to clarify the language of politics and economics so that they cannot retreat into obscure jargon and have to deal with real people confronting the problems of poverty and inequality; and thirdly, to recover a legal procedure that will enable the use of tools to be controlled so that non-convivial uses are prevented. These are not idealistic and drastic proposals, but, with a little willingness, quite sensible and practicable.

It is in the social and political contexts of the minimal state, in which mutual aid and conviviality prevail, that appropriation too can flourish and people can assume responsibility for the character of the places in which they live. But since the minimal state is so remote from present political circumstances, which are marked by the continuing aggrandisement of state and corporate authority, it may be that it should be dismissed as a mere pipedream. Then we can concentrate on more immediate and probably constructive thoughts and actions, perhaps working for an economy based on conservation, or opposing the practices of large corporations, or even using expertise in the tradition of paternalistic humanism to improve the environments of those poorer than ourselves. Such actions are undoubtedly invaluable in particular contexts, and they may produce quick and tangible results. Yet if there is no clear understanding of deeper attitudes and beliefs, such as those of scientific humanism, and no identification of more distant goals and ideals, such as those of environmental humility, then these pragmatic actions can easily be reduced to stop-gap measures or even be subverted into means of promoting precisely that which they are meant to oppose. The minimal state, in which there is co-operation and a timeless way of building, may not be part of our immediate or even our distant future, but it nevertheless offers a standard by which we can judge current practices for making and maintaining places, and a goal towards which we can direct our efforts.

Environmental Humility

Environmental humility suggests a way out of the vicious circle of using ever more rational practices of management and planning to correct the destructive consequences of rationalistic management and too much planning. It does this, first, by emphasising the individuality of places, communities and landscapes, for individuality is not susceptible to analysis and manipulation. It does this also by stressing the need for a sensitivity in seeing that can lead to the development of a compassionate intelligence which respects things and persons as they are. And it does this, above all, by acknowledging appropriation, or the fact that everything has value simply by virtue of its existence and that human beings have an obligation to tend and care for things both non-human and man-made. The use of appropriation and compassionate intelligence and individuality for making environments cannot be precisely delineated because that would reduce them to simplistic formulations like those of the rationalism to which they are deeply opposed. However, it is possible to suggest some of their general implications, for instance places designed so that they are responsive to the needs of their most sensitive users, especially children and the elderly. The further implications are more radical and suggest a complete restructuring of ways of designing and making buildings and landscapes so that there is no longer a dependence on specialist advice and techniques. But this return of responsibility to individuals and communities is unlikely to happen except in the context of the minimal state in which the rights and obligations of autonomous individuals are accepted as paramount. In the minimal state geographical humility could prevail.

The likelihood of this actually happening is slight. There is, in fact, a long history of proposals for self-effacing custodianship of the world and its contents, respecting not only the individuality of fellow human beings but of everything that exists. Few of these have had any enduring social and economic expression, though they have persisted as philosophical and spiritual ideals. The theme that it is misguided to impose one's will on others or on nature, and that one should strive to co-operate with others and with environments, can be identified in the earliest Greek philosophy, in Gnosticism, in the teachings of Lao Tzu and Zen Buddhism, and more recently and prosaically in the writings of Kropotkin, Illich, Mumford, Ward, Goodman and Schumacher. Each of these adopts a different perspective, but they are consistent in maintaining that while we may offer direction, assistance and protection we should not enforce authority and controls. There are, however, few if any places where such a philosophy is actively practiced.

None the less, it is inconceivable that appropriation could have no effect on what is made and done because any deeply held and clearly thought out understanding must manifest itself in deeds and action. Though environmental humility and its predecessors may never have attained expression on a large social scale, they do constitute ideals which are worth reiterating and adapting as social and environmental circumstances change. In these ideals there is no room for arrogance based on expertise or for authority stemming from some abstract conception of rights; there is equally no room for an unthinking subservience which abandons obligations to specialists; and there is no room for the exploitation and unfeeling manipulation of either people or environments. But there is scope for craftsmanship, for autonomy, for being responsible for the environments in which one lives and works, for the quality without a name, and for guardianship. Environmental humility is not easily practiced nor is it likely ever to achieve a widespread expression in landscapes. It is simply an ideal and a possibility worth contemplating.

The Last Landscape of Humanism

Modern landscapes, those which have been made in the twentieth century and are being made now, are the crowning achievement of humanism. They are an embodiment of what Descartes called 'the plumb-line of reason', an expression of the enormous and powerful achievements of rational analysis and design. Roads are wider and straighter, buildings bigger and better heated, machines faster than ever before. We who are fortunate enough to occupy these modern built-environments are, in general, healthier, better-fed and more comfortable than any of our ancestors. In the developed world at least the humanist ideal of rational knowledge used in the service of man has become reality.

Yet in its realisation the ideal seems less complete, less attractive than it should be. If we dare to ask what is *not* the purpose of human life the reply might reasonably be that it is not to be futile bomb or cannon fodder, that it is not to die because of someone else's incompetence or arrogance, that it is not to live in perpetual despair and hunger, that it is not to be subject in either public or private life to the dictates of others, that it is not to be a consuming unit in a market for manufacturers, and that it is not to be a mere statistic manipulated to serve some abstract end. Yet all of these are actualities or very real possibilities—if not for us then for many people in the world. Humanism has done nothing to reduce such obvious distortions of human life; indeed through its deep implication in science and technology it has tended to exacerbate them. Of course, it can be argued that this has happened through an abuse of humanism and reason. If so, it means that there is nothing in humanism to prevent such abuse.

The landscapes of scientific humanism are monumental achievements, huge and often spectacular in both their scale and design. But they are also frequently awful, dwarfing people, lacking detail, allowing no involvement except that which is prescribed in the plans. They are a manifestation of rationalism pushed to its limits and already turning against itself, becoming restrictive rather than enlightening. In such modern landscapes humanism in any sense is already disappearing. The future to which they point is one with a landscape of a perfect and an efficient order, with occasional loud and glossy parts for retailing and entertainment; a landscape in which all the details of life will be planned for a population too sated with material luxuries to notice or to care about the loss of values and of freedom. The means of control will have become invisible: microwaves, central computer records, secret shelters for government and military officials, electronic surveillance and distant missile silos. In the final phase of rationalistic humanism, when reason will have been pushed to its limits by men in the service of men, the landscape will be either a vast and perfectly managed prison or a graveyard. The modern landscape will have been the last landscape of humanism, and perhaps the last landscape of all.

I do not expect environmental humility to hold great sway against scientific humanism. It is after all only an attempt to clarify a non-manipulative ideal for seeing and maintaining places. It is a way that has a sound philosophical foundation, which allows and adapts human skills that have a long tradition, which can identify an appropriate means of making places and a sympathetic social and political context. But non-manipulation, co-operation and caring are not strong attitudes with which to confront control, competition and efficiency. Nevertheless, should environmental humility, or some similar attitude, come to prevail in the world, then landscapes would become once again what they were before the advent of humanism and the invention of the idea of landscape – the unselfconsciously accepted contexts for everyday life. They would be neither set apart as objects for contemplation nor deliberately manipulated for human benefit. Humanism would be replaced by a broader and deeper humanity that attends to all Being and makes landscapes an inseparable part of existence. In such a case the ideas of both humanism and landscape would have been transcended and, in this case too, the modern landscape would have been the last landscape of humanism.

But much more probable than the transcendence of humanism through the adoption of environmental humility, and less depressing than its destruction through an excess of rationalism, is its continuation much as it is now. Landscapes will be added to and changed in a piecemeal fashion within a cloak of planning regulations and consumer enticements. The remnants of older humanist landscapes – those of the Renaissance and the Enlightenment, and even of the paternalism of the nineteenth century – will be diligently preserved. New office towers, power stations, pintable arcades, shopping malls, factory farms and public-housing complexes will continue to be built in spite of protests by some outspoken groups and individuals; continuing attempts will be made to use scientific research to improve standards of living, though no doubt some will benefit more than others.

As long as it permits personal pleasure and sadness, and allows freedom of expression, this piecemeal approach to making landscapes is tolerable even if its results are sometimes annoying and distressing. However, toleration does not demand passivity and complacency. The modern landscape should be described and criticised whenever it threatens the freedom that comes with taking responsibility for one's environment, whenever it promotes inequality or threatens values, and wherever it demonstrates manipulation through detached expertise. It should also be appreciated for the comforts and conveniences it provides – not everyone is so fortunate. The modern landscape may be the last landscape of humanism but it is our landscape, and we must make of it what we can.

POSTSCRIPT

Humanity subdues inhumanity as water subdues fire. Nowadays those who practice humanity do so as though with one cup of water they could save a whole wagonload of fuel on fire. When the flames were not extinguished they would say that water cannot subdue fire. This is as bad as those who are inhumane.

Mencius, 371-289 BC, Book 6A, s. 18

BIBLIOGRAPHY

Note: In order to maintain some sense of the chronology of ideas about landscape and humanism I have referenced books by the date of original publication. The date of publication of the particular edition used is given at the end of the bibliographic entry. Ruskin's multi-volume work *Modern Painters* has posed special difficulties. It was first published over a period of seventeen years, but since I have used primarily Volume III published in 1856 I have for convenience ascribed that date to all volumes. Furthermore, I unwittingly used two different editions of *Modern Painters*, one by George Allen, London, 1904, the other by George Routledge, London, no date of publication given but probably 1905. There is a discrepancy of about ten pages in the page numbering of these two editions.

Abler, R., Adams, J.S. and Gould, P. (1971) *Spatial Organisation: The Geographer's View of the World*, Prentice Hall, Englewood Cliffs, NJ

Alexander, C. *et al.* (1975) *The Oregon Experiment*, Oxford University Press, New York

——(1979) *The Timeless Way of Building*, Oxford University Press, New York

Amsterdams Historisch Museum/Art Gallery of Ontario (1977) *The Dutch Cityscape in the Seventeenth Century and its Sources*, Amsterdams Historisch Museum/Art Gallery of Ontario, Amsterdam/Toronto

Banham, R. (1960) *Theory and Design in the First Machine Age*, The Architectural Press, London

——(1976) *Megastructure: Urban Futures of the Recent Past*, Harper and Row, New York

Barrell, J. (1972) *The Idea of Landscape and the Sense of Place 1730-1840*, Cambridge, Cambridge University Press

Barrett, W. (1972) *Time of Need: Forms of Imagination in the Twentieth Century*, Harper and Row, New York

——(1978) *The Illusion of Technique*, Anchor Press, Doubleday, Garden City, NY

Benevolo, L. (1967) *The Origins of Modern City Planning*, Routledge and Kegan Paul, London

Berger, P. (1963) *Invitation to Sociology: A Humanistic Perspective*, Doubleday, Garden City, NY

Blackham, H.J. *et al.* (1965) *Objections to Humanism*, Penguin, Harmondsworth, Middlesex

Blake, P. (1964) *God's Own Junkyard*, Holt, Rinehart and Winston, New York

Blake, W. (1803) 'Auguries of Innocence' in J. Bronowski (ed.), *William Blake: A Selection of Poems and Letters*, Penguin, Harmondsworth, Middlesex, 1958

Blythe, R. (1979) *The View in Winter*, Harcourt, Brace, Jovanovich, New York

Booth, C. (1902) *Life and Labour of the People of London*, Macmillan and Co, London

Cassirer, E. (1944) *Essay on Man*, Bantam Books, New York, 1970

Chisholm, M. (1975) *Human Geography: Evolution or Revolution?*, Penguin, Harmondsworth, Middlesex

Chomsky, N. (1967) *American Power and the New Mandarins*, Pantheon Books, New York

Chorley, R.J. and Kennedy, B. (1971) *Physical Geography: A Systems Approach*, Prentice Hall International, London

Clark, K. (1949) *Landscape into Art*, John Murray, London

Clark, S.R.L. (1977) *The Moral Status of Animals*, Clarendon Press, Oxford

Cobb, E. (1969) 'The Ecology of Imagination in Childhood' in P. Shepard and D. McKinley (eds), *The Subversive Science*, Houghton Mifflin, Boston

—— (1977) *The Ecology of Imagination in Childhood*, Columbia University Press, New York

Cole, J.P. and King, C.A.M. (1968) *Quantitative Geography*, John Wiley, London

Corbett, P. (1972) 'Postscript' in S. Godlovitch, R. Godlovitch and J. Harris (eds), *Animals, Men and Morals*, Taplinger Publishing, New York

Cox, K. (1972) *Men, Location and Behaviour*, John Wiley, New York

Crosby, T. (1973) *How to Play the Environment Game*, Penguin, Harmondsworth, Middlesex

Cullen, G. (1961) *Townscape*, The Architectural Press, London

Cumberland, B. (1886) *The Northern Lakes of Canada*, Hunter, Rose and Company, Toronto

Denham, Sir J. (1642) 'Cooper's Hill' in H. Kenner (ed.), *Seventeenth*

Century Poetry, Holt, Rinehart and Winston, New York, 1964

Descartes, R. (1637) *Discourse on Method and the Meditations*, Penguin, Harmondsworth, Middlesex, 1968

Deskins, D.R. (ed.) (1977) 'Geography, Humanism, Analysis and Social Action', Proceedings of a Symposium, Michigan Geographical Publication No. 17, Department of Geography, University of Michigan, Ann Arbor

Dillard, A. (1974) *Pilgrim at Tinker's Creek*, Harpers Magazine Press, New York

Dresden, S. (1968) *Humanism in the Renaissance*, McGraw-Hill, New York

Eckbo, G. (1969) *The Landscape We See*, McGraw-Hill, New York

Ehrenfeld, D. (1978) *The Arrogance of Humanism*, Oxford University Press, New York

Ehrlich, P., Ehrlich, A. and Holdren, J. (1973) *Human Ecology*, W.H. Freeman, San Francisco

Engels, F. (1845) *The Conditions of the Working Class in England*, Panther Books, St Albans, 1969

Entrikin, N. (1976) 'Contemporary Humanism in Geography', *Annals of the Association of American Geographers*, vol. 66, no. 4, pp. 615-32

Feyerabend, P. (1978) *Science in a Free Society*, NLB, London

Fitzgerald, B.P. (1974) *Developments in Geographical Method*, Oxford University Press, London

Foucault, M. (1970) *The Order of Things: An Archaeology of the Human Sciences*, Tavistock Publications, London

Freeman, K. (1962) *Ancilla to the Pre-Socratic Philosophers*, Basil Blackwell, Oxford

Friedlander, M. (1963) *Landscape, Portrait, Still-Life*, Schocken Books, New York

Fromm, E. (ed.) (1966) *Socialist Humanism*, Doubleday, Garden City, NY

Gay, P. (1970) *The Enlightenment: The Science of Freedom*, Weidenfeld and Nicolson, London

___(ed.) (1973) *The Enlightenment: A Comprehensive Anthology*, Simon and Schuster, New York

Giedion, S. (1948) *Mechanisation Takes Command*, W.W. Norton, New York, 1969

Glazebrook, G., *et al.* (1969) *A Shopper's View of Canada's Past*, University of Toronto Press, Toronto

Goethe, J.W. (1970) *Italian Journey (1786-88)*, translated by W.H.

Auden and E. Mayer, Penguin, Harmondsworth, Middlesex
Goodman, P. (1969) *New Reformation: Notes of a Neolithic Conservative*, Vintage Books, New York
Grigson, G. (1962) *Gerard Manley Hopkins*, Longmans, Green and Company, London
Gropius, W. (1935?) *The New Architecture and the Bauhaus*, The MIT Press, Cambridge, Mass., 1965
——(1955) *Scope of Total Architecture*, Harper and Row, New York
——(1968) *Apollo in the Democracy*, McGraw-Hill, New York
Hamerton, P.G. (1890) *Landscape*, Roberts Brothers, Boston
Harris, K. (1978) 'Fundamental Ontology and the Search for Man's Place' in M. Murray (ed.), *Heidegger and Modern Philosophy: Critical Essays*, Yale University Press, New Haven
Hayek, F.A. von (1955) *The Counter-Revolution of Science: Studies on the Abuse of Reason*, Free Press of Glencoe, New York
Heidegger, M. (1947) 'Letter on Humanism' in D.F. Krell (ed.), *Martin Heidegger: Basic Writings*, Harper and Row, New York, 1977
——(1954) *What is Called Thinking?*, Harper and Row, New York, 1968
——(1966) 'Only a God Can Save Us', a *Der Spiegel* interview reprinted in *Philosophy Today*, vol. 20, Winter 1976, pp. 267-84
——(1971) *Poetry, Language, Thought*, Harper and Row, New York
——(1977) *Basic Writings*, D.F. Krell (ed.), Harper and Row, New York
Herbert, R.L. (ed.) (1964) *The Art Criticism of John Ruskin*, Doubleday, Garden City, NY
Hoffer, E. (1952) *The Ordeal of Change*, Harper and Row, New York
Hofstadter, A. (1970) *Agony and Epitaph*, George Braziller, New York
Horkheimer, M. (1947) *The Eclipse of Reason*, Oxford University Press, New York
Hoskins, W.G. (1955) *The Making of the English Landscape*, Penguin, Harmondsworth, Middlesex, 1970
Houghton, W.E. (1957) *The Victorian Frame of Mind*, Yale University Press, New Haven
Huizinga, J. (1949) *The Waning of the Middle Ages*, Doubleday, Garden City, NY, 1954
Huxley, J. (ed.) (1961) *The Humanist Frame*, George Allen and Unwin, London
Hyams, E. (1971) *Capability Brown and Humphry Repton*, Charles Scribner's Sons, New York
Illich, I. (1973) *Tools for Conviviality*, Harper and Row, New York
——(1976) *Limits to Medicine*, Marion Boyars, London

Jackson, J.B. (1953) 'Commentary', *Landscape*, vol. 3, pp. 28-9
___(1970) *Landscapes: Selected Writings of J.B. Jackson*, E.H. Zube (ed.), University of Massachusetts Press
James, W. (1901) *The Varieties of Religious Experience*, Collier Books, New York, 1961
___(1912) 'The Essence of Humanism' in *Essays in Radical Empiricism*, E.P. Dutton, New York, 1971
Jonas, H. (1966) *The Phenomenon of Life*, Dell Publishing, New York
___(1974) *Philosophical Essays*, Prentice Hall, Englewood Cliffs, NJ
Jonson, B. (1616) 'The Forrest' in H. Kenner (ed.), *Seventeenth Century Poetry*, Holt, Rinehart and Winston, New York, 1964
Kenner, H. (ed.) (1964) *Seventeenth Century Poetry*, Holt, Rinehart and Winston, New York
King, L.J. and Golledge, R. (1978) *Cities, Space and Behaviour: The Elements of Urban Geography*, Prentice Hall, Englewood Cliffs, NJ
Kitson-Clark, G. (1962) *The Making of Victorian England*, Methuen, London
Klee, P. (1961) *The Thinking Eye*, Lund Humphries, London
___(1964) *The Diaries of Paul Klee*, F. Klee (ed.), University of California, Berkeley
Knight, R.P. (1795) *The Landscape: A Didactic Poem addressed to Uvedale Price*, republished by Gregg International, Farnborough, Hants, 1972
Krishnamurti, J. (1973) *Beyond Violence*, Harper and Row, New York
Kropotkin, P. (1898) *Fields, Factories and Workshops Tomorrow*, C. Ward (ed.), Harper and Row, New York, 1974
___(1902) *Memoirs of a Revolutionist*, Doubleday, Garden City, NY, 1962
___(1914) *Mutual Aid*, P. Avrich (ed.), New York University Press, New York, 1972
Kurtz, P. and Wilson, E.H. (1973) 'Humanist Manifesto II', *Current*, vol. 156, pp. 28-36
Kurtz, S.A. (1973) *Wasteland*, Praeger, New York
Lamont, C. (1949) *The Philosophy of Humanism*, Frederick Ungar Publishing, New York
Langer, S.K. (1966) 'The Social Influence of Design' in L.B. Holland (ed.), *Who Designs America?*, Doubleday, Garden City, NY
Lasch, C. (1978) *The Culture of Narcissism*, W.W. Norton, New York
Lewis, C.S. (1968) *A Mind Awake: An Anthology*, C.S. Kirby (ed.), Harcourt, Brace and World, New York
Lewis, P. (1976) 'Axioms of the Landscape', *Journal of Architectural*

Education, vol. XXX, no. 1, reprinted in D.W. Meinig (ed.), *The Interpretation of Ordinary Landscapes*, Oxford University Press, New York, 1979

Lewis, P. and Marsh, B. (1979) 'Slices through Time: The Physical and Cultural Landscapes of Central and Eastern Pennsylvania' in R.A. Cybriwsky (ed.), *The Philadelphia Region*, Association of American Geographers, Washington, DC

Ley, D. and Samuels, M. (eds) (1979) *Humanistic Geography*, Maaroufa Press, Chicago

Louch, A.R. (1966) *Explanation and Human Action*, University of California Press, Berkeley

Lynch, K. (1971) *Site Planning*, MIT Press, Cambridge, Mass.

Mack, M. (1969) *The Garden and the City: Retirement and Politics in the Later Poetry of Pope 1731-1743*, University of Toronto Press, Toronto

Maritain, J. (1936) *Integral Humanism*, Charles Scribner's Sons, New York, 1968

Marx, K. (1844) *The Economic and Philosophic Manuscripts of 1844*, International Publishers, New York, 1964

Maslow, A. (1968) *Toward A Psychology of Being*, van Nostrand Reinhold, New York

——(1971) *The Farther Reaches of Human Nature*, The Viking Press, New York

Meinig, D. (ed.) (1979) *The Interpretation of Ordinary Landscapes*, Oxford University Press, New York

Mencius (371-289 BC?) 'The Book of Mencius' in Wing-Tsit Chan (ed.), *A Source Book in Chinese Philosophy*, Princeton University Press, Princeton, 1969

Merleau-Ponty, M. (1947) *Humanism and Terror*, Beacon Press, Boston, 1969

——(1964) 'Cezanne's Doubt' in *Sense and Nonsense*, Northwestern University Press, Evanston

Moncrieff, P. and Rizvi, S. (1974) 'The Broiler Marketing Question', *Agricultural Economics Research Council of Canada*, Ottawa

Monod, J. (1970) *Le Hasard et la Necessité*, Editions du Seuil, Paris

Mumford, L. (1961) *The City in History*, Harcourt, Brace and World, New York

——(1964) 'The Myth of the Machine' in *The Pentagon of Power*, Harcourt, Brace, Jovanovich, New York

Murray, M. (ed.) (1978) *Heidegger and Modern Philosophy: Critical Essays*, Yale University Press, New Haven

Nelson, G. (1977) *How to See*, Little, Brown and Company, Boston

Newton, N.T. (1971) *Design on the Land: The Development of Landscape Architecture*, The Belknap Press of Harvard University Press, Cambridge, Mass.

Nozick, R. (1974) *Anarchy, State and Utopia*, Basic Books, New York

Olsson, G. (1975) *Birds in Egg*, Michigan Geographical Publications No. 15, Department of Geography, University of Michigan, Ann Arbor

Panofsky, E. (1940) 'Art as a Humanistic Discipline' in *Meaning in the Visual Arts*, Doubleday, Garden City, NY, 1955

Partridge, E. (1958) *Origins: A Short Etymological Dictionary of English*, Routledge and Kegan Paul, London

Percy, Walker (1967) *The Moviegoer*, The Noonday Press, New York

Peters, M. (1972) 'Nature and Culture' in S. Godlovitch, R. Godlovitch and J. Harris (eds), *Animals, Men and Morals*, Taplinger Publishing, New York

Pope, A. (1734) 'Essay on Man' in J. Butt (ed.), *The Poems of Alexander Pope*, Methuen, London, 1950

Pushkarev, B. (1966) 'Scale and Design in a New Environment' in L.B. Holland (ed.), *Who Designs America?*, Doubleday, Garden City, NY

Richards, J.M. (1972) 'Lessons from the Japanese Jungle' in G. Bell and J. Tyrwhitt, *Human Identity in the Urban Environment*, Penguin, Harmondsworth, Middlesex

Richardson, W.J. (1967) *Heidegger: Through Phenomenology to Thought*, Martinus Nijhoff, The Hague

Riis, J. (1968) 'How the Other Half Lives' in F. Cordasco (ed.), *Jacob Riis Revisited*, Doubleday, Garden City, NY

Ruskin, J. (1856) *Modern Painters*, volumes I to V (George Allen, London, 1904) (see note at beginning of bibliography)

___(1856) *Modern Painters*, volumes I to V (George Routledge, London, 1905?)

___(1880?) *The Crown of Wild Olive*, The Mershon Company, NY

Sarton, G. (1931) *The History of Science and the New Humanism*, Indiana University Press, Bloomington, 1962

Sartre, J-P. (1946) *Existentialism is a Humanism*, Methuen, London, 1964

Sauer, C.O. (1925) 'The Morphology of Landscape' in J. Leighly (ed.), *Land and Life: A Selection of the Writings of Carl Ortwin Sauer*, University of California Press, Berkeley, 1967

Schaefer, F.K. (1953) 'Exceptionalism in Geography', *Annals of the Association of American Geographers*, vol. 43, no. 2, pp. 226-49

Schumacher, E.F. (1977) *A Guide for the Perplexed*, Fitzhenry and

Whiteside, Toronto
——(1979) *Good Work*, Fitzhenry and Whiteside, Toronto
Scott, G. (1914) *The Architecture of Humanism*, Methuen, London, 1961
Simmonds, J.O. (1961) *Landscape Architecture*, McGraw-Hill, New York
Singer, P. (1975) *Animal Liberation*, Random House, New York
Skinner, B.F. (1971) *Beyond Freedom and Dignity*, Bantam Books, Toronto
Steiner, G. (1971) *In Bluebeard's Castle: Some Notes Towards the Redefinition of Culture*, Faber and Faber, London
Stinson, R. and Stinson, P. (1979) 'On the Death of a Baby', *The Atlantic*, July 1979, pp. 64-72
Stoddard, L. (1926) *Scientific Humanism*, Charles Scribner's Sons, London
Thomson, J. (1730) *The Complete Works of James Thomson*, J.L. Robertson (ed.), Oxford University Press, London, 1908
Tocqueville, A. de (1945) *Democracy in America*, volume II, Vintage Books, New York
Towndrow, F. (1933) *Architecture in the Balance: An Approach to the Art of Scientific Humanism*, Chatto and Windus, London
Tuan, Yi-Fu (1976a) 'Humanistic Geography', *Annals of the Association of American Geographers*, vol. 66, no. 2, pp. 266-76
——(1976b) 'Reflections on Humanistic Geography', *Journal of Architectural Education*, vol. XXX, no. 1, pp. 3-5
Tunnard, C. (1978) *A World with a View*, Yale University Press, New Haven
Tunnard, C. and Pushkarev, B. (1963) *Man-Made America: Chaos or Control?*, Yale University Press, New Haven
United States, Department of Agriculture (1970) *Contours of Change*, USDA Handbook, Washington DC
——(1977) 'The Chicken Broiler Industry', Department of Agriculture Report No. 381
Venturi, R. *et al.* (1977) *Learning from Las Vegas*, MIT Press, Cambridge, Mass.
Versenyi, L. (1965) *Heidegger, Being and Truth*, Yale University Press, New Haven
Ward, C. (1978) *The Child in the City*, Pantheon Books, New York
Wasserman, J. (1947) *My Life as a German and a Jew* cited in H. Miller, *Remember to Remember*, New Direction Books, Norfolk, Conn.
White, E.B. (1966) *One Man's Meat*, Harper and Row, New York

Williams, R. (1975) *The Country and the City*, Paladin, St Albans

Williams-Ellis, C. (1928) *England and the Octopus*, Portmeirion, Penrhyndeudraeth, 1975

Woodward, Sir Ll. (1962) *The Age of Reform 1815-1870*, Clarendon Press, Oxford

Wordsworth, W. (1798) *Selections from Wordsworth*, D.C. Somervell (ed.), J.M. Dent, London, 1920

Yeates, M. (1974) *An Introduction to Quantitative Analysis in Human Geography*, McGraw Hill, New York

Zube, E.H., Brush, R.O. and Fabos, J.G. (eds) (1975) *Landscape Assessment: Values, Perceptions, Resources*, Dowden, Hutchison and Ross, Stroudsberg, Penn.

INDEX